"When I was growing up in the educated in taboo subjects. My parents never even said the word was already married. I was behind the curve when it came to subjects such as sex, abuse, suicide, anxiety, and depression. But I'd venture to guess that most people are not very knowledgeable about what God's Word says about taboo subjects because, frankly, we do not discuss them, even in church. Pastor Novotny tackles these subjects head-on. He explains them in a detailed but clear way, always shoring up his discussions with the foundation of God's Word. It's about time that Christians discuss taboo ideas and learn what God has to say about them. This is a book that I wish I'd had many years ago!"

—DR. NANCY FLORY

Senior Editor at *The Stream*

"Whether you are a family being torn apart by the practices of the day or a ministry leader guiding others, *Taboo* lays bare today's gut-wrenching issues that are dividing us from the ones we love (or should love). Exposing all their confusion and messiness and pain, Mike takes us on a journey to hear directly from God where truth and love meet on every issue. You might not hear what you want, but you will hear God's heart with compassion and clarity. From there, you can go forward with Him."

—KIM WIER

Host of *The Art of Friendship* podcast and author of *Everyday God*

"I genuinely believe that *Taboo* by Mike Novotny is a must-own for every Christian, as well as for any non-Christian seeking answers. Moreover, I assert that this book should grace the bookshelves of every Christian pastor. I commend the way the book skillfully navigates the delicate intersection of faith and the forbidden. Brushing aside the questions that arise from the topics covered in this book or responding to them with frivolity does not contribute to bringing peace and clarity to those seeking answers.

With insight and compassion, Mike challenges readers to confront taboos, not for the sake of scandal but to address real issues that everyone, Christian or not, has either faced directly or indirectly. As Christians, it is crucial to provide biblical responses—not merely cultural ones—to these questions. The book prompts readers to reconsider topics they may have thought were straightforward, offering a balanced approach from a fresh perspective. *Taboo* strikes a balance between truth and love in addressing these hot-button issues, providing valuable guidance for decision making and discernment as readers navigate life and assist others with similar questions."

—TIM FERRARA

Pastor, podcaster, and founder of Discerning Dad

"Living and working in Hollywood, it's been my experience that the vast majority of people who leave the Christian faith leave because their local church refused to discuss many of the very issues Mike Novotny tackles in his new book, *Taboo*. People have questions, and fortunately, Mike understands that God is big enough to handle our greatest challenges. Thank you, Mike, for writing the book, and thank you for creating a timely resource that I believe will have an incredible impact on today's culture."

—PHIL COOKE, PhD

Media producer and author of *Ideas on a Deadline*

"*Taboo* is the book that brings much-needed sunlight to our dark, Christian world. Mike Novotny shines the light of Jesus in places where comfort doesn't exist and, in doing so, allows God's grace to replace the hopelessness that our hidden sins create. In *Taboo*, Mike brings everything to the table including the kitchen sink. Anxiety. Depression. Sex. Porn. Addiction. Politics, just to name a few. The great thing about *Taboo* is that Mike doesn't just introduce these topics and then leave the reader hanging there but takes the reader to the issue through the lens of God's Word and provides solutions, bringing restoration at the end of each chapter. You and I may not have all these issues, but if you're a human, you know someone who does, and that's where *Taboo* and you come in. Read the book and then share the book. *Taboo* is part of everyone's solution in the same way that Jesus is the answer to every question. Jesus is the light, and if we bring everything into the light, then darkness won't exist. Mike has given us all a tool in *Taboo* to help shine the light of Jesus."

—DAVE MACDONALD
Christian Podcaster

"Mike Novotny's book *Taboo* is a game changer. It delves into crucial yet often avoided subjects, offering profound insights into life and faith. I highly recommend it for those ready to engage in important conversations and foster growth in their faith journeys. It's a must-read for the Church."

—SUE DETWEILER
Author, speaker, and founder of Life Bridge Global

"The chaos of this world has left many of us with unanswered questions. How do we talk to *that* person? How do we love others as Christ does? Mike Novotny is a forerunner in tackling hard issues with love, truth, and humor that break down the walls that keep us divided. *Taboo* will help every person feel heard and gain confidence in loving people who hold differing worldviews."

—MATT CLINE
Director of Restored Ministry

"'What we feel is not the basis of our faith.' In a time when Christians are discouraged from speaking truth in a politically correct charged society, Mike Novotny does a masterful job of discussing taboo topics with grace and wisdom. In his book *Taboo*, Mike brings the Word of God into tough conversations, showing its relevance to difficult topics we face in our culture today."

—DENISE PASS
Author of *Make Up Your Mind*

"Mike Novotny's newest book, *Taboo*, will challenge, confront, and comfort you all at the same time. Without watering down the truth, *Taboo* brings the grace of God to the most complicated situations facing Christians today, such as addiction, abuse, politics, purity, and more. A message full of grace and truth is exactly what American Christianity needs today!"

—PAT WILLIAMS
Cofounder of Orlando Magic and author of *Every Day Is Game Day*

"*Taboo: Topics Christians Should Be Talking About but Don't* lays a solid, biblical foundation to address how the Church should tackle difficult, hot-button topics many struggle with today. Pastor and author Mike Novotny tackles these taboo topics with grace and humility. He lays out clear spiritual truths and challenges us all not to just take his word for it but to open our Bibles and see what God has to say. Mike challenges us to love without hesitation, to have greater intimacy with God than with sin, and to face these tough questions directly."

—DEBBIE KITTERMAN
Speaker, podcaster, founder of Dare2Hear Ministries and Sound the Call, LLC

"*Taboo* is an essential resource for tackling hard topics Christians don't normally feel comfortable talking about. Pastor Mike delivers timeless biblical truths with grace, love, and respect for all who are impacted by these difficult issues."

—BRIAN DAVISON
Lead vocalist for Koiné Music Ministries and president of Koiné Worship Media

"Satan likes it when we shy away from specific topics. It's these issues especially that must be addressed and brought out into the open. As we have learned from practical experience, there's nothing like daylight and the truth of God to overcome, purify, and disinfect. As Pastor Mike addresses in his new book, *Taboo: Topics Christians Should Be Talking About but Don't*, it's a reminder to be countercultural. It's the current culture that has us mired in chaos and confusion—certainly something God does not author. Thank you, Pastor Mike, for pulling back the curtain on the deception of this age."

—BILL MARTINEZ

Host of *The Bill Martinez Show*

"Talking about the hard things does not get easier until it does. Mike Novotony gives us tools to practice the hard conversations until we can have them and help one another grow, heal, and ultimately trust God through the hard things. Mike always goes back to the Bible to let us view God's Word when it comes to our life experiences. *Taboo* reminds us that trusting God with the hard things is an act of obedience alongside those action steps that keep us exercising in faith."

—DAWN RAE

Cohost of *Dawn and Steve in the Morning*

"There are a lot of topics that Christians don't feel comfortable talking about. Mike Novotny isn't afraid to go there and apply biblical truth with grace and love. *Taboo* is a great resource if you're looking for biblical answers to hot-button issues."

—STEVE HILLER

Cohost of *Dawn and Steve in the Morning*

"We need to talk about these subjects! Pastor Mike Novotny has written an easy-to-read book that addresses every hidden issue in life and will be healing for many. The book can be read in the privacy of a home or in a group Bible study. Whatever the case, Pastor Mike's bold look at these issues is much needed."

—LISA BURKHARDT WORLEY

Award-winning author and documentary film producer

TOPICS CHRISTIANS ANXIETY DEPRESSION RACE MARRIAGE ADULTERY SHOULD POLITICS ABORTION HOMOSEXUALITY BE TALKING TRANSGENDERISM SEXUAL INTIMACY DIVORCE SUICIDE ABOUT ALCOHOL PORNOGRAPHY BUT DON'T

TABOO

MIKE NOVOTNY

Published by Fedd Books

Printed in the United States of America

LCCN: 2023920105

ISBN: 978-1-957616-55-1

CONTENTS

DEDICATION

This book is dedicated to our church family. You not only allowed but also encouraged me to grab God's Word and talk about what most Christians don't talk about. Without you, these pages simply wouldn't exist.

INTRODUCTION

Many years ago, on an April 24, I walked into a counselor's office and admitted my addiction to pornography. I remember feeling awkward and self-conscious as I passed people in the hallway that led to his office, wondering if they might be wondering what I was doing that day. Did they know my struggle? Would they guess my sin? Would they think differently of me if they guessed correctly?

I didn't know the answers to those questions, but I did know that I needed help. It would have been, by definition, insanity to keep doing what I had been doing and expect a different result. I was stuck and unable to save myself from old patterns and sinful behaviors. And, by God's insane grace, and through talking to a counselor, I got help.

WE ARE NOT TALKING ABOUT THE REAL ISSUES WE ARE FACING. AND THAT'S NOT HELPING.

I wanted to start this book with my story because it supports a deep belief I have about life, namely, that not talking is not helping. In too many

Christian churches and homes, we are not talking about the real issues we are facing. And that's not helping.

In every Christian community, there are people who tend to experience anxious and depressed thoughts as a default state. People who have wondered if anyone would miss them if they were gone, who silently (or not) look down on other ethnicities, who realize they are attracted to their same sex, who feel trapped in the wrong bodies, who are on the edge of an affair, whose search history is filled with pornography. People who are being abused, people who are abusing, people who believe divorce is an option, people who believe divorce is never an option, people who know more about modern politics than ancient Scripture, people who are living together because they're terrified of marriage, people who are married who have no clue what they're doing, and people who crack open a beer (or five) every day when they get home from work.

That is us. In the church. In your church. In your home. And—here's my point—not talking is not helping. As awkward and cringeworthy as those conversations can be, avoiding them will not resolve them. In fact, secrecy and shame have a way of making bad things get worse.

SECRECY AND SHAME HAVE A WAY OF MAKING BAD THINGS GET WORSE.

Which is why I'm so happy you picked up this book. For the past decade, I have tried to open the Bible and tackle the toughest, most taboo topics that modern Christians are facing, not with three or four sentences in a sermon but rather with three or four sermons in a series. Since issues of race, relationships, mental health, and sexuality are so complex, I have decided to slow down and spend some time letting God speak grace and truth into the areas of our lives where we feel stuck and don't quite know what to do.

What follows are chapters based on lots of those sermons. And by "lots," I mean lots! I have searched my files to find every taboo sermon I have ever preached in hopes of providing you with a one-stop resource for your toughest questions and your most complicated situations.

Struggling with anxiety? There's a chapter for that. Got a depressed friend? There's a chapter for that. Feeling frustrated by politics (or a family member's idolatry of their preferred political party)? There are chapters on that. Questioning your sexuality? There are even more chapters on that. Did your daughter move in with her boyfriend? Check. Concerned about your brother's relationship with alcohol? Check. Wondering if he's in hell after taking his own life? Check.

I believe you will find the vast majority of the words that follow to be timeless and applicable to the issues you are facing today, tomorrow, and in the years to come.

My prayer is that this book helps you find the message you need when you need it most. There's no rush to read from start to finish (unless you're one of those people). Just jump straight to the topic that you are facing right now or are curious about at this moment. Let Scripture shape your thoughts, guide your actions, and reveal the forgiveness you can know through Jesus.

Talking helps. Even if we are talking taboo. May God bless you as you do.

"All Scripture is God-breathed and is useful for teaching, rebuking, correcting and training in righteousness, so that the servant of God may be thoroughly equipped for every good work" (2 Timothy 3:16,17).

PART 1

ANXIETY, DEPRESSION, AND SUICIDE

Chapter 1

HOW TO DEAL WITH ANXIETY

Not long ago, I had an illogical but emotional experience with anxiety. I was standing in the living room of a good guy who was helping me fix some bad habits with my voice. As I struggled with a few of the exercises, I could feel my brain and body starting to unravel. At one point, I noticed my toes were curled, clenched vertically in my shoes. "You okay?" the guy asked me, but I didn't know what to say besides, "I'm really sorry, but I have to go." I *had* to, and I did. Looking back, there was nothing about it that was logical, but there was something undeniably powerful.

Have you ever felt the power of anxiety? According to the National Alliance on Mental Illness, anxiety is the number-one mental health struggle in America, chronically affecting about 20 percent of adults and a rising number of children.[1] Statistically, in every row at church, every circle of friends, and every extended family are people with anxiety.

Ongoing anxiety is not just the nerves you feel before a first date or a big presentation; it's more like a "what if?" snowflake that snowballs into an avalanche of worry. It's the thought you can't stop thinking, a roller-coaster ride with one loop that never stops—the one that gets stuck in your head and goes around in your stomach and keeps you up at night. Twenty percent of us feel just like that.

And it happens in church too. A lot. Even though Christians know we shouldn't worry, we still do. Even though Christians know we should trust God to take care of it, we still don't. She worries about her safety, even though she's not in any real danger. He worries about dying young, even though he's not actually sick. She worries about being good enough for God, even though she's perfect through Jesus. He worries that his struggle with worry is proof that he isn't really that sorry, and maybe he's not that worthy, and maybe God is that angry.

So, how do you deal with your anxiety? Or theirs? Telling anxious people, "You're fine. It's fine. Just don't worry!" doesn't work. We need more than that. Thankfully, God offers more than that. I want to share a bunch of Bible passages and wisdom from some solid Christians from my church who deal with anxiety most days. Let's learn together how to deal with anxiety.

Two things before we dive in. First, some people have wondered if it is biblical to say that anxiety is sinful or somehow a weakness in our faith. One woman recently reached out and compared anxiety to having cancer, a purely physical struggle that has nothing to do with her sinfulness or holiness. Others have pointed out that a certain type of anxiety is actually a good thing since it drives us to take action to fix a problem. These are fair questions that deserve a biblical response.

The Greek word from the New Testament that we often translate as "anxious/anxiety" can, in fact, be a godly thing. In 1 Corinthians, Paul says that married Christians are "concerned" about how to make their spouses happy and that believers should be "concerned" for each other (7:33; 12:25). If I am concerned that my marriage is struggling and that concern causes me to serve my wife, I am thinking in a God-pleasing way. If you are worried about a member of your family who is straying from Jesus and that worry leads you to pray, reach out, and encourage him to stick with his Savior, God is pleased. To prevent confusion, most translations refer to this state of mind as "concern" rather than "worry" or "anxiety" in order to emphasize the positive nature of this way of thinking.

But that same Greek word most often has a negative/sinful context. It's the kind of worry that doesn't change anything but only spins in our heads and makes us afraid. Or it's the anxiety that focuses on all the terrible things that could happen instead of on the powerful God who is in charge of every detail of our future. That, according to the Scriptures, is a moral no-no. It fits into the "do not" list of God's law, which makes anxiety/worry/fear a sin.

There is, no doubt, a physical component to how our minds work, one that can be affected by medication, as I will mention soon, but that doesn't undo God's will for his children to "not be anxious about anything" (Philippians 4:6). We most often worry when we lose sight of God and all that he has done for us through his Son.

I know that might feel discouraging to you, because your constant battle with anxiety is, therefore, a constant battle against sin, one that you lose more often than you would like. But as I will soon show you, Jesus' grace is always greater than our greatest sins. Therefore, we can have tremendous compassion on fellow Christians who face this struggle, and we can call them to stronger faith and comfort them with Jesus' mercy.

GOD'S WORD CAN HELP US GROW TO KNOW WHAT TO DO AND TO WHOM TO GO WHEN WE FEEL ANXIOUS.

Second, dealing with anxiety is like dealing with impatience, pride, or any other spiritual weakness. It's not a "light switch" fix but instead a process, like how fruit grows and matures slowly over time. So, the next few pages probably won't "cure" anyone's anxiety, but God's Word can help us grow to know what to do and to whom to go when we feel anxious.

Now that we've clarified those two issues, let's get back to God's plan for how to deal with anxiety. First, breathe. This might sound like heresy, but if you're super anxious, it might be better to start with breathing than with your Bible. That's because of your amygdala. Ever heard of it? That almond-shaped thing in your brain appears to be God's way of keeping you safe from danger.

If a roaring lion prowled out in front of you, your amygdala would trigger your body into a fight-or-flight reaction. It would send signals to pump adrenaline into your system, taking blood from your prefrontal cortex and your digestive system and rushing it into your muscles so you could sprint out a door or grab a chair and start swinging at your predator. Because in such terrifying moments, you don't need to do complex thinking or digest your lunch; you need to live!

However, your amygdala is famous for false alarms. It goes off even when there's not a lion within 100 miles. A random thought can trigger the same physical responses, which is why worry makes your stomach ache or prevents you from thinking logically. So, if your brain is freaking out, I could grab my Bible and try to reason with you, but you're not ready to reason. This is why the first step to dealing with your anxiety is breathing. Deep breathing literally uses your nervous system to tell your amygdala: "It's okay. You're okay. You're not running from a lion. You can stop and slow down and think again."

One counselor compared it to a glass jar filled with liquid and glitter. Worry has a way of "shaking the jar," making your thoughts frantically swirl around in your head. That's why you need to breathe. To calm down your glitter. Breathe in . . . and out . . . in . . . and out . . . to prepare your brain for the Bible. Breathe, remembering how the Creator created your body. That's the first step to dealing with anxiety.

Second, pray. There are thirty passages where words like *anxious* or *worry* show up, and two of them specifically tell you to pray. Paul wrote, "Do not be anxious about anything, but in every situation, by prayer and petition, with thanksgiving, present your requests to God" (Philippians 4:6), and Peter added,

"Cast all your anxiety on him because he cares for you" (1 Peter 5:7). Notice God's love for his anxious kids. Your Father doesn't want you to be anxious about anything. He wants you to cast off "all your anxiety." Why? Because he cares that much for you. Your constant worries might wear down your friends, your mom, or your husband, but not God. What a thought! God never gets tired of talking to you. If you're anxious a lot, God isn't rolling his eyes and saying, "You again?" He cares constantly about you. All of you. Every thought. Every time. So, pray and ask him to take your worry away.

BRING GOD INTO THE ROOM. OR BETTER YET, RECOGNIZE THAT HE'S ALREADY THERE. PRAY.

That's what a member of my church family does. There's a woman from my congregation who recently told me that anxiety has been part of her story for a long time. I asked her to tell me how she deals with it, and she gave me permission to share her response. She said that her anxiety was a survival mechanism during her dangerous childhood, but it stuck around even after the danger was gone. How does she fight back? She emailed, "I don't. I don't handle it because I cannot. It is only through Christ that victory is found." I love that. When you're one-on-one with the father of lies, it's hard to win the mental fight. So, bring God into the room. Or better yet, recognize that he's already there. Pray. That's the second step to dealing with anxiety.

The third step is to seek. In the Bible, eight of the thirty uses of worry words show up in Jesus' classic teaching in Matthew 6 and Luke 12, the spots where Jesus says, "Do not worry about your life" (Matthew 6:25) and "Seek first [God's] kingdom and [God's] righteousness" (verse 33). When you get stuck on some terrible thought, seek. "Seek" means to hunt for. To go after. To remember. Seek God's kingdom and God's righteousness.

This is such good news. God's kingdom is where God is the King, where he uses his authority to bless you with safety. As a child of the King of all kings, your Father will keep you safe from all the stuff outside the walls of the kingdom.

The lion might be prowling out there, roaring lies, telling you you're not worthy or that God is angry, but that liar can't take you away from the kingdom. Jesus died on a cross so you would be safe from condemnation—so you would be right here with God and always right with God. That's what his righteousness is, namely, the gift of being right with our Father through the blood of his Son. That gift is yours not because you are such a trusting, perfect Christian but because Jesus was perfect in your place. Let me repeat that: you are right with God, not because you are perfect or your faith is perfect but because Jesus was perfect.

YOU ARE RIGHT WITH GOD, NOT BECAUSE YOU ARE PERFECT OR YOUR FAITH IS PERFECT BUT BECAUSE JESUS WAS PERFECT.

I received good advice from a brother in the faith when I sought guidance on this topic. He said, "Make sure [people] know Jesus loves them even when they're not trusting him as they ought." Neither life nor death, neither the present nor the future, not worries or anxiety, nor anything else in all creation can separate us from the love of God in Christ Jesus. (See Romans 8:38,39.)

This is why Psalm 94:19 is golden: "When anxiety was great within me, your consolation brought me joy." My anxiety might be "great," but God is still here, comforting me with his unfailing love. He's not going to fail me, even if I fail him. He saved me once, and he's coming back to save me from this, to bring me into his heavenly kingdom. Seek passages like that, and you'll find a great way to deal with anxiety.

This brings me to my final point. First, breathe. Next, pray. Then, seek. Finally, group. Stay connected to a group of Christians who can keep you connected to the promises of Jesus.

I loved the email from a fellow Christian who is doing better than ever in fighting her anxiety. Her secret? She answered that question by emailing, "Group, group, group, group, group." (I think she was trying to make a point.) When you're stuck in your own head, it's easy to forget to breathe, to pray, and to seek, but that's why God gave us each other. That's why doing life together and being real with each other is so essential. I might be stuck, but you can snap me out of it. You can bring me back to Jesus.

Proverbs 12:25 says, "Anxiety weighs down the heart, but a kind word cheers it up." A kind word from a friend, pastor, or group is God's way of helping you deal. A friend who says, "Okay, let's breathe for a second." A father who says, "Can I pray that God would take this away?" A group who guarantees, "You're good. King Jesus isn't going to give up on you or give you to the enemy." Group is the supercharged way that God helps us with everything, anxiety included.

So, if you want to deal with anxiety, remember these four steps: Breathe. Pray. Seek. Group. It won't cure anxiety by tomorrow, but it will help.

There is a framed picture that hangs in one of the bedrooms in my home, a visual reminder of how to deal with these battles in our brains. It shows Jesus holding a little lamb in his strong arms and scarred hands, clutching that vulnerable animal close to his heart. When my own family fights those old battles against "what if?!" and "what about?!" we try to fix our eyes on that picture and remember Jesus. We might be so mentally weak, but he is loving and strong. Does that picture "fix" it? Sometimes. Does it keep us closer to Jesus? Always.

May you, in all your faith and fear, believe that Jesus is as close to you as he could possibly be.

STUDY QUESTIONS

1. Evaluate this statement: The church services that are most helpful to anxious people are those that focus on what Jesus has done for us instead of what we should do for Jesus.

2. Study 1 Peter 5:1-11, the context of one of the Bible's most famous passages about anxiety. What do Peter's words add to this chapter's message?

3. Studies suggest that volunteering is a wonderful way to combat anxiety and depression. Scripture adds that serving others is a wonderful way to imitate the servant heart of Jesus. How might you give a bit of your time and talents in the year to come? Pray over that question and ask your Father for guidance.

Chapter 2

GOD'S TO-DOS FOR THE DEPRESSED

The guys had never seen Dan depressed. But after he lost his job, Dan seemed to lose his passion for life. His friends tried their best to help. They invited him out, but Dan stayed in. They texted job openings to help their buddy get back on his feet, but Dan never followed up. They prayed for and with him, but Dan barely mumbled an "Amen." Frustrated, the guys did what any confused Christians would do. They Googled it. "Overcoming depression," they typed into the search bar. That's when they realized what their friend needed to do: Exercise. Eat right. Stick to the medication. Don't drink (depressants don't help the depressed). Volunteer.

After scribbling down their internet findings, Dan's hopeful friends shared Google's wisdom. They pleaded with Dan to listen to their list and act upon it.

Except Dan didn't. His eyes glazed as they lectured him on how to get better. All those to-dos never got done.

Ever been there? Over 8 percent of American adults battle depression every year. I don't mean the cloudy emotional days that we all experience but rather the storm of sadness that clouds the forecast for weeks. Depression comes from the Latin *depressio*, which means "a pressing down," which can result from any number of causes.

Maybe that pressing down runs in your family's DNA, or maybe it surprised you after the birth of your first child. Maybe depression is the snowbird who spends the winter months in your mind. Maybe losing your job or battling cancer or grieving a loss has left you depressed.

If so, I bet you know all about the to-dos that Dan's friends discovered—that long list of things you should do to get your joy back. Do take your Zoloft (there's nothing unchristian about good medicine). Do talk out your thoughts at therapy. Do set goals, even if you don't feel like it. Do exercise, even if you have to wipe the tears off the treadmill. Do eat right, even if you have no appetite. Add to that list all the spiritual steps that Scripture urges us to take. Do attend church and do pray and don't skip your devotions and don't forget God's promises. Do remember the blessings of your baptism. Don't avoid the comfort of the Lord's Supper.

That's good advice. But do you know the problem? When we're depressed, we don't get much done. Mary Keith, a Christian who's battled depression, admits, "I didn't usually trust God, make a gratitude list, or recite Scripture. My shield of faith was often lying next to me on the ground."[1] She knew what to do. It just didn't get done. And all her not-done to-dos made her more depressed.

WHEN WE'RE DEPRESSED, WE DON'T GET MUCH DONE.

That's why in this chapter, I want to share God's to-dos for the depressed. They're found in Psalms 42 and 43, two ancient songs written by what appears to be a depressed believer. In the dim light of his depression, he scribbled a song and then asked his church's director of music to use it. The title of Psalm 42 says, "For the director of music."

Can you imagine that conversation? A man who hasn't shaved in a few days shuffles up to the choir director, hands him a tear-stained papyrus scroll, and mutters, "Have the whole church sing this."

The director glances at the lyrics and nervously replies, "This? I was hoping for something a bit more uplifting."

But God wanted this song sung. His Holy Spirit inspired every chorus and every verse. And in the middle of this minor key, there's a note you need to hear. It's God's to-dos for the depressed.

Psalm 42 starts:

> As the deer pants for streams of water, so my soul pants for you, my God. My soul thirsts for God, for the living God. When can I go and meet with God? My tears have been my food day and night, while people say to me all day long, "Where is your God?" (verses 1-3)

"Where is God? When will I see God?" These are the questions depression forces down our throats. "Where is God right now? Why doesn't God fix this? This marriage, this family, this bankruptcy, this injustice, this cancer, this chemical imbalance?" And like an overheated deer, exhausted from running, panting for water, we thirst for God and his blessings, for anything better than this.

What do you do when your very soul is parched and your faith is dying of thirst? The songwriter knows: "These things I remember as I pour out my soul: how I used to go to the house of God under the protection of the Mighty One with shouts of joy and praise among the festive throng" (verse 4). Ah, that sounds better. The author is, as we would say today, counting his blessings. Shouts of joy. Praise. Worship in God's house. When you count your blessings—forcing your mind to see just how good God has been to you—depression doesn't stand a chance. Right?

Not quite. Did you catch the past tense in verse 4? "I used to. I used to go to the house of God and rejoice. But that was then. This is now."

Maybe you are currently in a dark valley, looking back at the blessings you had in the past. "I used to have a good life. We used to be happy. I used to be healthy. I used to love my work." But then the reality of now erases the blessing of back then, and "used to" presses down on your spirit.

That's when the chorus comes in, the words the author will repeat three times before the song is done. It appears to be his to-do that will fix his depression, so pay close attention. He sings, "Why, my soul, are you downcast? Why so disturbed within me? Put your hope in God, for I will yet praise him, my Savior and my God" (verse 5). This is soul music. He turns and talks to his own soul: "Why are you depressed? Why are you so down? You know what you need to do. Put your hope in God! He's 'my God' and 'my Savior,' my personal Lord and not some distant deity. This is the God who rescued *me* from danger. So, don't forget the day you came to trust in this God. Remember your own salvation story." Do that, and depression doesn't stand a chance.

Or maybe it does. Look at the very next lyric: "My soul is downcast within me" (verse 6). Wait, what? Didn't he just say something about God being his personal Savior? Yeah, but he's still sad. According to this Spirit-inspired verse, depression isn't cured with a catchy chorus. In fact, the rest of the song makes that point. In verse 7, he sings: "All your [God's] waves and breakers have swept over me." "I'm drowning, God, and you send one thing after another. I'm down, then out, then down and out, and you kick me again. I get sick and then broke, and then it goes from bad to worse." (Ever had a season in life when your heart moans, "Seriously, God? You're going to let this happen to me now?")

Things get better in verse 9: "I say to God my Rock." That's a vital truth when your world has been shaken. God is your Rock. Everything in life is shifting sand, but God is faithful and solid. Maybe the author is finding his spiritual footing.

Until the next line reverts to this: "Why have you forgotten me?" (verse 9). "I prayed a thousand times, Father. Did you forget to listen? Did my messages go into your junk mail?"

But before the question pulls him away from God, he jumps back to the chorus in verse 11: "Put your hope in God." Whew. That's better. Until the next verse: "Why have you rejected me?" (Psalm 43:2). Despite all that "my Savior" and "my Rock" talk, the sorrow of his heart outvotes the convictions of his head.

Until he gets back to the chorus: "Put your hope in God" (Psalm 43:5). Back to where we were before and before that.

EVERYTHING IN LIFE IS SHIFTING SAND, BUT GOD IS FAITHFUL AND SOLID.

If the song added a few verses, you can probably guess how they would go. From faith to fear and back to faith. From convictions to accusations and then more accusations and convictions. Psalms 42 and 43 almost seem like they were written by two separate people, one who trusts in God and another who doubts him. Or maybe both people live within us all.

Depression isn't simple. You don't say, recite, or pray the right thing, and depression respectfully leaves. No, depression is a back-and-forth battle that rarely has a quick-and-simple solution.

So, what should I tell you? Pray more? Run to your Rock more? Put your hope in God more? There might be some truth in that biblical list, but how likely are you to get the entire list done? That's why I want to tell you about something better, something that actually works, something that Psalms 42 and 43 offer to the careful reader.

A chiasm.

Ever heard of a chiasm? (I wouldn't be shocked if you haven't, because my computer kept trying to autocorrect it!) A chiasm is a common technique in ancient song writing, a way to express the point of your poetry. In modern pop music, we put the point in the chorus. Justin Bieber sings the same thing seventy-eight times in the chorus until you know the words by heart. In other words, you get the point by noting what is repeated.

But ancient poets would put the point of their messages in the middle. A chiasm is like a song sandwich where all the lyrics are good, but what comes in the middle is the best.

If you look at this song, which covers Psalms 42 and 43, and find the middle, Psalm 42:8, you will discover an essential message—God's to-dos for the depressed.

Check it out: "By day the LORD directs his love, at night his song is with me."

So. Good.

Remember the last time "day" and "night" appeared in this song? When the author ate his own tears day and night (42:3). In the middle of his deep depression, in the midst of all the crying and sleeping and moping, what is the Lord doing? Directing his love.

The Hebrew word "direct" is the same word as "command." God commands us in the Ten Commandments—do this and don't do that. But in this verse, God is commanding his love. God is looking down on his sad sons and his depressed daughters, and he is commanding his unfailing love like a general speaking to an obedient soldier: "Go! Help her! Go! Bless him!" Day and night, 24/7, God is directing love to the depressed. Because God's to-dos are not something you do. They are something God does for you.

Let me repeat that so you don't miss it—God's to-dos for depression are not something you do for God. They are something God does for you.

You, in your weakness, might not get that list done, but God, in his strength, always will.

My youngest daughter has an epic stuffed animal collection. It's mostly sloths, but her favorite by a long shot is an eighteen-inch-tall snuggly, squishy version of Jesus. Nearly every night, my baby girl begs me for a "Jesus story," a Bible story, or a made-up daddy story with Jesus as the star. Most nights, Jesus comes to my daughter to snuggle with her, talk to her, and help her with whatever she is going through. She never has to get out of bed to get to Jesus, because Jesus always comes to her.

GOD'S TO-DOS FOR DEPRESSION ARE NOT SOMETHING YOU DO FOR GOD. THEY ARE SOMETHING GOD DOES FOR YOU.

What I am trying to say—no, what God is trying to say in these psalms—is that heaven sends unfailing love to unworthy people. No one can read Psalms 42 and 43 and say that the author has perfect faith. He wavers like the weather. He doubts as much as he trusts. Yet God, day and night, still sends his unfailing love.

Dear depressed person of God, our Father has not changed. When depression tempts you and me to be doubtful, moody, lazy, foolish, and even accusatory toward our holy Father, God responds with what none of us deserve: his love. If that feels unfair, you are right. It is pure, unadulterated grace. It is love that is unearned and undeserved given by a God who, for some inexplicable reason, is kind to sinners.

But how exactly does God love us in our depression? First, he directs his love through Scripture. Did you ever notice how there is no Bible translation called the NDV: New Depressed Version? Thank God! God is not going to water down his Word even if you spent the morning in the fetal position in your bed. God isn't going to edit his love because you feel unlovable. God's mercy is new every morning, no matter what your emotional state was this morning.

GOD RESPONDS WITH WHAT NONE OF US DESERVE: HIS LOVE.

"Never will I leave you; never will I forsake you" (Hebrews 13:5) is true regardless of how many healthy habits you got done this week. Neither angels nor demons nor anything else in all creation (depression included) will be able to separate us from the love of God that is in Christ Jesus (Romans 8:38,39). The most faithful, reliable way that God directs his love to your heart is through his unchanging promises, which are waiting for you in his Word.

Second, God directs his love through your loved ones. Writer Mary Keith remembers the day when her friends Niccole and Scott showed up at her apartment unannounced. Mary wasn't all that fun to be around due to her mental health, yet her friends still came. "We brought dinner!" they announced with a smile. "You don't want to cook when things are sucky." At night, Mary would cry out to God, "Where are you?" But then she realized, God was there in Niccole and Scott. God was working through her friends, directing his love toward her heart.[2]

If you know someone who is depressed, your presence might be the best present. Be there. Be there when they do something. And be there when they don't. Bear with them. Ask God to give you the faith to love the depressed. Show them, by your presence, the love that has been commanded by heaven itself to reach them in their time of need.

In addition, God directs his love through doctors. Some Christians don't believe that. They believe if you just had enough faith, you wouldn't need medication. But would you tell a diabetic or a friend with a broken leg, "You don't need insulin or a cast—just pray"? No, God directs his healing love through doctors and prescription medication.

Hear me: Taking medicine is not a sign of mediocre faith. By God's grace, we understand better than ever before how the chemicals in our brains function and what can, and often does, go wrong. You don't have to choose between your church and your doctor. You can, with a clear conscience, enjoy the blessings of both.

Finally, and most important, God directs his love through Jesus. Do you remember Jesus' first sermon? In a synagogue in Nazareth, Jesus unrolled the scroll of Isaiah and read chapter 61: "The LORD . . . has sent [Jesus] to bind up the brokenhearted" (verse 1).

To bind up and bandage someone's brokenness, you need to get close to them. That's what Jesus did. He left heaven and came down to be with us when we needed him most. Jesus was a man of sorrows, a Savior who wept and begged his friends to stay with him in his time of greatest need (Matthew 26:38). A day later, like a panting deer, Jesus cried out from the cross, "I am thirsty." Then he questioned, in words that remind us of Psalm 42, "Why, God? Why have you forsaken me? Where are you right now?"

BEING WITH YOU WAS AT THE TOP OF GOD'S TO-DO LIST.

Why did Jesus do that? Why would Jesus suffer all that? So that you would know that your God is willing to meet you in your deepest darkness. There is no place so depressing, not even a shameful cross, where Jesus was not willing to go in order to be with you. Wherever you are and however you are, Jesus is there, the love that God sent down from heaven.

Jesus came to do the Father's will. And the Father wanted you to never be alone. Being with you was at the top of God's to-do list.

A chiasm. I told you it was good. Because when we struggle with depression, what we need most is not a list of things to do. It's a reminder of what God has already done through his only Son.

STUDY QUESTIONS

1. Why do you think God recorded the experiences of depressed believers like Job, Jeremiah, and David in your Bible?

2. Think deeply about Titus 2:11-14. Why is grace the greatest motivator when it comes to doing the right thing, even when we feel down and discouraged?

3. Challenge: Remind a depressed friend about what God has done for them through Jesus.

Chapter 3

TALKING TABOO: SUICIDE

I watched the Netflix series *13 Reasons Why* before I heard about the controversy—before I was aware that the National Association of School Psychologists released its first-ever warning for a television show.

13 Reasons is a show about a girl who commits suicide and leaves behind tapes with all her reasons why. I watched . . . and I wept. I cringed at the bullying and the betrayal and the rumors and the rape, but I cried when Hannah Baker finally did it, a scene so graphic that Netflix edited it out two years after its release. I shook when Hannah's mom walked into the bathroom and found her baby girl bleeding in a bathtub. I thought of my own girls. I thought of my church family. I thought of us.

Because suicide isn't just a show. Suicide is one of the leading causes of death on earth. A majority of suicides involve major depression or substance abuse, but not all. Teenage girls are highly susceptible, but not as much as elderly men, the leading demographic of suicide.

But those stats don't matter as much as our stories. Like my great-grandfather who shot himself when he was exactly my age. Or perhaps your cousin. Or your classmate. Or your uncle. Or the time you tried. Or thought about it. When the depression got dark. When the addiction seemed inescapable. When the affair came to light. Maybe that's why suicide is a taboo topic. It's emotional, personal, vulnerable. It's something we don't share at the meet and greet at church. But the silent treatment isn't treating us well. Because we need compassionate answers to our questions. About heaven and hell. About what to say to someone who wants to. About what to say to ourselves. So, what does God say about all this? Let's open Scripture and try to understand suicide from a biblical point of view.

There are five suicides described in the Bible. For example, King Saul and his armor-bearer, a double suicide found near the end of 1 Samuel. Wounded in battle, Saul is terrified about being captured by his enemies, so he falls on his sword, and his armor-bearer copycats the act. Next comes Ahithophel, a senior adviser to the wannabe king, Absalom. When his advice is ignored, Ahithophel immediately goes home, puts his house in order, and hangs himself. Then Zimri, Israel's seven-day king, flees to his hideout after committing a crime and eventually lights the match that ends his life. Finally, Judas, the guy who betrayed Jesus. Seized with remorse, Judas gives back the bribe to the religious leaders and hangs himself.

What do these stories teach us? That suicide has many causes. Fears about quality of life. Shame after sinful choices. Major reactions to minor events.

Some Christians would also say these stories teach us that everyone who takes his or her own life goes to hell. These five men seem to be unbelievers who didn't have a living and forgiving God to give them a reason to live.

But is that assumption true? Can we say with biblical certainty that anyone who dies by suicide has eternally separated themselves from God? The problem with that interpretation is that these five stories are descriptions, not prescriptions. Do you know the difference? A description describes what happened, right or wrong, true or false, the exception or the rule. A prescription prescribes what God wants, what God thinks, what God desires.

For example, the fact that Jesus was baptized in a river is a description, not God's prescription that all baptisms must be in rivers. Just because Jesus has a friend named Thaddeus doesn't mean you need to find a buddy by the same name, since that is a description and not a prescription of what God wants all Christians to do. Based on that distinction, making blanket statements about heaven and hell based on the five descriptions of Judas and company would be a faulty interpretation.

To get clearer answers, we need to look at clearer passages. Is there any passage that says suicide condemns you to hell? Pastor Kurt Ebert, who later wrote about the tragedy in his family, is interested in that question. He was downstairs when he heard the gunshot. Scrambling to his feet, he ran to the stairs, where he met his son Nathan. Nathan was clutching his chest, pleading, "I'm sorry, Dad. I love God. I'm sorry." And then he died. Did Nathan give up heaven when he pulled the trigger?

The answer—No. Nathan did not miss out on seeing Jesus. Why not? Because suicide is not mentioned, not even a single time in the Bible, as being an unforgivable sin.

SUICIDE IS NOT MENTIONED, NOT EVEN A SINGLE TIME IN THE BIBLE, AS BEING AN UNFORGIVABLE SIN.

It is true that suicide is always a sin, the devastating result of a lack of faith. The question is, which kind of faith does a person lack when they decide to end his or her life—*Faith* (with a capital *F*) in Jesus or *faith* (with a small *f*) in the promises of God? Every Christian knows the difference. Like you, I have Faith in Jesus, but, like you, my worry and fear prove I can lack faith. And just like a lack of small-*f* faith can lead a Christian to worry or fear, it can also lead to despair and suicide. This means a Christian with Faith can be forgiven for his lack of faith, even if the result is suicide.

I think of this distinction in the story of Jesus and the father who had Faith but not enough faith. This desperate dad had a demon-possessed son, leading him to beg Jesus for a miracle. He pleaded, "If you can do anything, take pity on us and help us" (Mark 9:22). Jesus immediately noticed the "if," a subtle sign that this man did not have as much faith as he should have.

After a gentle rebuke, the father responded with a line that is worth memorizing: "I do believe; help me overcome my unbelief!" (Mark 9:24). How can one man "believe" and yet struggle with "unbelief" at the same time? Because there is a difference between Faith and faith, between believing in God and believing everything that God says.

This is a vital truth as we process the tragic deaths of Christians who commit the irreversible sin of suicide. Do they lack faith? Without a doubt. If they perfectly trusted all the promises of God, they never would have ended their own lives. But can we say that they all lacked Faith, that none of them really believed they were sinners saved by the work of Jesus Christ? No. We cannot say that.

JESUS DOESN'T FORGIVE ONLY SOME STUFF BUT ALL THE STUFF, SUICIDE INCLUDED.

That's why there's no asterisk in 1 John. Jesus' friend writes, "If we confess our sins, [God] is faithful and just and will forgive us our sins and purify us from all unrighteousness" (1:9). Catch that word? *All.* Jesus purifies us from *all unrighteousness*. Jesus doesn't forgive only some stuff but all the stuff, suicide included.

But wait. The verse said, "If." If we confess our sins. And not every suicide is like Nathan's, where the final seconds included a remorseful confession. What if you don't confess? What if you don't verbally repent?

Good questions. Let's test that logic with a few examples unrelated to suicide. If, after church, you got into an argument in the car with a family member and, in the middle of your defensiveness and pride, got T-boned by a semi, would you go to hell? You didn't confess your sin just yet, so . . . ? No. Don't panic. Christians don't lose their connection to Jesus every time they sin until they verbally confess that sin to God. If that were true, we would flip-flop between being saved and being lost a hundred times a day!

What proves that you are not a Christian is not that you sinned but that you, as the book of Hebrews says, "deliberately keep on sinning" (10:26). Instead of struggling or wrestling with sin, you just do it. And you don't care. And you're glad you did.

People who commit suicide are committing a sin. But is it possible that a depressed Christian could struggle with suicide and then do it? Absolutely.

When over seven hundred family and friends gathered for Nathan Ebert's funeral, the pastor preached a sermon with this theme: "He did what?" Nathan did what? The pastor's son did what? The preacher didn't dance around the taboo issue. But the sermon ended with a similar question. He did what? Jesus did what? He loved Nathan. He forgave Nathan. He saved Nathan. Yes, yes, he did exactly that. Because all the messiness and darkness of life cannot separate us from the love of God that is ours through Faith in Jesus Christ.

I know Satan could twist what I just said and push you over the edge. "Life is terrible. Heaven is incredible. So, why not?" That's why I want to give you a reason why not. Scratch that. The Netflix show gave us 13 reasons why Hannah Baker did it. I want to give you 13 reasons why you shouldn't. I know depression doesn't like logic, but I want to overwhelm you and your loved ones with reasons why being alive is worth it. Ready?

Reason 1—*God loves you.* God so loved the world that he gave his one and only Son (see John 3:16). Do you know who is in that world that God loves so much? Depressed people. You might feel like no one loves you, like no one cares, but God himself loves you. Your ex might not love you. Your classmates might not love you. You might not love you. But this I know—God loves you.

Reason 2—*God has a plan for you*. Ever heard that coffee-cup verse, "'I know the plans I have for you,' declares the LORD"? You know who wrote that? A depressed prophet named Jeremiah. He once asked, "Why did I ever come out of the womb?" (Jeremiah 20:18). He didn't see the point of his life. But God did. Just think of that famous passage that has inspired countless Christians. A million coffee cups are proof God can work through depression. And God can work through you. He can encourage through you; teach through you; parent, give, and bless through you. He has plans for you.

Reason 3—*This emotion will end for you*. After Pastor Rick Warren's son killed himself, Rick released a video pleading with those considering suicide. Emotions are like waves, he said. They come and sweep over you. But then they pass. No emotion can last forever in this life. That's true. There will be agonizing days and horrible nights, but they won't last forever. The devil wants you to believe it will always be like this, so he urges you to end it. But he is the father of lies, not the lover of life (see John 8:44). The truth is this pain, as unending as it may seem, will pass.

Reason 4—*We would love the real you*. A pastor named Peter Preus never asked for prayers for his depressed wife until after she took her own life. He feared what people would think of the pastor's family. But now he knows. He knows the vast majority of people in the family of God would love the real you. In fact, when members of my church emailed me and described their depression and anxiety, I loved them even more.

Reason 5—*Suicide is sin*. Throughout this chapter, I have intentionally used the phrase "commit suicide" instead of the softer substitute "die by suicide," because suicide is a spiritual crime that breaks the sacred laws of God. "You shall not murder" (Exodus 20:13), God commands, and the murder of yourself is included. "You are not your own; you were bought at a price" (1 Corinthians 6:19,20). You didn't knit yourself together in your mother's womb, so you don't own you. Your life is God's. To begin. To end. Your best life. Your worst life. A quality life. A deteriorating life. It's all God's life. That's why suicide is sin.

Reason 6—*Suicide is selfish*. Most suicidal people don't want to end their lives but instead to end the pain. But suicide does the exact opposite. Suicide passes on the pain with compounded interest. Someone will find you. Someone will blame themselves. Everyone will point fingers at who should have done this and who should have seen that. Someone will live with a thousand questions. Don't do that to them. Love "is not self-seeking" (1 Corinthians 13:5). And suicide is just that.

Reasons 7, 8, and 9—*I need you. We need you. They need you*. As a pastor, I want to help the depressed, the embarrassed, the jobless, and the hopeless at my church. But there are some demons I have yet to fight. So, in order to help them, I need you. The best part of writing this was learning from some trusted friends at church who told me about their thoughts of self-harm. I never knew until they opened up. I'm a better pastor because of their struggle. This is a better chapter because of their stories. I need you to help us.

We need you. You are a uniquely wired, essential member of Jesus' church. Paul writes, "Those parts of the body that seem to be weaker are indispensable" (1 Corinthians 12:22). You might feel weak, but you are like that muscle we don't even know we have until we pull it and realize how important it is.

They need you. In a world where someone is trying to kill themselves every few seconds, they need you. There are people in your family, at your work, in your life who don't have capital-F Faith. They might assume God couldn't love them. They might assume they don't belong in church, because only faithful, joyful, hopeful people can go to church, right? They need you, a living, breathing, walking, talking example that our Father loves his depressed daughters and his broken sons.

Reason 10—*God knows too.* Do you ever feel so overwhelmed with sorrow that you feel like dying? Like it's not safe to be alone? Jesus knows that feeling. The night before his death, he admitted to his friends: "My soul is overwhelmed with sorrow to the point of death. Stay here and keep watch with me" (Matthew 26:38). Jesus has been there. In the darkness. In the pit. Scared. When you pray to Jesus, you pray to a God who gets it, a God who knows. He has been tempted in every way, just as we are. When you cry out, Jesus nods, "Me too. Me too." Jesus knows.

Reason 11—*God is with you.* Maybe your ex isn't with you. Maybe you lost a baby or a spouse. Maybe your good reputation is gone. Or your ability to care for yourself. Or your career aspirations. Or your hopes and your dreams. Maybe they all left you. But not God. "Never will I leave you; never will I forsake you," he promised (Hebrews 13:5). Even in the valley of the shadow of death, your Good Shepherd is with you.

Reason 12—*God's got you.* When King David was in the pit of despair, he cried out, "My times are in your hands" (Psalm 31:15). He knew his drama was in God's hands. And yours is too. I know you don't have this life figured out, but he does. And his hands, the same hands that were pierced for you, are good hands to be in.

Reason 13—*God forgives you.* Do you know the saddest thing about Judas? Jesus had already forgiven him. If he would have waited just two days, he could have gathered with Peter the Denier and Thomas the Doubter. Judas the Betrayer could have discovered forgiveness from the risen Jesus. Because Jesus forgives it all. Maybe you feel shame because of what you did. Maybe you are carrying deep wounds from what happened to you as a kid. Maybe you live with the regret of not doing more, not seeing the signs, not saying something before it was too late. Maybe you feel unforgivable. Not to God. God forgives you. Yes, you.

There are your 13 reasons why life is still worth living. Can I encourage you to come out into the light of confession and community? And when you hear that confession, can I beg you to immerse your loved one in the light? Get help, get medication, get counseling, and give them reasons to live in the light with Jesus.

The Golden Gate Bridge is all too famous for suicide. That's why you will find a sign posted there that reads, "There is hope. Make the call." The church should have a sign like that. There is hope in Jesus. Call upon his saving name. Call out to his followers for help in your time of need. You don't need to hide or fake it. We would love to help and heal and pray for the real you. Suicide does not have to be taboo. We can bring our greatest darkness into the presence of the God who is light.

"In [Jesus] was life, and that life was the light of all mankind. The light shines in the darkness, and the darkness has not overcome it" (John 1:4,5).

STUDY QUESTIONS

1. What was your view of suicide before reading this chapter? Which passages confirmed or changed your thinking?

2. Which of the "13 Reasons Why Not" struck you as especially powerful? How might you use that reason with a suicidal friend?

3. Challenge: If you love someone who has thought about committing or has already attempted suicide, share this message with them. Follow up a few days later to encourage and pray with them.

PART 2

SEXUAL INTIMACY, HOMOSEXUALITY, AND TRANSGENDERISM

Chapter 4

SEX IS GOOD

One night I thought I was being a good Samaritan . . . but actually, I was picking up a prostitute. She was hunched over, shivering on a brutally cold Wisconsin winter night.

"Are you okay?" I asked out of my car window.

"No," she said, "my car just broke down at that gas station."

"Can I give you a lift home?"

"That would be amazing," she said as she hopped into my car.

I said, "Hi, I'm Mike," and we weren't a block down the road when she asked, "So, Mike, are you a freak?"

"Excuse me?"

"Are you a freak? Do you like to have sex?" (Remember that question as I finish this story.)

I said, "Yeah . . . with my wife."

She realized nothing was going to happen, so we talked about life and raising kids until she asked, "So, Mike, what do you do?"

"Well," I smiled, "I'm a pastor."

I wish you could have seen her face. "Just my luck," she groaned. I invited her to church on Christmas Eve, dropped her off, and had an incredible story for my wife the next morning.

Now go back to her question for a second: "Do you like to have sex?" That's a good question. Because it gets to the heart of what sex is. Can a Christian like it? Desire it? Enjoy it? Those are questions that go unanswered for most Christian kids. Because mostly what we hear in Christian churches and homes is "Don't!" or "Wait!" Sex talks are awkward at best and often include shock-and-awe presentations of unwanted pregnancies, incurable STDs, and the addictiveness of porn. In some families, you can't even say the word. Like a curse word, you can only spell it: S-E-X.

The problems of this approach are immense. If all you've heard during your formative years is, "Don't! Sex is sinful! Shameful! Unchristian!" you've literally wired your brain to equate sex with sin. And getting married can't and won't flip that switch. If you've spent decades hearing (or assuming) "Good girls don't do that," then what will you think when you do that? So much of good sex is based on believing sex is good. The best sex is not a series of physical steps but the ability to be naked and unashamed. To be connected and comfortable. To be safe and loved. And none of that can happen unless we believe sex is, by its very nature, good.

YOU'VE LITERALLY WIRED YOUR BRAIN TO EQUATE SEX WITH SIN.

This is why I want to take you back to the place where we first find sex in the Bible. *In the beginning, before there was sin or shame, there was sex.* And that sex was good. Look back at the first chapter of the Bible, Genesis 1: "So God created mankind in his own image, in the image of God he created them; male and female he created them" (verse 27). God made man and woman, Adam and Eve, in his own image. That meant these people were like

God; they were good like God, holy like God, sinless like God. In the beginning, God created two good people.

And guess what he did next? Right after the creation of human beings, the Word says, "God blessed them and said to them, 'Be fruitful and increase in number'" (verse 28). "Be fruitful. Increase in number. Have sex. You're welcome." We go from creation to procreation in one verse. And what does God think about his new creation? Three verses later, we read, "God saw all that he had made, and it was very good" (verse 31). What was very good? All that God made. And what did God make? Sex. Highlight this: SEX IS GOOD.

**WHAT WAS VERY GOOD? ALL THAT GOD MADE.
AND WHAT DID GOD MAKE? SEX.**

This should be obvious, but we have this weird Christian culture that's scared of sex. We see the danger of sinful sex, so we only talk about the sinful side of sex. But there's another side. A good side. A godly side. And that side is where God starts. Just think it through: Who made our bodies? God! Who made the parts of our bodies? God! Who came up with the idea of sex? God! Who invented sexual pleasure? God! If you believe that God is good and if you believe God is the Maker of heaven and earth, then you believe, by your own confession, that sex is good.

A few years ago, a pastor preached a message called "Sex to the Glory of God," encouraging married couples to enjoy sex often as a way to praise and worship God. Sometime after the message, an older couple had the pastor over for dinner. They enjoyed a meal together, and then the wife gave the pastor the token tour of their home. She showed him the kitchen, the family room with the pictures of the grandkids, the basement, and the bedrooms. But she paused outside the master bedroom, smiled at the pastor, and said, "And this is the worship center." Yes! That Christian got it. Sex is not a necessary evil. Sex, when done selflessly between spouses, is worship. A way to tell God how much he is worth.

Nothing proves that point better than Song of Songs. Ever heard of it? It's tucked away in the Old Testament, but you should read it because it proves sex is not just for procreation but for recreation, for connection, for intimacy. Read 1:2: "Let him kiss me with the kisses of his mouth." That's quite an opening line. "Take me away with you—let us hurry! Let the king bring me into his chambers" (1:4). To play *Fruit Ninja*? Nope. For sex. To which their religious friends say in 1:5: "We will praise your love more than wine." No frowns. No shame. "Go for it!" their friends shout.

And then you get to chapter 7: "Your stature is like that of the palm, and your breasts like clusters of fruit. I said, 'I will climb the palm tree; I will take hold of its fruit'" (verses 7,8). How's that for a life verse?! Parents, I know that's a bit much, but do you know what the father in Proverbs 5 said to his son? "May you rejoice in the wife of your youth. A loving doe, a graceful deer—may her breasts satisfy you always" (verses 18,19). And God inspired him to say that!

What's the point? That sex is good. Yeah, we can mess it up. Yeah, we can make it selfish and scarring, but sex is not bad. Or wrong. Or dirty. Or demonic. Sex is from God. And God is good. All the time.

So, what does this mean for you and me? Let's apply this teaching to three groups—singles, married couples, and parents. Singles, be carefully excited about sex. If you're dating or hope to be married one day, it's okay to be excited about sex. In chapter 6 I'll explain the "careful" part, because sex is fiery. For now, be excited. Look forward to it. You can be excited about one day marrying and having kids. And you can be excited about one day marrying and having sex. Because if God blesses you one day with marriage, he's going to show up at your reception, give his blessing to this gift, and smile, "You're welcome."

Married people, learn to see sex as good. If he wants sex or she desires sex, that's good. That's from God. In the next chapter, I'll talk about why good sex takes good work, and why you can't make love without lots of nonsexual love first. For now, start to talk about sex as something good. If talking about your bodies, desires, or this part of your marriage feels awkward, that's okay. There are lots of good resources out there. Read and listen with discernment, but I'd recommend the book *Sheet Music* by Kevin Leman; the book *Friends, Partners, & Lovers* by Kevin A. Thompson; and the podcast called *Sexy Marriage Radio* with Shannon Ethridge. Read, listen, and talk together about the good gift of good sex from a good God.

READ, LISTEN, AND TALK TOGETHER ABOUT THE GOOD GIFT OF GOOD SEX FROM A GOOD GOD.

Parents, if you're married, tell your kids (with a smile) that Daddy and Mommy have sex. Let their first memories of sex not be porn or a playground story. Let it be, "Daddy loves Mommy. Mommy loves Daddy. Daddy and Mommy love sex." Of course, it will get awkward. When puberty hits, and you try to talk about sex, your teenagers will want to stab themselves in the eardrum with a butter knife—but they will listen. And they will remember. And when they see some cheap version of sex, some idiot who wants sex without love, they will remember what they've seen and heard at home their whole lives. Sex is something for people who have vowed to love and respect and say, "You first" until death do us part. That's what makes sex so good. Parents, scrap "the talk" and start to talk about sex. Your children, before you know it, will need it.

But no matter who you are, please know this: sex is not just good; *sex is forgivable*. If you've made bad choices with God's good gift of sex, there's grace and forgiveness for you from Jesus. I know that because of a story Jesus told about a man who didn't just pick up a prostitute but had sex with her. And not just once. But when he came home to his father, alone and ashamed, when he confessed, "Father, I have sinned," Jesus said the father ran to his son and hugged him. He threw a feast and forgave him. The kid came home dirty and ended up dancing.

Do you know why Jesus told that story? So that the sexual sinners in his "church" would know they were forgiven. And you are too. Confess your sins to Jesus, sexual sins included, and you can end up dancing. No guilt. No shame. No scarlet letter. Just grace. Just mercy. Just Jesus.

STUDY QUESTIONS

1. What did your parents and/or your church teach you about sex when you were growing up? Did they prepare you to recognize sex as a good gift from a loving God? If so, how? If not, why not?

2. Read Song of Songs and underline all the passages that prove that sex is a good gift from a great God.

3. On average, kids in America will be exposed to hardcore pornography by age eleven. Before their first click happens, what would you want to teach your children/nieces/nephews/etc. so they see porn as a pathetic substitute to the amazing gift God desires sex to be?

Chapter 5

SEX IS WORK

There are three good reasons to talk about sex—because the world is, because parents aren't, and because God does.

The world teaches us so much about sex, most of it foolish, fictional, and dangerous. And most of our parents didn't teach us much about sex besides "Don't!" or "Wait!" But God says so much about sex. On the first page of the Bible, God brings up sex, and things get steamy in Song of Songs. God gave the gift of sex and said, "It is very good." That's our biblical foundation.

But you know sex isn't always good, even in marriage. I sent a survey about sex to my church members and asked, "If you could ask God any question about sex, what would you ask him?" The most common response was this: "Why are we so sexually different? Why does one spouse want sex more than the other?" Multiple people asked, "Why do guys want sex so much more?" It's not always the husband with the higher desire, but in almost every couple, there is one who wants more sex than the other.

Which is a huge issue. There's something unique about sex that's so personal and powerful and emotional. When two people are on two different pages, sex can stop being good. The higher desire can feel rejected, disrespected, ignored, even unloved. If he or she is the only one who initiates sex, that person might wonder if he or she is desirable, attractive, or good enough. At the same time, the lower desire can feel pressured, exhausted, constantly trying but never satisfying. A couple with different desires can feel broken, messed up, and incompatible.

A COUPLE WITH DIFFERENT DESIRES CAN FEEL BROKEN, MESSED UP, AND INCOMPATIBLE.

Our culture doesn't help. The world of music and movies and Netflix shows us lots of sex, and that sex is easy. One flirtatious look, one raised eyebrow, one innuendo, and—boom—sex is happening. One author calls this "fiction sex," but the world doesn't warn us that way. Instead, it suggests good sex is natural, biological, eventual. So, when sex turns out to be challenging or frustrating, you start to wonder what went wrong.

I get that. Trust me. My wife said I could share this: The hardest part of our marriage has been this difference in desire. We have an amazing marriage—can I brag about it to God's glory? We try to pray every day, date every week, get away every quarter, and vacation every year. I make her breakfast every day. She packs my lunch before work. We are on the same page with parenting, money, faith, and family. By God's grace, neither of us has endured sexual abuse, and both of us were virgins until our wedding night. But guess where we were seven years into our marriage? A counselor's office. For what? To figure out how we could love each other so much but be so different when it came to sex. Over the years, we've learned so much and grown so much closer. Here's what I really want you to know, even to expect: SEX IS WORK. Good sex—true connection, intimacy, and pleasure—is work.

That's what the very first recorded sex in Scripture says. In the last chapter, we saw the invention of sex on page 1 of the Bible: "Be fruitful," God told Adam and Eve. "Multiply and make babies. Be naked but not ashamed." But we don't hear of sex actually happening until a few pages later. And the way God describes it is everything. Look at Genesis 4:1: "Adam made love to his wife Eve." He made love. He didn't just have sex or (how would the kids say it?) get it on or get some or do the nasty or have relations or make whoopee or bow-chicka-wow-wow (man, we have a lot of ways to talk about sex!). No, Adam made love. There is no good sex without love. Love is patient, love is kind, love is not self-seeking, love always protects, and love always perseveres. Love does what is best for the other, no matter what. (See 1 Corinthians 13.) Sex is bad when it's not good love. Which is why Adam made *love* to his wife.

But there's more. This passage was originally written in Hebrew, and the Hebrew literally says, "Adam yadah'd his wife." *Yadah* literally means, "He knew." It's the same verb as to know the answer to a question. Adam knew his wife, Eve. That's how the Jews would talk about sex. He knew her. The first time we see sex in the Bible is not just about pleasure or passion; it's about knowing someone.

This is why one author tells college students, "Your parents are better at sex than you are." That gets their attention! "My parents? Ew. No way." Why would the students say that? Why would they think they know more about sex than their parents? Because their world has taught them that sex is acrobatics, not intimacy; the shape of your body and not the state of your mind. No one has told them that the best sex is when a man "yadahs" his wife. Something that takes time, honesty, listening, forgiveness, and love.

Think of it like this. I've never played a violin before. Ever. I've never even held one. I've seen people play violins. I've even Googled "tips for playing violin." But if I picked up a violin and started playing, would it sound good? Of course not! We would never expect that. So why do we expect it from sex? Why would we use the phrase *honeymoon sex* as slang for the best sex ever? Why would we think hormones, passion, and danger would make sex better than knowledge, practice, and love? No, God says Adam knew her. He knew her. That's what made sex good.

GOD SAYS ADAM KNEW HER. HE KNEW HER. THAT'S WHAT MADE SEX GOOD.

If you're married, I won't be giving many tips on good sex in this book, but I will say this: With sex, knowledge is power. Powerful sex happens when you know your spouse. When you've studied her for years. When you've learned what makes him tick. When is she most energetic and interested? In the morning? At night? After working out? When is she the least distracted? After her to-do list is done? After the kids are in bed? How spontaneous is he? Do you need to just go for it or give her time to prepare? Does talking or praying or cuddling make her more intimate? Does a flirty text during his workday spice things up? Is she a slow cooker or a microwave? Is his love language a compliment posted on Facebook or a back rub after work? Does doing her chores before she gets home (a.k.a. "chore play") make her more interested in sex? Does she need tons of affirmation of her beauty after kids have changed her body? Is he battling depression because of work stress and needing a morning distraction? This is what it means to "yadah": "I know you. Through the years, I know who you are and how you think and the best way to serve you, to love you. Which is why I know how to make love to you."

By the way, if you're dating, God wants you to start thinking about sex. This isn't just a time of "Don't!" and "Wait!" This is a time to learn, to study, to gain knowledge about yourself and maybe your future spouse. Talking and loving and serving one another in nonsexual ways gets you ready to, one day, have really good sex.

This reminds me of that turkey. A few years ago, I was on a field trip in Green Bay and saw these female turkeys pecking seeds for lunch. And who shows up during the meal? Tom Turkey. I should have taken a picture because old Tom came in strutting—chest all swollen and feathers out. He strutted past all the ladies, did a 180-degree turn, and strutted past them again. And guess what? They didn't even look. Not a single lady turkey stopped eating! No lovin' for Tom that day. He didn't "know" those ladies very well.

Men, don't be that turkey. We dudes think taking off our shirts and flexing will do the trick, but that's because we're not "yadahing." We're forgetting that for most women, sex is mental. They have things on their minds, projects to finish, problems to think through. So, serve her well, and she can relax and let go, which is what makes sex good. Ladies, this is true for you too. Most men are visual. You can work like mad to have a beautiful home and a great family, but most men are visual. The way to our hearts is not through our stomachs. It's through our eyes. Remember that, and you can "yadah" your husband.

Now I'm not just squeezing this idea out of one little word in Genesis 4; Paul makes a similar connection in Ephesians 5. On the other end of your Bible, Paul (who was joyful and satisfied despite not having sex, by the way) connects sex with serving one another. Paul quotes Genesis 2: "For this reason a man will leave his father and mother and be united to his wife, and the two will become one flesh" (Ephesians 5:31). *One flesh* is a reference to the sexual and emotional union of husband and wife. But back up a few verses, where Paul writes this: "In this same way, husbands ought to love their wives as their own bodies" (verse 28). Men, how much do you love your bodies? Answer: A lot. You know your body, and you serve your body well. You know when your body is hungry or thirsty or cold or hot. And so you go to the kitchen, pour a glass of water, grab a sweatshirt, or roll down the windows. You "love" your body by meeting its wants and needs as soon as possible, which is how a husband is to love his wife. He comes to know what she wants, what she needs, and then tries to meet those needs and fulfill those wants as soon as possible. So before Paul gets to one-flesh sex, he talks about love.

Which is how wives love their husbands. Ephesians 5:21: "Submit to one another out of reverence for Christ." *Submit* means to put someone else first. Put him first. Learn what makes him feel loved and how he likes to make love, and put him first. That's the good work that leads to good sex.

Which I think is the answer to the questions: Why are sex drives so different? Why does he want it more? Why aren't we exactly the same? Here's my answer: So you can (make) love. Just like different personalities, different communication styles, and different strengths force us to choose to love, sex is often the same way. Your spouse might be more or less interested than you are. Which makes sex your chance to love, to show how much she means to you, to serve him well. There are few things that matter more to God than loving your neighbor as yourself, even if your neighbor is the one you married.

But I can't finish this chapter until I talk about the most important teaching of all: *Sex is forgivable*. Because of Jesus, a virgin born of a virgin, sex is forgivable. Thank God. Because there are those who didn't do the work. And sex was not good. Not to God. We didn't do the work of waiting for marriage, waiting for God's timing. We didn't do the work of loving and serving, and we rushed it and pressured her. We didn't do the work of prioritizing and initiating, and he felt dismissed.

So many of us have sinned sexually. But sex is forgivable. Paul told me so. Paul can't help but tell his Christian friends (who had major sexual baggage!) about Jesus. "Husbands, love your wives, just as Christ loved the church and gave himself up for her to make her holy, cleansing her by the washing with water through the word, and to present her to himself as a radiant church, without stain or wrinkle or any other blemish, but holy and blameless" (Ephesians 5:25-27). The "church" is everyone who believes in Jesus as his or her Savior. Jesus gave himself up for you. Jesus made you holy. Jesus cleansed you in Baptism and washed away every sexual sin. Jesus presented you radiant, not broken or unworthy. Jesus sees you without stain or wrinkle or blemish. Jesus declares you holy and blameless.

MANY OF US HAVE SINNED SEXUALLY.
BUT SEX IS FORGIVABLE.

Which means when you see him, he won't blame you. He won't shame you. Because he already forgave you. Because Jesus did the work on the cross, the work of waiting and sacrificing and serving. He knew what we needed: someone to deal with our sins. He knew it, and he loved us enough to give it. So, yes, sex is good. And, yes, good sex takes work. But know this: no matter how good or bad sex has been for you, sex is forgivable.

STUDY QUESTIONS

1. Think of the last depiction of sex you saw in a movie or television show. What did it teach you to expect about the ease/difficulty of good sex? Did the people involved "know" each other, love each other, and respect each other? If not, why didn't the producers script sex more accurately?

2. Agree/Disagree: Selflessness is the key ingredient to good sex.

3. Read Ephesians 5:25-27. What word from those verses would bring the most comfort to someone who feels ashamed for messing up God's plan for sex?

Chapter 6

SEX IS FIERY

Now I want to write about why, when it comes to sex, Christians are so different. I don't have to tell you that, right? Nowhere is the gap between Christians and our culture more obvious than in the bedroom. While they find common ground on certain aspects such as consent, age, and possibly adultery, their perspectives diverge on nearly everything else.

Can you hook up with no-strings-attached sex? Can you explore your sexuality through pornography? Can dating couples have sex? Or engaged couples? Culture says, "You can! You should!" But Christianity dares to say, "Not yet. Not until your vows. Sexual pleasure is a good gift that God only gives to a man and his wife." Which sounds crazy, right? Poor Christians are missing out on all the fun. No wonder people assume we're against sex.

By the way, this isn't new. Two thousand years ago, Christians were called out for being sexually different. Demosthenes, a writer from the fourth century B.C., described what that culture was like: "We have [concubines] for pleasure, female slaves for our daily care [sex] and wives to give us legitimate children." But not Christians. One man. One woman. One flesh. That's it. One critic of Christianity noted the difference: "[The Christians] share their food but not their wives." So followers of Jesus have always been different when it comes to sex.

But just because it's clear in Jesus' teaching doesn't mean it's easy for Jesus' people. For some of my church family, this has been the hardest part about following Jesus. There are desires and urges that feel like needs. Saying no to lust, porn, premarital sex, and adultery can be agonizing. Trying to tell your date what you believe about sex can be a fast way to end a relationship. Working not to end up in the same place with your girlfriend is a struggle, a battle, a war. So why would God do that?

JUST BECAUSE IT'S CLEAR IN JESUS' TEACHING DOESN'T MEAN IT'S EASY FOR JESUS' PEOPLE.

If sex is God's good idea and a way to find pleasure and connection, why would God limit sex for so few people to enjoy? Why would God ask us to live up to standards so few of us could keep? Why would Jesus ask you to be so different?

Good questions. And, because I read every single Bible passage that uses the words *sex* or *sexual*, I found a good answer. There are seventy-seven total, almost evenly split between the Old and New Testaments, written to believers living in B.C. Canaanite culture and A.D. Greek/Roman cultures. And guess what I found? All seventy-seven passages are . . . warnings!

There are lots of positive ways the Bible talks about sex, but when the word *sex* is used, 100 percent of the time God is warning us about the dangers of sex outside of marriage. Here's the point I want to explore: SEX IS FIERY.

In other words, God thinks about sex like the fireplace in my house. We love making fires in our family room. The look of the flames. The warmth of the fire. A good fire on a cold night is the best. But that same fire scares me. When the fireplace door is swung open, I get nervous. Are my kids far enough away from the hot glass? Is there anything close that could catch fire? These concerns are not unfounded. Because fire is wild. The same thing that warms and comforts also catches and destroys, so I fear the fire. I know people who've gotten burned, who lost everything in a house fire, so I'm careful with it. As a father, I have rules about who can make a fire in our house and when and how. Not because fire is bad, but because fire is fiery.

Just like sex. Is sex bad? No. Should Christians never have sex because it might turn out bad? No. But should Christians have a healthy fear of sex wherever, whenever, with whomever? Absolutely. A loving Father wouldn't design it any other way. That's why I want to share three of the seventy-seven reasons why our Father warns us about sex. Like the passages, this will be pretty heavy, but my prayer is that, despite the challenge of obeying, and our regular need of forgiveness, you will trust God's countercultural design for sex.

The first passage comes from the book of Proverbs, which is an Old Testament book of wisdom. Proverbs portrays how wise people live. And Proverbs talks a lot about sex. In fact, for nearly three entire chapters, a dad talks to his kids about sex. He affirms that sex is good (actually telling his son to enjoy his wife's body and be intoxicated by their love). But mostly this dad warns about sex gone bad. Here's what he says about adultery: "Can a man scoop fire into his lap without his clothes being burned? Can a man walk on hot coals without his feet being scorched? So is he who sleeps with another man's wife; no one who touches her will go unpunished" (Proverbs 6:27-29). Notice the logic here. "I love you, son. I don't want to see you get burned. But sexual sin will burn you."

Why does this dad say this to his son? Why does he repeat it in Proverbs 5, 6, and 7? Why did God inspire so much ink on this one topic? A previous pastor at my church had this saying that stuck around, even years after he left. "STP = LTP." Know what that means? Short-Term Pleasure = Long-Term Pain. Yeah, it will feel good now. It's sex! But the pleasure won't last. The consequences, however, will. This dad mentions shame, disgrace, and the fury of those who are hurt by our sexual sin. Why is God so restrictive? Because sex can hurt you.

Ever experienced that? Maybe you messed around with someone's boyfriend in high school, and it amplified the drama in *your* life. Maybe you were just having fun, and *you* ended up with a STD. Maybe you didn't plan to get pregnant, but *you* did. Maybe you believed your porn was private, but then *you* got caught or *you* got hooked or *you* didn't really know how real sex worked. Maybe you gave your body to someone who wasn't willing to work, serve, respect, or protect you, and he broke *your* heart. Maybe *you* really messed up your family. Maybe *you* felt the shame of saying yes when you should have said no.

Many years ago, I taught a class of teens about sex. And, of course, one of the students brought a friend, his first time ever at our church (I'll call the friend Keandre). I didn't know Keandre's story or background, but I sensed he didn't know much about the Bible. The whole time I taught, I wondered what he thought about the Bible and sex. (I remember reading Song of Songs and seeing the expression on his face!) But when I paused and asked for questions, Keandre's hand went up.

"Yes?" I dared to ask.

"Pastor," Keandre shared, "the world would be better if everyone followed that. There would be no families who don't have a dad around and no people having kids before they're ready."

Wow . . . this kid didn't know a lot about Christianity, but he knew our culture's habits hurt us.

Which is what God sees. Sure, some unmarried people could have sex and have fun. These proverbs aren't promises of stuff that happens every time. They are probabilities. I'm positive there are times when two people have sex and don't get hurt. Just like there are times when you leave the fireplace door open and the flames don't spread. Just like there are times you don't wear your seatbelt and are just fine. Just like there are times you don't look both ways yet cross the street in one piece. But God's mercy doesn't negate his wisdom. Because when we all think we'll be fine, when we all feel like we'll be the exception to God's rules, when we're convinced we'll just have fun and no one will get hurt, we do get hurt. Lots of us do.

But not just us. Sex can hurt others too. Check out God's second reason for being sexually cautious: "It is God's will that you should be sanctified: that you should avoid sexual immorality; that each of you should learn to control your own body in a way that is holy and honorable, not in passionate lust like the pagans, who do not know God; and that in this matter no one should wrong or take advantage of a brother or sister" (1 Thessalonians 4:3-6).

GOD WANTS US TO LEARN SEXUAL SELF-CONTROL.

God wants us to be sanctified, which means set apart from our culture, distinct and different like Jesus. God wants us to learn sexual self-control (and he said *learn* because that's not natural for most of us). God doesn't want us to see sex like pagans. Why not? Because "in this matter" (sex), you can wrong a brother or a sister. In other words, sexual sin doesn't just hurt you. Sex can hurt them.

The biggest fear I had about talking on the subject of sex at our church was the kinds of people who would hear it. Maybe a twenty-year-old guy would be really interested in the subject, but what about the seventy-year-old woman watching on TV? However, my fear dissipated after I asked people to email Time of Grace with any questions they might have about sex. Want to guess who emailed the most? Older women. Email after email of heartbreaking stories of sex that hurt. And I should have known that. Because that seventy-year-old woman was twenty when the sexual revolution was hot and heavy, when America decided to keep the fire but dismantle the fireplace. And people got burned.

Maybe you know this pain. Is there anything that comes close to the hurt caused by sexual sin? The affair, the addiction, the abuse? According to the National Sexual Violence Resource Center, 81 percent of women and 43 percent of men reported some form of sexual harassment or assault in their lifetimes.[1] And that's just sexual violence. Add pornography to the mix. Sit with me in my office as she cries, "I thought he was attracted to me." See the looks in their eyes as they try to recover from another relapse discovered in the search history. Porn kills. Because sex can hurt. Your short-term pleasure can cause long-term pain.

But the biggest victim of sex isn't them or you. It's God. Look at the third reason: "Therefore God gave them over in the sinful desires of their hearts to sexual impurity for the degrading of their bodies with one another. They exchanged the truth about God for a lie, and worshiped and served created things rather than the Creator" (Romans 1:24,25). For the sake of sex, some of us give up God. We worship a created thing—sex—instead of the Creator—God. We trust in sex to make us happy instead of God. And that's how sex becomes our god. Sex can hurt him.

The worst thing that can happen in the bedroom is that you close your Bible—you stop listening to God. You exchange his truth for your truth, his wants for your wants, his Word for your word. And if someone tries to talk to you about the affair, the sex before marriage, the dating history, or your sexual identity, you won't hear it. Not even if Jesus said it. That's the proof. It's the proof you don't like sex or even love sex; you worship it. When you refuse to let the Lord get the last word, you are a sex slave. And, unless you change, you cannot be set free.

So why would we change? Why would we let Jesus have the last word on sex? Why would we trust our heavenly Father if this Christian way is crazy? If the three reasons I've given don't convince you, here's something better: *Sex is forgivable*. When Jesus, who is God, came to this earth, he didn't hurt you. Despite all your sins, doubts, and sexual failures, he didn't hurt you. Instead, he loved, forgave, and died for you.

THE WORST THING THAT CAN HAPPEN IN THE BEDROOM IS THAT YOU CLOSE YOUR BIBLE—YOU STOP LISTENING TO GOD.

That's what I want to tell the twenty-year-old who emailed me with her story: *"My boyfriend and I are both continuously going to church together, setting boundaries, seeking help, reading the Word together, and praying together; yet we keep engaging in sex, which leaves us both frustrated and convicted. . . . I feel dirty, guilty, and just unworthy of what God has for me. . . . I just don't know how God sees us right now, and I just feel so ashamed and like God is upset with us. Does he forgive people who keep engaging in the same sin although they claim to love him and follow him?"* Does God forgive people like that, people like you and me?

Despite the dark, rebellious part of our pasts, Jesus loves us. His cross put our sins to death, and his resurrection from the dead reconnected us to God. What Jesus did for us was so powerful and so perfect that this is how God feels about us. He is not ashamed. Not embarrassed. Not fed up. He knows your story, yet his love is unstoppable and unconditional. Christ gave himself for the church to make her holy, to make us so flawless God himself could delight in us.

Know this: Christianity is different from our culture. Not just with sex, but with salvation. Jesus may be cautious with sex, but he is crazy generous with forgiveness. And grace. And mercy. And patience. And love. God knows this is hard, but our Father knows what's best for us. And the proof is in his Son, the Savior, who went through short-term pain so we can have eternal pleasure. Yeah, it might be hard to deny ourselves, to keep fighting, keep repenting, but where else would we want to be except with Jesus?

STUDY QUESTIONS

1. Study 1 Corinthians 6:12-20. List at least three reasons why Paul is so cautious about sexual immorality.

2. Evaluate this statement: The Bible sets people up for guilt and shame by having such a high standard for sexual purity.

3. Spend some quality time meditating on Proverbs 5 to 7, three chapters written by a caring father to his beloved son. Imagine that the father is your Father and that the son is you, God's child. How do these chapters reveal God's heart for you when it comes to his strict boundaries on sexual pleasure?

Chapter 7

GAY & GOD: DIFFERENT DOESN'T DETER LOVE

The email said it all: "Hey, Pastor . . . When I was 14, I came out as a lesbian. Today I have an amazing marriage and want to start a family. I want my children to grow up in the church and hear God's Word. I would like to know if my wife and I and my future children are welcome [at your church]."

This email and this woman are why I needed to write about this topic and why you and I need to really take a look at it. Because this isn't just about wedding cakes, county clerks, and the latest celebrity who comes out as nonbinary. It's about people. People like the writer of this email. People God loves. It's about the young gay man who loves to go to church—is he welcome? It's about the flesh-and-blood brother of one of our brothers in the faith—should we celebrate his coming out or call it sin? It's about the lesbians who want to adopt—what will this chapter say about their love? LGBTQ+ people aren't "out there." They're here. They're us. They're the ones we love.

But the answer to this email is not so simple. Not in this divided-down-the-aisle debate. Is she welcome at church?

"Well, everybody can come."

"But you have to judge her sin, right?"

"But how can it be sin if God made her gay?"

"God didn't make her gay. She chose it."

"No, she didn't. And didn't Jesus say, 'Don't judge!'?"

"But Jesus also said, 'Repent'!"

"But John 3 says God loves the world."

"But Leviticus 18 says it's an abomination."

"But Leviticus also says you can't eat shrimp!"

"You're ignoring the passages."

"You're ignoring the people."

With reasons like this on both sides of the debate, I think God feels like Stretch Armstrong, pulled to opposite extremes.

Here we are in the middle of the debate, the one about being gay and what God thinks about it. For the next four chapters, that's what we're going to do. But before we open a Bible and dig deeper, I need to tell you four things:

First, I'm not winging this. I'm not copying and pasting a sermon I heard about Sodom when I was a kid. No, I have dedicated countless hours to studying the passages, surpassing the attention I have given to any other written or preached material. I've read eight books on this subject written by straight conservatives, gay conservatives, gay liberals, and former liberal lesbians who are now straight conservatives. I have interviewed six pastors, five of whom believe homosexuality is not a sin. I have dialogued with members of Rainbow Over Wisconsin and Positive Voice, pro-LGBTQ+ organizations. All were incredibly gracious to a total stranger, and I want to portray their beliefs in an equally gracious way.

Second, for full perspective, you have to read all four "Gay & God" chapters. To read one chapter would not be fair to you, me, or God. So please give this topic the priority it desperately needs in your heart because God needs you to love his people and passages more deeply than you ever have before.

GOD NEEDS YOU TO LOVE HIS PEOPLE AND PASSAGES MORE DEEPLY THAN YOU EVER HAVE BEFORE.

Third, in full disclosure, in 1999 in Waunakee, Wisconsin, I kissed a girl. It was my first kiss. The only woman I've kissed besides my wife. A month later, that woman came out as a lesbian. I've kissed two girls. One married me. The other married a woman. I don't know what to make of that, but I thought you should know.

Finally, *I know this matters*. Remember that email from the lesbian seeking a home church? Her email won't let me forget how much this matters. To tell a woman in love that God doesn't like her love is no small thing, and to tell billions of Christians over the past two thousand years that they were wrong about God is no small thing. This is about God and it's about people, and there's nothing more important than God and his people. Agreed?

Now, let's talk about love. Jesus once said, "Everyone will know that you are my disciples, if you love one another" (John 13:35). That's why the book *unChristian* by David Kinnaman unsettles me. It's the published results of a survey done of thousands of sixteen- to twenty-nine-year-old non-Christians.

When asked what phrases describe present-day Christianity, 75 percent said, "too involved in politics," 85 percent "hypocritical," 87 percent "judgmental," and—the number-one answer—91 percent agreed "anti-homosexual." The authors conclude, "The primary reason outsiders feel hostile towards Christians . . . is not because of any specific theological perspective [including sexuality], [but] our 'swagger.' . . . They say their aggression simply matches the oversized opinions and egos of Christians. . . . We have become famous for what we oppose, rather than who we are for."[1] One gay pastor whom I met said the same thing: "Mike, for most gay people, the church is public enemy number one."

That's why we need to start with an old, old story about love, a story about a very religious man who loved people and loved these passages, or so he thought.

Check out Luke 10 with me: "On one occasion an expert in the law stood up to test Jesus. 'Teacher,' he asked, 'what must I do to inherit eternal life?'" (verse 25). The person asking here is an "expert in the law," a Bible passage protector, a guy who thought about God all day long. He wants eternal life. He wants to be good enough to go to a better place and be with a perfect God. So he asks, "Jesus, what do I do?"

"'What is written in the Law?' [Jesus] replied. 'How do you read it?'

"He answered, '"Love the Lord your God with all your heart and with all your soul and with all your strength and with all your mind"; and, "Love your neighbor as yourself."'

"'You have answered correctly,' Jesus replied. 'Do this and you will live'" (verses 26-28).

The expert recites a passage from Deuteronomy: "Love God with everything you are" and a passage from Leviticus: "Love them like you love yourself." Bingo! Jesus smiles: "Keep loving God like that and people like that and you will live forever."

The expert in the law nods, but then he pauses because his conscience has a question: "But he wanted to justify himself, so he asked Jesus, 'And who is my neighbor?'" (verse 29). Don't call this guy a weasel just yet, because he's thinking of the passage. The passage he quoted says this: "Do not seek revenge or bear a grudge against anyone among your people, but love your neighbor as yourself" (Leviticus 19:18). Among *your* people. The Jewish people.

Most Jews saw a loophole in the love passage. They quoted those words—*among your people*—so many times they believed they didn't have to love other people. Gentiles, non-Jewish people? Oh no. Gentiles were different, unclean, impure. Or Samaritans? Israel's neighbors to the west were different ethnically, morally, and sexually. They were different. John 4:9 actually admits, "Jews do not associate with Samaritans." Why not? Because they were different, and the passage says, "Love your people." People like me. Right, Jesus?

"In reply Jesus said: 'A man was going down from Jerusalem to Jericho, when he was attacked by robbers. They stripped him of his clothes, beat him and went away, leaving him half dead'" (Luke 10:30). A guy gets jumped. He's outnumbered and alone, bullied and beaten, abused and embarrassed. But thankfully—whew!—thankfully, two God-fearing men are on their way, men who love the passages about loving people. A priest, a full-time church worker, is coming. And a Levite, an assistant to the priests, is right behind him. Help is on the way!

"A priest happened to be going down the same road, and when he saw the man, he passed by on the other side. So too, a Levite, when he came to the place and saw him, passed by on the other side" (verses 31,32). They both passed by. Why? Was it because the man was different? Dirty to their clean? Naked to their clothed? Dangerous to their safety? We don't know why they didn't love him, but we know they didn't.

> "But a Samaritan, as he traveled, came where the man was; and when he saw him, he took pity on him. He went to him and bandaged his wounds, pouring on oil and wine. Then he put the man on his own donkey, brought him to an inn and took care of him. The next day he took out two denarii and gave them to the innkeeper. 'Look after him,' he said, 'and when I return, I will reimburse you for any extra expense you may have.'" (verses 33-35)

The Samaritan saw him, and yeah, the beaten man was different. But different didn't deter the Samaritan. He took pity on the man. He went to him. He helped him. He interrupted his schedule for him. He spent money on him. He went over and above for him. The man on the side of the road was different, but that didn't deter the Samaritan's love. That's why this was a good Samaritan.

So Jesus asks, "'Which of these three do you think was a neighbor to the man who fell into the hands of robbers?' The expert in the law replied, 'The one who had mercy on him.' Jesus told him, 'Go and do likewise'" (verses 36,37). How do you get eternal life? You love God and you love people. Which people? All people. In other words, if you want life with God, don't let *different* deter your love.

Do you love your neighbors? All of them? That question makes me think about my first year at seminary. My unofficial job at the seminary was to make people laugh. Three buddies and I would make up songs and skits and entertain the students at lunch. One day I wrote a song that took a shot at another seminary student's sexual orientation. I can still remember it. I expected the laugh that edgy humor sometimes gets. But the guys didn't laugh; they hissed. When the song was done, the classmate left with tears in his eyes.

It wasn't the first sin. My school years were filled with gay jokes; limp-wristed, lisping impressions of gay men; foul uses of *fag* and *dyke* and "That's gay." I mocked and joked and stood around while others did the same. I was the expert in the law. I read my Bible every night, and I wore a WWJD bracelet for my senior pictures. I wonder if I wore it when others needed help and I passed by on the other side? Oh, I loved *some* people, "my people," but not all people, not different people.

DO YOU LOVE YOUR NEIGHBORS? ALL OF THEM?

And you? Are you like me, like the priest in Jesus' story, who does nothing when others are shaming a girl because she might not like boys? Are you like me, like the Levite in Jesus' story, who just passes by when transgender kids are hurting because you don't want to get your holy hands dirty? Are you like me, like the robbers in Jesus' story, who strip gay men of their joy and rob them of their dignity when you look at them with disgust? Are you homophobic? Do you feel something around LGBTQ+ people that you don't feel around other people? Do you display those nonverbals that make it clear love is not on your mind? Do you want to see gay athletes fail and gay marriages crash just to prove that "your people" are right?

A colleague of mine was a passionate supporter of reaching out to the Muslim community. Despite all the differences, he and his wife loved Muslims. But then their daughter came out as a lesbian, and his wife hated it. She hated the homosexual agenda and the gay rights movement. She hated gay people. Until one day, the pastor said to his wife, "How can you show so much love to Muslims and have so much hate toward homosexuals?"

You see, Christian people have a problem. Sometimes those of us who claim to love a passage the most love people the least. That means we don't really love the *passages* at all. We love our version of the passage, the version that allows us to be comfortable, to be right, to be bigots.

But, according to the Law (as mentioned in Luke 10:26-28), if you don't love, you don't have life. If you don't love your different neighbors, you can't inherit eternal life. If you're a conservative Christian and you haven't loved lesbians, the passage says you can't have life. If you're a lesbian and you haven't loved conservative Christians, the passage says you can't have life. People who pick and choose their neighbors can't be neighbors with God.

SOMETIMES THOSE OF US WHO CLAIM TO LOVE A PASSAGE THE MOST LOVE PEOPLE THE LEAST.

But Jesus' biggest reason for telling this story was not to make sure we loved more; that was a point, but not *the* point. The point was to strip all of us of the belief that we are good enough. The point was to help even experts see no one has actually loved God or their neighbor that much, not all the time. The point was to turn us into the wounded man, half dead, and then tell us this: Jesus is *the* Good Samaritan.

We were dying. Spiritually, our own sin mugged us and stripped us of eternal life. We couldn't get down the road toward God. The legs of our love were broken, our patience was punctured, our compassion infected. Empty religion came walking by and kept its distance. We weren't good enough for the rule-keeping, sexually pure club for saints. But then Jesus came, and he was different. He is the Son of God; we are the sons and daughters of men. He is impartial; we are picky. He is spotless; we are sinners. He is whole and holy; we are broken. But the difference didn't deter him at all. The Son of God came to sinful people . . . before we were better . . . before we repented right or believed right or acted right . . . before our relationships were biblical or our love corrected.

God demonstrates his love for us like this: While we were still sinners, Jesus came walking down the road. And he saw us. He saw you. And he had pity. Compassion. He went to us, and he fixed us. He healed our wounds. It would cost him more than a few silver coins. It cost him his life. He would get jumped, abused, embarrassed, stripped, and killed on a cross. Why? So that *by his wounds we could be healed* (see Isaiah 53:5).

The expert in the law thought he was good and wanted advice on how to be better. Jesus said, "You're bad, but a good God didn't let *different* deter his love!"

THE GOSPEL COMPELS US TO STOP PICKING AND CHOOSING AND START LOVING WHOMEVER, WHEREVER, WHENEVER.

That is what changes us. It's called the gospel, the good news of God's love for bad people. The gospel compels us to stop picking and choosing and start loving whomever, wherever, whenever. Despite her partner. Despite his politics. Despite the differences.

The gospel, the good news of God's love for the different, is what will turn your street, your work, your school, your church into a "gayborhood." Know what that is? A gayborhood is a neighborhood where gay people are loved. Wikipedia calls it an "oasis" in an otherwise hostile environment. Shouldn't our Christian churches be oases like that? Shouldn't they be known for love and not for hypocrisy and politics? Churches where the unchurched say, "I don't know about everything they stand for, but I know they stand for love."

What will that look like this week? The theologian Martin Luther said Christians should love God so much that they befriend their neighbor in every bodily need. So, befriend a bisexual. And if there's a bully's fist and a bisexual's cheek at your school, place your face in between the two. Luther also said Christians should love God so much they defend their neighbor. So, if your church friends are chuckling at the transgender kid, pack up your PB&J and eat lunch with the one who needs defending. If your girlfriends are giggling about him being gay, rain on that hate parade. When a gay couple moves into the next apartment, be the first neighbor to love them. When a gay man starts at the company, be the first coworker to include him. When your sister comes out, be the first family member to call her, not to fix her or change her or share every passage about sexuality, but to care for and love her. If you've sinned, apologize to those you've excluded.

NO MATTER WHAT YOU THINK, JESUS IS TELLING YOU TO LOVE.

Oh, I know! I haven't written a word about whether God is okay with being gay. I haven't written about the morality of sexuality, about faith and repentance and same-sex attraction. That's why you need to keep reading. But this much is indisputable. No matter what you think, Jesus is telling you to love.

Love like Ed Dobson. Ed Dobson was a pastor who knew and believed the passages that called homosexuality a sin. Which is why some were surprised when the host of a gay radio talk show invited him in as a guest. Some in Pastor Dobson's church feared the church would be overrun by homosexuals. Dobson's reply, "Terrific. They can take their place in the pews right next to the liars, gossips, materialists, and all the rest of us." Then he added, "When I die, if someone stands up and says, 'Ed Dobson loved homosexuals,' then I will have accomplished something in my life."[2]

I'm not sure what you believe about the morality of sexuality, but I am sure of this: our Good Samaritan, Jesus, loved us despite our differences. Now he sends us down the road looking for people who are different, because different will not deter our love.

STUDY QUESTIONS

1. Read Luke 10:25-37. Have you ever thought of Jesus as the Good Samaritan? What did he have to go through to show his love for you?

2. Agree/Disagree: Most Christians hide behind Bible passages to excuse their homophobic hearts.

3. Consider how you've talked about or treated LGBTQ+ people in the past. What do you wish you could do differently so your love would have looked more like Jesus' love for you?

Chapter 8

GAY & GOD: L(OVE) G(OSPEL) B(IBLE) T(RUST)

"But what do you think?" the young gay man asked me. "Do you think it's a sin?"

No matter how much you love LGBTQ+ people, that question will come up eventually. Is God okay with being gay? Try that as the icebreaker at your next holiday gathering! It's a dangerous question, isn't it? Some people don't care if God's okay with it because they're not. To them, being gay is gross, disgusting, unnatural. While I wish I could change their minds, I have to admit this chapter isn't really for them. Other people don't care if God's okay with it because they're okay with it. To them, embracing your sexual orientation is beautiful and natural, and anyone who quotes a passage and says otherwise is intolerant and abusive. While I wish I could change their minds too, I have to admit this chapter isn't really for them either.

No, this chapter is for those who do care. They care about the passages because they care about God. They love Jesus and they trust what he says, no matter what. In this chapter, I want to answer this question: Is God okay with same-sex attraction? I want to answer it because I know there are people who'll read this book who feel same-sex attraction and they don't know what to do. Does God want them to embrace those desires or deny them? Can they talk about those desires and be loved, or should they hide them? Their consciences tell them, "This is wrong!" But are their consciences right?

I don't want to share what I think, what the church used to teach, or what the latest survey says. No, I want to tell you what God says.

Here's why—because God is good. The reason you should believe whatever you're about to learn is because God is good and what you're about to read comes from him. If God is the Good Samaritan, who isn't deterred by our differences, by our sin, then he is good. If the God we meet in the Bible is the One who doesn't count our sins against us, who forgives us for the sins we try to hide, who is happy with us despite all the moral reasons we are disappointed in ourselves, then God is good. If Jesus gave up his life on a cross for you when everyone else gave up on you, then God is good. The reason I want to look at some Bible passages is because they're from the same book that tells me about that cross. I believe the passages are good because the God who wrote them is too.

Let's look at what God says by going back to his Word. In Genesis 19, Leviticus 18, Leviticus 20, 1 Corinthians 6, 1 Timothy 1, and Romans 1, God appears to address same-sex behavior. What does he say?

Let's start with Genesis 19, the story of Sodom. Do you know it? Sodom stinks. God says its stench wafts up to heaven and turns his stomach. God sends angels in disguise to investigate. A man named Lot welcomes them into his home, but that's when the men of Sodom pound on the door. "Where are those men?!" they demand. "Bring them out so we can have sex with them." When they try to break down the door, the angels step forward, strike the sex-crazed mob blind, and rush Lot's family out of Sodom just as fire falls from heaven and destroys them all. And if you grew up in church, that's all the proof you need. God burns up gays. Case closed, right?

Not exactly. Type "Sodom" into a Bible search engine, and you might be surprised. For example, Ezekiel 16:49, "Now this was the sin of your sister

Sodom: She and her daughters were arrogant, overfed and unconcerned; they did not help the poor and needy." Arrogance. Pride. Selfishness. Jesus' brother says in Jude 1:7, "Sodom and Gomorrah and the surrounding towns gave themselves up to sexual immorality and perversion," and I'd call gang rape immoral and perverted, wouldn't you? So did God destroy Sodom because its men were arrogant, proud, selfish, and perverted or because they were arrogant, proud, selfish, perverted, and gay? The answer: we don't know. In the case of Sodom, God doesn't say much about a marriage that is faithful, monogamous, and gay.

I BELIEVE THE PASSAGES ARE GOOD BECAUSE THE GOD WHO WROTE THEM IS TOO.

Leviticus 18 and 20 seem less cloudy. Leviticus 18:22 says, "Do not have sexual relations with a man as one does with a woman; that is detestable." Leviticus 20:13 says, "If a man has sexual relations with a man as one does with a woman, both of them has done what is detestable." Well, there you go. *Detestable* isn't a neutral adjective. But there's a slight hiccup. Do you know what it is? Leviticus 18:22 is found in the book of . . . Leviticus. And if there's one book in the Bible that we don't pay much attention to, it's Leviticus.

Jennifer Knapp said it best. When the Christian contemporary artist came out as a lesbian, she challenged, "The conservative evangelical uses what most people refer to as the 'clobber verses' to refer to this loving [same-sex] relationship as an abomination, while they're eating shellfish."[1] Knapp was quoting Leviticus 11, which prohibits eating at Red Lobster. But it's not just that. Leviticus 1–7 are about animal sacrifice, which we don't do. Leviticus 8–10 are about rules for priests, which we don't keep. Chapter 11 is about unclean foods, which we ignore. Chapters 12–15 are about which infections and bodily fluids make you unclean, which you don't even want to read about. Chapter 16 is about a holiday we don't celebrate. Chapter 17 is about God's issue with raw meat, which we ignore with every rare burger. But then we get to Leviticus 18 and say, "But this one, this passage about gay guys—that one still applies."

It seems like we should just leave Leviticus in the Old Testament with those old rules. But wait. Remember last chapter where I mentioned that Jesus affirmed a quote about loving your neighbor? Remember where it came from? Yup. Leviticus 19:18. It's there, along with do not lie, do not play favorites, and do not hate. We don't want to throw those out too, do we?

Do you see the problem? How do we know which of these passages are for God's people back then and which are for God's people today? How do we pick and choose? Here's the good news—we don't. In the New Testament, God picks. God tells us which passages were for back then (like he did with shellfish) and which are for his followers today by repeating them in the New Testament. So, is this passage repeated?

As we move into New Testament territory, we run into the most hotly debated Greek word of our time: *arsenokoitai*. The New Testament was originally written in Greek, and more ink has been spilled over the real meaning of this word because of these two passages. First Corinthians 6:9,10: "Do not be deceived: Neither the sexually immoral nor idolaters nor adulterers nor *arsenokoitai* nor *malakoi* nor thieves nor the greedy nor drunkards nor slanderers nor swindlers will inherit the kingdom of God."

God is saying, "Be careful! People will try to deceive you! But sin is sin, and sin is serious to me. You can't accept any of this, live in this, be proud of this, love this, and yet claim to love me. You won't inherit the kingdom of God."

First Timothy 1:9,10 makes the same point: "We also know that the law is made not for the righteous but for lawbreakers and rebels, the ungodly and sinful, the unholy and irreligious, for those who kill their fathers or mothers, for murderers, for the sexually immoral, for *arsenokoitai*, for slave traders and liars and perjurers—and for whatever else is contrary to the sound doctrine." Who is living contrary to God's will? Liars and murderers and the sexually immoral and *arsenokoitai*.

So, what in the world does that word mean? Bishop Gene Robinson, the first openly gay bishop in a major Christian denomination, wrote, "The Greek word *arsenokoitai* is an even greater mystery. It is found nowhere else in Scripture. . . . We have nothing . . . to give us guidance as to its meaning. . . . Do we really want to base our condemnation of an entire group of people on a shaky translation of an unknowable Greek word? A reasonable person, not to mention a compassionate Christian, would not."[2]

Bishop Robinson is right. This exact word is only used in these two passages. But he's wrong in saying we have no guidance to its meaning because *arsenokoitai* is a Greek compound word. *Arsen* means "male." *Koitai* means "a man who sleeps with." Put the two words together and you have "a man who sleeps with a male."

While Robinson might call the translation shaky, the extreme majority of translators from all different denominations don't agree. The New International Version translates, "those who practice homosexuality." The English Standard Version, "men who practice homosexuality." The New American Standard Bible, "homosexuals." The Holman Christian Bible, "anyone practicing homosexuality." Dozens of other translations say exactly the same.

And that's not all. Remember those two passages from Leviticus? It turns out that the Hebrew Old Testament was translated into Greek just before the New Testament was written. Guess what words the Greek writers used to translate Leviticus 18 and Leviticus 20? Yup. You shall not have sex with (*koiten*) a man (*arsen*). Paul put the words together in the New Testament and repeated the sexual ethics of the Old.

Roy is a Christian who deals with same-sex attraction every day. That's why I value his words on this particular word: "Naturally, over the years, I've spent a lot of effort trying to discover a 'spin' on these passages which would enable me to embrace a gay relationship. But each time I've tried to do so, I've found that my conscience clobbers my pro-gay arguments. . . . Having studied Greek, it seems to me fairly self-evident that *arsenokoitai* is a compound word referring to those offenders condemned in Leviticus 18:22. . . . Suppose I have an Old Testament text which says, 'it is unlawful to lay bricks,' and I have a New Testament text that says, 'bricklayers are lawbreakers.' It would seem inconceivable to me to say that 'Greek scholars don't know exactly what *bricklayer* means.'"

THE WORDING OF 1 CORINTHIANS 6 AND 1 TIMOTHY 1 HELPS US SEE THAT HOMOSEXUALITY IS NOT GOD'S WILL FOR OUR SEXUALITY.

See his point? The wording of 1 Corinthians 6 and 1 Timothy 1 helps us see that homosexuality is not God's will for our sexuality.

That leaves us with Romans 1:25-27. Look at Paul's words:

> They exchanged the truth about God for a lie, and worshiped and served created things rather than the Creator—who is forever praised. Amen. Because of this, God gave them over to shameful lusts. Even their women exchanged natural sexual relations for unnatural ones. In the same way the men also abandoned natural relations with women and were inflamed with lust for one another. Men committed shameful acts with other men, and received in themselves the due penalty for their error.

In the final weeks of the Bible 101 class that I teach at my church, I read this paragraph to people from all different spiritual backgrounds and then ask, "What is that saying?" While it's offensive to some and challenging to us all, I've only ever gotten one answer: "God doesn't like it."

I'm not sure about Sodom, but the rest of Scripture is clear. It's the reason why Christians for thousands of years have not doubted, questioned, or denied this.

I know, there's so much I haven't told you. I haven't taught you the context of these passages. I haven't addressed why Romans 1 isn't about abusive older men having sex with boys or why Leviticus isn't about raping conquered armies. I haven't addressed every scholarly objection from LGBTQ+ supporters. If you want to dig further with me, I'd love to, but now you know what I believe and why I believe it.

Two weeks ago, I was talking with a young gay man. He was humble and kind and generous to me. I talked about the church's failure to love, about Christian homophobia, about my sin against LGBTQ+ people, and about my failures as a pastor. But at the end of the conversation, he asked me, "What about you? Where do you stand?" I said, "I've studied this more than anything I've ever studied, and I can't get around it. I can't get around the passages. On this issue, I can't say God is okay with it."

I know. I haven't said everything that needs to be said just yet, and that might confuse or frustrate you. I know I haven't addressed the sins Christians commit against LGBTQ+ people. I haven't addressed the objections either, such as: Didn't God make some people gay? Are you saying gay people can't be God's people? Didn't Jesus say not to judge? Aren't you a sinner too?

That's why I urge you to keep reading. I will get there, but for now, I want to remind you of what I've already expressed. God is good. Do you know how I know that? Because of Leviticus. Have you read Leviticus 16? It's about this odd old ritual where a priest would confess his sins on the head of a goat and then send it off into the wilderness. God put people's sins on a goat. Isn't God good?! But that was meant to be a picture of Jesus. Did you know Jesus took your sins away? The big ones, the ugly ones, the shameful ones, the sexual ones, the things I wouldn't dare to write down here. Do you know what he does? He takes them as far away from you as the east is from the west. God is good!

I WANT TO REMIND YOU OF WHAT I'VE ALREADY EXPRESSED. GOD IS GOOD.

In 1 Corinthians 6:10,11 God says *arsenokoitai* and drunks and greedy people can't inherit his kingdom. Ever been drunk? Ever had a budget that had nothing to do with God? Me too. But in the very next verse, Paul says, "But you were washed, you were sanctified, you were justified in the name of the Lord Jesus Christ" (verse 11). Jesus got rid of our greed. He sanctified us from our sexual sin. God is good!

In 1 Timothy 1:9,10 God says that *arsenokoitai* and liars are living contrary to God. Ever lied? Me too. But five verses later, Paul writes, "Christ Jesus came into the world to save sinners—of whom I am the worst" (verse 15). What a verse! I am the worst sinner I know. The worst. But I am the kind of person Jesus came to save, and you are too. Turn to him and there is nothing, nothing you have ever done that will get in the way of you and God. God is so good!

Don't forget Romans 6. We all worship created things instead of God. We love a relationship, a job, an opinion, a feeling more than God every single day. But listen to where Romans goes: "The wages of sin is death, but the gift of God is eternal life in Christ Jesus our Lord" (verse 23)! Sinners deserve to be separated from God, to die spiritually, but God has a gift: eternal life in Jesus. It's for sinners because sinners are all that there are! God is so good!

I don't know how God's passages are challenging you today, but I do know this: whatever you've done, God is good. His greatest joy would be for you to turn to him and find out why because no one will ever love you like this God. No one will ever be faithful to you like this God. No one will ever bring you more joy, comfort, friendship, affection, hope, peace, or life than the God who says, "You've sinned, but I won't let that stop my love." If these passages point out your sin, let me point you to the God who loves sinners, even the worst of them.

If you already knew all of this, if this confirms what you already believed about sexual morality, I ask you to remember these letters as you share the message—LGBT. Every letter matters, and the order of the letters matters even more.

I AM THE KIND OF PERSON JESUS CAME TO SAVE, AND YOU ARE TOO.

The L stands for *Love*. It's the one and only place to start. Love LGBTQ+ people. Laugh with lesbians. Serve all sexual orientations. Be the guy who loves gay people. Love your neighbors. All of them. You're not allowed to even mention Leviticus until you've truly loved.

The G stands for *Gospel*. It's the passage you need to start with. Remember how I started with how good God is? Show LGBTQ+ people why you love God, why you love the Bible, why you are willing to turn from anything that gets in the way of knowing and experiencing God's love. Help them see the God who is better than anyone and anything.

The B stands for *Bible*. This is the tough part. It's what I covered in this chapter, but it's not the place to start. You shouldn't post this on Facebook. You shouldn't publicly share your views on gay marriage. You shouldn't try to convince gay non-Christians to stop living like they are.

There's a time, after lots and lots of love and lots and lots of gospel, when you can talk to LGBTQ+ friends who profess Christianity about biblical sexuality.

The T stands for *Trust*. Trust the Holy Spirit no matter if your gay brother says thank you or hates you or if people repent or reject you. I know some of you are ready to put this book down and never pick it up again. You hate this. You're disgusted with me. I thought of you as I wrote, but I trust it's never wrong to encourage you in following God. Yes, the cross is heavy. Yes, you have to deny yourself. But this is the only place to find grace, to find undeserved, unstoppable love. I trust this was not a mistake.

LGBT. Love first. Gospel next. The Bible follows. And trust it works. That's what Christians need to do with what they've learned in this chapter.

That's what changed Rosaria. As a lesbian professor at Syracuse, Rosaria Champagne hated how Christians hated. She knew what Christians were like from the protests and the threatening letters she received, but then she met Pastor Ken and his wife, Floy. Ken invited Rosaria over for one of Floy's home-cooked meals and listened. They loved. It wasn't a gimmick or a bait-and-switch. It was just love, and then Ken prayed.

LGBT. LOVE FIRST. GOSPEL NEXT. THE BIBLE FOLLOWS. AND TRUST IT WORKS.

Rosaria wrote, "I had never heard anyone pray to God as if God cared, as if God listened. . . . I felt as though I was treading on something real, something sincere, something important, something transparent. . . . Ken's God seemed alive." Ken prayed to God as his Father, because Jesus made Ken God's son. That's the gospel.

For the next two years, Ken opened the Bible. As Rosaria wrestled with her sin and God's grace, a war raged in her heart. Another pastor assured her she could honor God by living an honorable lesbian life. "He told me that I could have Jesus and my lesbian lover," Rosaria wrote. "This was a very appealing prospect. But I had been reading and rereading Scripture, and there are no such marks of postmodern 'both/and.'"

That's the Bible.

Then it happened. Here's how Rosaria describes it: "That morning I emerged from the bed of my lesbian lover and an hour later was sitting in a pew. . . . You never know the terrain someone else has walked to come worship the Lord. . . . Two incommensurable worldviews clashed together: the reality of my lived experience and the truth of the word of God. . . . In this crucible of confusion, I learned something important. I learned the first rule of repentance: that repentance requires greater intimacy with God than with our sin. . . . And sometimes we all have to crawl there on our hands and knees."[3]

Rosaria did. Because of Ken and Floy's love and the gospel and the Bible and the trustworthy work of the Spirit, she came just as she was, and Jesus accepted her that way.

STUDY QUESTIONS

1. Before this chapter, what did you believe about the morality of homosexuality? Why did you believe that?

2. After this chapter, what do you believe about the morality of homosexuality? Why do you believe that?

3. Fill in these blanks according to this chapter. Why is the order of these words so important?

   L_________ G_________ B_________ T_________

Chapter 9

GAY & GOD: BUT WHAT ABOUT . . . ?

The online article about gay and God was short, but the comments below were not. "God created me gay. I'm living God's will by being who he created me to be." "In the church we are taught to make our sins feel lighter by judging. . . . But love and acceptance is what Jesus preached." "I [am gay but I] still have faith and I will . . . get to heaven."

Those comments raise some good questions. Are LGBTQ+ people born that way? Does God make people gay? Are Christians judging when Jesus said not to? Can LGBTQ+ people go to heaven? So far in this "Gay & God" section, God has taught us to love people, all people, despite their differences. God has taught us to love passages, all the passages, despite their difficulty. But those two foundational points don't answer all our questions. So what about . . . ?

In this chapter, I want to cover four of the biggest questions about being gay and following God. Here's the passage I want to guide us with: "Trust in the LORD with all your heart and lean not on your own understanding" (Proverbs 3:5).

Whenever we talk about something controversial, it's essential to trust that God, who is righteous, is also right about this. So, with all your heart, trust him. Wherever the passages lead you, trust him. Even if culture, the church, or you disagree, trust him, because this is the Lord. This is the Good Samaritan God who doesn't let our sin stop his love. This is the God who loves us before we get better, before we fix ourselves, before our sexuality is on the straight and narrow. There is no one like the Lord. With that trust, let's address some tough questions.

Question one is a game changer: Are you born gay? The great twenty-first-century theologian Lady Gaga sang a song about God not making mistakes; she was born the way she is. The logic seems solid. If we don't choose our sexual orientation, then it's how we were made. And if God made us, then God makes people gay. If God always does what's right, then acting on your orientation can't be wrong.

But have you ever witnessed an aisle 4 meltdown? A three-year-old wants the squeaky toy in aisle 4. Mom says, "Not today, Sweetie." That's when it happens. Shouting, screaming, writhing, whining, drooling on the store's tile floor. Where did the kid learn that? Did Mom model that behavior? Where did it come from? God's answer: the kid was . . . born that way.

The passage says it like this: "Surely I was sinful at birth" (Psalm 51:5). The apostle Paul added, "I know that good itself does not dwell in me, that is, in my sinful nature" (Romans 7:18). Nature. Sure, you can be nurtured, or taught, to sin. But you and I were already naughty by nature. Because of sin, we are born that way.

That includes our sexuality. Did you know that I am a natural-born polygamist? Don't panic. I love my wife. I haven't cheated on her. The truth is when a commercial comes on showing models in their underwear, I have to force myself to look away. I also have to fight the natural desire that 98 percent of men feel to lust after countless women, wedding ring be damned. I was born that way. When two teenagers are dating, they have to fight the natural desire to steal God's wedding gift of sex because they were born that way. When a wife feels lonely and her old boyfriend reaches out through social media with some old memories and some new feelings, she has to put that desire to death because she was born that way. Our emotions, reactions, inclinations, desires, and orientations are very natural. Eye for eye and tooth for tooth revenge is very natural, but that doesn't make it biblical.

I hope that fact raises your compassion. I hope that truth doesn't become your weapon but your reason to sympathize with LGBTQ+ people. Don't make the mistake he did . . .

EYE FOR EYE AND TOOTH FOR TOOTH REVENGE IS VERY NATURAL, BUT THAT DOESN'T MAKE IT BIBLICAL.

A few years ago, a well-meaning Christian man said something that made me want to hide under a pew. Our church invited a guest speaker to talk about his struggle with same-sex desires. The speaker was honest and vulnerable. He admitted that despite all the attempts, he couldn't pray the gay away. That's when the older Christian raised his hand. "How can you feel that way?" he yucked. "I can't imagine feeling that way about another man." There was little compassion in his voice because he forgot that our desires are not always our choice. Many Christians battle same-sex attraction with unwanted desires. They're in a war they didn't choose to enlist in. They need a band of brothers, a squad of sisters, fellow Christians to fight by their sides, to carry them when they're wounded, and to love them despite the difference in their desires.

I don't know if science will ever discover a gay gene, but I do know this: our bodies, brains, sexuality, and souls were affected by the fall into sin. God made a masterpiece when he made us, but sin scribbled on God's *Mona Lisa*. We are born in sin and need to be born again. That means our natural passions don't determine right or wrong. Only God's passages can do that.

That brings us to question two. We keep talking about this in the context of sin, and then we judge. But didn't Jesus say, "Don't judge!"? Being judgmental isn't very Christian, is it? Aren't we all sinners? What right does one sinner have to judge another? Wasn't rapper Tupac right when he rapped that only God could judge him?

That's a great question, and it might be right. Jesus did say, "Do not judge, or you too will be judged." But let's look at what Jesus said in context. Matthew 7:1-5 says:

> "Do not judge, or you too will be judged. For in the same way you judge others, you will be judged, and with the measure you use, it will be measured to you. Why do you look at the speck of sawdust in your brother's eye and pay no attention to the plank in your own eye? How can you say to your brother, 'Let me take the speck out of your eye,' when all the time there is a plank in your own eye? You hypocrite, first take the plank out of your own eye, and then you will see clearly to remove the speck from your brother's eye."

Jesus is concerned about that plank. He's concerned Christians will try to pick at the sins in others and pay no attention to the sins in themselves. That's hypocrisy! But notice what he says at the end. First, start with your plank, and then remove their speck. Catch that? Should Christians pick the specks out of other people's lives? Should Christians judge? Specifically, should Christians tell LGBTQ+ people what we learned in the last chapter of this book? The answer is . . . maybe. It depends on who you are and who they are.

If they're not Christians, you should not judge. Let me repeat that. Christ did not tell Christians to judge the world. Let me repeat that again. Jesus did not tell his disciples to tell people who aren't his disciples to start acting like disciples. Listen to Paul's words: "What business is it of mine to judge those outside the church? Are you not to judge those inside? God will judge those outside" (1 Corinthians 5:12,13).

What business is it of ours to judge non-Christians for their lifestyle, sexuality, definition of marriage, or sins? Answer: it is none of our business. It's why Jesus says to take the speck from your "brother's eye." A "brother" means a fellow son of God the Father, a fellow Christian. If he's not a brother, it's not your business to judge. So be careful what you post for the world to see. You're not being bold when you stand up for God's law on social media. Social media is the world. This is the church. Judge non-Christian behavior in the Christian church. If they're not Christians, what business is it of yours to judge? Answer: it's none of your business.

CHRIST DID NOT TELL CHRISTIANS TO JUDGE THE WORLD.

Does that mean we should stick to judging other Christians? Well, maybe. Even if they are Christians and there's a plank in your eye, you should not judge. If there's a sin you aren't taking seriously, aren't repenting of, aren't going to war against, you shouldn't say a word about anyone else.

When my classmate wrote a blog about this topic, one of the comments killed me. A woman wrote, "I went to college with you, and I saw what you and your friends did. You all got drunk and didn't seem too sorry about it. But you made sure everyone knew how bad it was to be gay." I wish she wasn't right. Looking back, Jesus would have told us, "Don't you dare judge. Until you take care of you, don't say a word about them." Because Jesus didn't want plank-faced Christians to pick at the speck in a bisexual's bed.

You shouldn't either. If you aren't fighting your selfishness in marriage, impatience with the kids, critical tongue, disrespect of our president, game-day buzz, selfish ambition, social media addiction, selective love, unspoken racism, grudge with your ex; if you aren't taking your sin seriously, you have nothing to say about theirs. Nothing.

But there is a third category. If you yourself are a repentant Christian, not perfect, but you're sorry and you're trying to change, then you should humbly, gently, lovingly judge someone who is LGBTQ+ and loves Jesus and loves the Bible. Jesus says, "First take the plank out of your own eye, and then you will see clearly to remove the speck from your brother's eye" (Matthew 7:5). In other words, repentant Christians should judge. We should judge ourselves, and we should judge one another. We should open a Bible and talk with our sister who came out, our friend from Bible study, our bisexual son who says he's saved. A speck in your eye can cause you to crash on the highway to God, so repentant Christians should point out that speck and help remove it in Christ's name.

Question three—Can you be a gay Christian? Can LGBTQ+ people be saved? Now there's a complicated question, so let me start with a simple story. It was my daughter's birthday. She came home from school with bags of sugar, birthday snacks, and gifts from her teacher piled in her arms. Then she rushed to the mailbox and found a birthday package of cool socks. "Daddy, I want to carry them!" she insisted, piling the socks on top of the gifts on top of the snacks on top of the sugar, and then she ran to the house to enjoy the gifts. Suddenly she paused. She looked at the doorknob. Her hands were heaping with things she loved, but unless she set them down, she couldn't get inside.

Christianity is like that. There's something you can't hold on to and end up inside God's house, a part of his family. Do you know what that something is? It's not sin. Sin doesn't keep you out of heaven. If it did, none of us would get in! It's not sexual sin. Sexual sin doesn't keep you out. If it did, none of us would get in! It's not same-sex sin. Same-sex sin doesn't keep you out. Not the desire. Not even the behavior. No, there is one and only one thing that keeps you outside of heaven—a hard heart.

Here's what God says: "Blessed is the one who always trembles before God, but whoever hardens their heart falls into trouble" (Proverbs 28:14). And "if we deliberately keep on sinning after we have received the knowledge of the truth, no sacrifice for sins is left" (Hebrews 10:26). And "no one who is born of God will continue to sin" (1 John 3:9). If you keep intentionally sinning, you can't get inside, no matter what you think. If you know the passage and don't tremble before it, you harden your heart, you fill up your hands with sin, you tell God, "I don't care what the passage says; I'm not letting this go," then you can't get in. There aren't "Seven Deadly Sins"—there's only one. The one you're not sorry for.

THERE IS ONE AND ONLY ONE THING THAT KEEPS YOU OUTSIDE OF HEAVEN—A HARD HEART.

Let me be clear. If you care about your sin, you're in! The struggle, the desire to follow the passage, the sorrow you feel when you act, when you kiss, when you hook up, that does not kick you out of the kingdom. No! The fact that it bothers you means your spiritual heart is still beating. It's not hardened by sin. It's filled with the Holy Spirit. Can you be drawn to any sin, commit any sin, be of any sexual orientation and be saved? Yes. If we confess our sins, God is faithful and will purify us from all unrighteousness!

However, if you don't battle sin, any sin, this sin, you can't get in. If you won't let go of the relationship, of the lifestyle, of the opinion—not even for God—you're locking yourself out. I couldn't possibly claim to love you if I didn't tell you that. I know accepting that lifestyle brings all sorts of good things into your life: companionship, love, self-acceptance, an armful of good things. But there is something, someone so much better, and I don't want your hands to be so full that you don't get to see him face-to-face, because he so wants to see you.

I'm not God. I don't know which LGBTQ+ people know the truth and which don't. I don't know if your gay friend knows and is hardening his heart or if he's confused by the interpretations he reads online. I don't know if she's ignorant of the passages or unrepentant in the face of them. God will be the final judge of our hearts. Our job is simply to love every person and love every passage, even the passages that tell us to repent.

That brings us to our final question—Why this? Why now? How did sexual orientation become the issue, the one that divides families, churches, denominations? Why didn't Christians debate this for thousands of years until now? I think I stumbled upon that answer when I interviewed a gay pastor from Wisconsin.

Pastor Allen and I had an amazing talk about being gay and following God. My heart broke when he told me the story of being blackmailed into coming out by a member of his own church. (How's that for loving people?) He helped me understand how Christians hurt LGBTQ+ people and don't even know it. I definitely didn't want to do that. So I said, "Allen, if you were in our church, what would you think if I said this—'We all struggle with sin. With impurity, worry, impatience, homosexuality. You do. I do too. But we can struggle together. Jesus forgives us, and we can walk together and fight temptation as the family of God'"? I thought it was humble, grace-filled, community-minded, and hopeful, not hypocritical. But Allen didn't agree. He said, "You are attacking the core of my being."

That's when it hit me. He believes his sexuality is the core of his being. To say it's wrong is to say he's wrong. To call it sin is to take away his very identity, and I think that's it. The real issue is not sexuality; it's identity. In our culture, the greatest value is to be you. Be true to yourself, we preach.

Live your truth. Embrace who you are. Love yourself. Never be afraid to be yourself. March to the beat of your own drum. That's your true identity.

This is why we struggle. One day we realize we're gay. We have these desires or someone we love comes out. Desiring another woman is who she is. Culture has taught us to say, "Be yourself. Be true to you." But Jesus said, "Deny yourself. Take up your cross. Lose your life and follow me, and you will find a life that's even better." That's hard to say because the last thing in the world we want to do is to attack anyone's identity.

Pastor Allen was wrong. The core of our being is not our sexuality. No, the core of a Christian's being is Christ. This passage says it best: "Christ . . . is your life" (Colossians 3:4). Jesus Christ is the core of my being. Nothing else. He is all I need. I can deny that desire, the one Jesus says is sin, and I still have my identity. I still have a relationship status—a redeemed child of God. I still have a family—brothers and sisters in the faith and a perfect Father in heaven. I still have a community—countless Christians who are denying their sinful natures and finding perfection in Jesus Christ. The psalmist said, "Earth has nothing I desire besides you" (73:25). In Jesus we find something better than our truth. We find the Truth. We find a new identity. One that no one can take away.

Ethan, a young man who had left the church to embrace the gay lifestyle, once presented to a group of pastors. He told his story of walking away from the passages in an attempt to be true to himself before coming back in repentance, and he admitted that he didn't suddenly love women. He fought the sinful nature inside him. One of the pastors asked, "So what do you consider yourself? Gay? Ex-gay?" Ethan paused, then responded, "Well, I don't really like labels, but I guess if I had to choose one, I'd pick 'redeemed child of God.'" Yes. His identity was not his sexuality. It was Jesus. And if Jesus is your identity, he can take anything and you'll still have everything.

Are you born gay? Should Christians judge? Can LGBTQ+ people be saved? Why this? Why now? These are tough questions, and God's answers are not always easy to swallow. That's why I need to tell you one last story.

A few years back, a Christian preacher became an instant success. After only a year or two, thousands of people showed up, but then he preached *that* sermon. The passage that made the people angry. Some were confused. Most were offended, and almost everyone left. Not one or two families, but thousands of people left. The preacher watched his megachurch dwindle down to a small group because of a single sermon. So with a sad heart, he asked the few who remained, "Do you want to leave too?" One member of the church, named Pete, said, "Where are we going to go? You have the words of eternal life." Do you know the name of that pastor? Jesus. Jesus preached some hard things, but those who didn't lean on their own understanding trusted him and found the words of eternal life.

IN JESUS WE FIND SOMETHING BETTER THAN OUR TRUTH. WE FIND THE TRUTH.

I know this is hard. I know there are churches where preachers will tell you to protect America and judge the culture. I know there are churches where you won't be told to deny yourself and take up your cross. But where else will we go? What other book will tell us about a God who is so good to love sinners like us? What other message gives so much hope to people who've messed it all up? What other Lord would love enough to give his own Son for you? So let's deal with the tough questions, trusting in the Lord with all our hearts.

STUDY QUESTIONS

1. What have you found challenging about this teaching so far? How does Proverbs 3:5 help calm your fears as you work through those challenges?

2. As you think back to your experience, have you been a "good judge" as Jesus described in Matthew 7:1-6? Why or why not? What will be different about your judging in the future?

3. Name three reasons why finding your identity, value, and purpose in Jesus Christ is essential for embracing God's truth about sexuality. Use Psalm 73:25 for help if needed.

Chapter 10

GAY & GOD: AND!

Sometimes pastors do dumb things. Like Andy. When his church remodeled their worship space, Andy snuck in after hours to check the progress. That's when he saw the I-beam—an eighteen-inch steel beam stretched from corner to corner of the construction, twenty feet up off the ground. Andy thought, "I want to walk across that!" Like I said, sometimes pastors do dumb things. Minutes later, Andy was tiptoeing his way across the steel beam, twenty feet closer to heaven (and one step away from it!). Halfway across, he panicked. He realized what was at stake if he stepped too far left or too far right. If Andy didn't take the exact right step, the result would be disaster.

I think you've probably felt like that as you've read these "Gay & God" chapters. I don't think writing them was a dumb idea, but without a doubt, it has been a biblical balancing act, a balance between loving all the people in this world and loving all the passages in God's Word. God has taught us to love people. All people. Different people. Different should never deter a Christian's love, but step too far in the direction of people, and it's easy to fall away from the passages. The passages God wrote. The passages about sexual morality. The passages about repentance. The passages about judging correctly. Step too far in the direction of a few passages, and it's easy to step away from loving people.

How's your balance? If I asked your gay friends about you, what would they say? Would they talk about your love of people, your kindness, hospitality, and willingness to stand up to those who hate? Or would they talk about your love of passages, the passages you shared about being gay and following God? What are you known for: standing up for people OR standing up for passages? Which is easier for you: refusing to let go of your love for LGBTQ+ people OR refusing to let go of your love for God's inspired passages? Most Christians are "OR" people, but too much is at stake to stay that way.

If you're anything like me, you've been living an OR life for far too long. You've been quoting passages forever, but you haven't befriended a gay person . . . ever. LGBTQ+ people have little evidence that you actually love them. Yet if you don't love all people, you don't really love all the passages. Perhaps you've been loving LGBTQ+ people, but you've drifted from the passages. You've been quoting Lady Gaga, but not our Lord God. You've focused so much on not offending those you can see that you've offended the One you can't. You've been so concerned about acceptance that you've forgotten about eternity. But if you don't love all the passages, you don't really love people because God wrote the passages out of love for people! Oh, it's dangerous to be an OR person.

Don't you wish we could see how Jesus did it? Don't you wish there was a time when Jesus had to choose between loving a person and loving a passage so we could see what all this looks like in real life? Guess what. There is an example! One day, Jesus' enemies forced him to choose. Here's what happened . . .

After thirty years of carpentry, Jesus comes out and claims to be the Christ, the Messiah, the Savior of the world, the Son of God. That is controversial enough, but he also loves people, all people. Every prostitute in town knows Jesus doesn't want their bodies, but he does want their hearts. Every drunk has seen Jesus at a party or six, because he is friends with the kind of people who get drunk. And that's what makes the conservatives mad. "What about the passages about purity, sobriety, and obedience? How can you be the Son of God if you ignore all the passages just to love all those people?" they think.

Their chance to expose Jesus arises when they apprehend "her," one of "those people," a married woman discovered in the company of another man, an adulteress who seemingly disregarded the teachings on sexual purity, monogamy, and the sanctity of marriage. Listen to what happens:

> At dawn [Jesus] appeared again in the temple courts, where all the people gathered around him, and he sat down to teach them. The teachers of the law and the Pharisees brought in a woman caught in adultery. They made her stand before the group and said to Jesus, "Teacher, this woman was caught in the act of adultery. In the Law Moses commanded us to stone such women. Now what do you say?" They were using this question as a trap, in order to have a basis for accusing him. (John 8:2-6)

This isn't hypothetical. This is an actual person. And the passage says the wages of her sin is death. Leviticus 20:10 says, "If a man commits adultery with another man's wife—with the wife of his neighbor—both the adulterer and the adulteress are to be put to death." That's not some conservative Jewish tradition. That's a passage from God given to the government of Old Testament Israel. "So, Jesus, what do you say? Do you agree with God? Do you love God's passage, or will you love this sinful person?"

Oh snap! If Jesus says to the sinner, "I love you just as you are," what about marriage and right and wrong and the countless passages where God says, "I don't approve of that!"? If Jesus says, "Well, if the passage says kill her . . ." What about love and mercy and compassion and forgiveness? What about this person, this actual person, whom God loves?

Which will Jesus choose? There seems to be no way not to fall off the beam to one side or the other. Until Jesus decides to play Pictionary. "But Jesus bent down and started to write on the ground with his finger" (John 8:6). Jesus starts to sketch. The Greek verb "to write" is used, at times, to refer to writing down an accusation. Is that what Jesus is writing? Is he drawing lines in the sand, stick figures with trembling hearts that worry, tiny hearts that have no compassion, green hearts that envy? I don't know, but Jesus doesn't speak; he just draws.

Then he says it—a passage so profound you've heard it even if you never go to church. The famous words you've memorized even if you don't know any others. Verses 7 and 8 say, "When they kept on questioning him, he straightened up and said to them, 'Let any one of you who is without sin be the first to throw a stone at her.' Again he stooped down and wrote on the ground." "You guys want to kill her? Okay. If you've never stumbled, fire away. If you've never ignored a passage, send a split-fingered fastball into her face. If you've never sinned, throw the first stone."

> At this, those who heard began to go away one at a time, the older ones first, until only Jesus was left, with the woman still standing there. Jesus straightened up and asked her, "Woman, where are they? Has no one condemned you?"
>
> "No one, sir," she said. (verses 9-11)

The men leave. The older ones have more sins to remember. Their stones drop lifelessly next to their sandals. Even the most forgetful Pharisees remember a sin or two. They all leave. They all admit they are passage breakers, sinners just like her.

But the tension isn't over because guess who's still there? Jesus. Guess what Jesus has never committed? Sin. Guess what Jesus has every right to do? Throw the first stone. What will Jesus choose? Now that the conservative hypocrites are gone, now that it's just Jesus, the friend of sinners, the supposed Son of God, what will he say? Will he defend the person or the passage? You don't want to miss it, because Jesus summarizes my last few chapters in fourteen words. Ready for it?

THERE IS NOTHING WE CAN CONFESS THAT GOD WILL NOT FORGIVE.

"'Then neither do I condemn you,' Jesus declared. 'Go now and leave your life of sin'" (verse 11). Wow. "I don't condemn you." Because you're a good person? Because you fixed what you broke? Because you've proven you've changed? No. "I don't condemn you because I forgive you," Jesus says. Because God is full of mercy and compassion. Because there is nothing we can confess that God will not forgive. Jesus says something so shocking you might think he has totally forgotten about the passage from Leviticus. "Go. I'm not going to kill you. I'm not going to condemn you. I'm going to forgive you because I love you."

I love rainbows. No, this is not a tangent. Do you know how a rainbow got its name? Because it appears after it rains, and it looks like a . . . bow. A bow is a weapon. It's something that fires an arrow at your enemy or your twelve-point buck. Huh. God made the beams of sunlight travel through water droplets and separate into colors so that a weapon appears in the sky.

Kind of weird . . . but have you ever noticed which way God's bow is pointing? Up! If OR people like me and you are down here, shouldn't the bow be pointing down? Shouldn't God be in the sky threatening to fire away at those who don't love people and the passages? Why would God point the symbol of his anger up at himself?

In his crazy love for people, God took the punishment for our sins. The passages of God's law said sinners deserve to die—the wages of sin is death. But God wrote other passages, passages about a Messiah, a substitute, a Savior who would pay the price and die for our sins. That's why Jesus could tell a marriage-wrecking woman, "I don't condemn you." Not because adultery didn't deserve condemnation but because Jesus would go on to be condemned in her place. Jesus did the same for you. If you've been a judgmental accuser or a Scripture-twisting excuser, Jesus was condemned for you. One passage says, "Christ also suffered once for sins, the righteous for the unrighteous, to bring you to God" (1 Peter 3:18). Every rainbow reminds us of this! The rainbow is not a symbol for the LGBTQ+ community. It's a symbol of Christianity. It's a reminder that the anger God should have felt toward OR people was shot up at the cross so Jesus could smile and say, "I don't condemn you." It's why I can tell my congregation at the end of a church service, "The Lord bless and keep you. The Lord make his face shine on you." His face shines. God smiles. "I don't condemn you. Go now in peace!"

AND. Highlight that word. Underline it. Make a circle of glue around it and drop a pound of glitter on it. Jesus said to the woman, "I don't condemn you," *AND* "Leave your life of sin." "I love you, and stop sinning. I love you, and leave that life. I love you, and you're ignoring the passages I love. I love you, and stop. I love you just as you are, and don't stay that way."

WWJC? Which will Jesus choose? Passages or people? Jesus' answer is *AND*. Christ loved people *AND* passages. Does Jesus love people in such shocking ways that conservatives have always questioned his values? Yes.

AND does Jesus love passages in such shocking ways that liberals question his compassion? Yes. Does Jesus love people, different people, people who don't seem to fit in most church circles? Yes. *AND* does Jesus love passages, tough passages, convicting passages—you-were-born-in-sin-so-deny-yourself-and-follow-me passages? Yes.

JESUS SAID TO THE WOMAN, "I DON'T CONDEMN YOU," *AND* "LEAVE YOUR LIFE OF SIN."

"So, Jesus, should we love people, all people, of every sexual orientation?"

"Yes, *AND* you should love the passage. All the passages. About every sexual orientation."

"Jesus, shouldn't we stand up for the passages?"

"Yes. *AND* you should stand up for the people. Every last one, because God loves them too." Christ wants Christians to love people *AND* passages.

When it comes to gay and God, there are a thousand steps too far to the right that will kill people. Embrace the classic, conservative position, and you will kill compassion and gentleness and biblical love. There are a thousand steps too far to the left that will kill people. Embrace the modern position, and you will kill the trustworthiness of God's Word and repentance and eternity. There is only one very narrow step to keep us all safe. You must avoid that side *AND* that side because so much is at stake.

AND. We can't change what we did, but we can choose what we'll do. With the Holy Spirit's power, we can be AND people. We can be the neighbors who invite the gay couple over for dinner AND eventually tell them about a God so good we would give up anything for him. We can be the students who say, "Amen!" to this sermon AND make sure "That's gay!" is expelled from our schools. We can be the church family who humbly confesses our sexual sins AND gently judges our Christian brother's sexuality. We can be the church who loves it when lesbians walk through our doors so we can show them love AND share the light of God's Word. We can be the Christians who confess our same-sex desires only to find unconditional love AND prayers for our hearts to change. We can be the kind of Christians who confuse 98 percent of the church because we don't fit in their either/or world. We are against sin AND we are for people, and we learned it from the Son of God himself.

CHRIST LOVED PEOPLE *AND* PASSAGES.

When we fall (and we will), when our steps aren't on God's straight and narrow, remember Jesus' first word to that woman. That's what we need to change. That's what changed Josh. Despite being a Christian, Josh's marriage wasn't so Christian. One night, seven years in, it hit bottom. Josh was frustrated with his wife, and he told her how selfish and self-absorbed she was. While she sat in the living room, he stood in the kitchen, yelling his accusations, wanting to wound her with the venom spewing out of his mouth. That's when it happened. Josh wrote, "I'll never forget: Andrea came around the corner. I was steeling myself for whatever she'd throw back at me and getting ready to fight. But she just came up and pulled me really close to her, and she began sobbing. She cried and cried and cried as she held me. She said, 'I don't know what happened to you, but I am not going anywhere.'" Josh confessed, "Those were maybe the most powerful words I'd heard in our relationship. I was at my absolute worst . . . [and she said] 'I'm not going anywhere.'"

I don't know what sin you've committed today. I don't know what people or passages you've ignored, but I do know this: We have a God who makes the best promises to the worst people. We have a God who says, "I'm not going anywhere. I don't condemn you." And nothing makes us want to leave our lives of sin like that.

Followers of Jesus have tried to maintain a biblical balance since the Christian church began. It has never been easy, especially in the area of sexuality and family. As Christians, we ask God's forgiveness for our missteps and flaws in both our beliefs and our behavior.

May God send his Holy Spirit into our hearts so that every member of God's family would love what God loves, love who God loves, and love how God loves until the King of love calls us home.

STUDY QUESTIONS

1. Read John's description of Jesus in John 1:14. How is the phrase "full of grace and truth" a preview of what Jesus would model in John 8:2-11?

2. How can you be an "AND" person? List some specific things you can work on.

3. The apostle Paul promised, "Where sin increased, grace increased all the more" (Romans 5:20). For everyone who struggles to say no to sin, sexual or otherwise, why are these words life-giving to the soul?

Chapter 11

GOD & TRANSGENDER

Few things in life can challenge us and, perhaps, change us quite like seeing an issue up close. For many folks, that is true when it comes to being transgender.

Throughout the 2010s, I learned little bits about being transgender from pop culture headlines. Bruce Jenner became Caitlyn Jenner. Jazz Jennings got a TLC show. Chaz Bono danced with the stars. Laverne Cox was nominated for an Emmy. But it's hard to truly grasp the depth of a situation until you see it not through a screen but up close with your own eyes and ears.

I had a conversation with a member of our church not long ago, and her inquiry about transgenderism during one of our Question & Answer Sundays came to mind. With her question still fresh, I reached out via text, kindly inquiring whether her question held personal significance and, if so, "could we talk." She answered yes and yes (and said I could share this story).

In one conversation, I got a glimpse of her struggle up close. Here was a woman I respected, a Christian who was connected to God's Word, a woman I had pastored for years, a woman who was wrestling with the image she saw in the mirror.

So I tried to put James' words into practice and be "quick to listen" (James 1:19). I learned how disturbing it felt for her to be called a girl when she didn't feel that girly (like if someone called me "lady" while walking down the street). And how thrilling it felt when someone assumed she was a guy based on the way she dressed. And how scary it was to tell anyone what she was going through.

As I listened, it was hard not to feel compassion for a daily struggle that I had never experienced. That's what happens when cultural issues become personal.

Maybe you've experienced that same struggle. You've wrestled with those same thoughts. Maybe you love someone who has been in the same shoes as the woman from my church—maybe your sister, cousin, coworker, or classmate. And maybe you are confused. You want to be like Jesus, full of unfailing love and unchanging truth, but transgenderism feels so new and so rushed that you aren't quite sure what it means to imitate Jesus in such moments.

That's why I want to talk about transgenderism. But I'm not sure I should. I think it's best discussed in the context of a relationship. If I could, I would wait until I have a solid, trusting relationship with you. I'd wait to talk trans until you really know me and I you, until after I told you how messed up I am and how much I still struggle with so much and why I need the grace of God. I'd wait until we figured out who Jesus is, what the Bible is, what the Christian life is like, until I had prayed with you, confessed to you, wept and laughed with you. Then I'd talk about something as personal as this. And I know you don't know me like that. Part of me wants to wait, but I also know that you have questions and are facing choices that can't wait for years. So I've decided to write this, praying that you'll know my heart in loving you and loving God.

My goal here is to cover three things. First, I'd like to share the basics of what transgenderism is. Second, I'd like to open the Bible and see what God has to say about the transgender people he loves. Finally, I'd like to talk about what we can do to be more like Jesus in our diverse and changing world.

First, what is transgenderism? To be transgender is to "cross over" genders (like a transatlantic flight crosses over the Atlantic). Why would you want or do such a thing? Because your brain doesn't seem to agree with your body. Because the gender you feel doesn't fit with the chromosomes you have. That feeling is called gender dysphoria. Euphoria is a good feeling. Dysphoria is the opposite. And to feel better, many people trans, or cross over, their gender.

EUPHORIA IS A GOOD FEELING. DYSPHORIA IS THE OPPOSITE.

It's like my bathroom doorknob. When I moved into our house five years ago, I noticed that the bathroom doorknobs on either side of a single bathroom door were different colors. They didn't match. Most doorknobs do, but apparently, a few don't. (A science teacher later told me that it had to do with the humidity inside the bathroom.)

That difference between inside and outside is what transgender people are like. Their bodies say one thing, but their brains say another. Their chromosomes and sexual organs say, "Male," but their feelings, thoughts, and emotions shout, "Female!" According to a 2016 survey by the Williams Institute, 0.6 percent of Americans feel that way.[1] That's a small minority, but you don't have to be in the majority to matter to God and, hopefully, to his people.

When gender dysphoria happens, there are a number of options that vary in effort, visibility, and reversibility. You could just deal with it and hope it goes away, which it does for many kids as they grow older. Or you could change your outfit to experiment with clothing normally worn by the other gender, hoping that what you see in the mirror feels better to your brain. Or you could change your ID and ask others to use a new name that lines up with your felt gender. Or you could change your hormones, taking puberty blockers or testosterone boosters that would alter your body in various ways. Or you could go all the way and surgically change your body, your facial structure, your voice, your private parts, etc., so that your body would match your brain.

Now, before you react to those options, there's something I need you to know about transgender people, something that deserves 110 percent of your attention, especially if you are a follower of the God who loves the entire world. The experience of gender dysphoria is so agonizing that, according to the American Academy of Pediatrics, 42 percent of trans teenagers have attempted to kill themselves.[2] Forty-two percent! And not just thought about it, but actually tried it. That means 42 percent of those precious souls have grabbed a razor blade or a bottle of pills or a gun and attempted to escape the brutal battle in their brains. The daily struggle of gender dysphoria is so heavy that trans teens will try to end their lives three times more often than their non-trans friends.

I need you to understand that. Before you minimize this with some crude joke like, "Well, I'm identifying as a unicorn today," before you post some snarky meme, remember that these kids are killing themselves. And they are watching us. They are reading our comments. They are listening to our reactions. They are trying to figure out if we'd listen, if we'd sympathize, if we'd love them. So, I beg you, if you have been less than loving toward trans people, repent and publicly apologize. Take down the posts. Sit down with your kids and confess you were not like the Christ who has compassion on people who are struggling (Matthew 9:36). Because you can have all the knowledge in the world, you can be right about every issue, but the apostle Paul wrote, "If I have a faith that can move mountains, but do not have love, I am nothing" (1 Corinthians 13:2). Let's be something. Because transgender people are not just out there. They're in our churches. In our homes. They need us to understand, to listen, to love before they join the 42 percent of their gender dysphoria peers. Would you make that commitment today?

If so, you are prepared for part two. What does God think about transgenderism and the transition between male and female (or vice versa)? The word *transgender* wasn't around in Bible times, so does the Bible have any answers concerning gender dysphoria, gender identity, and the morally approved options to deal with the disconnect? Short answer—yes. That's what we find way back in the beginning. Remember the first pages of the Bible, when God made man and woman unique and united? This contains most of what God thinks about our transgender questions.

THEY NEED US TO UNDERSTAND, TO LISTEN, TO LOVE.

First, God created us physically and sexually, male or female. "So God created mankind in his own image, in the image of God he created them; male and female he created them. God blessed them and said to them, 'Be fruitful and increase in number'" (Genesis 1:27,28). God defines gender as male and female, not as a feeling that exists within our minds but as a physical and sexual reality that can be seen via our bodies.

We see the proof of this in verse 28's command to "be fruitful." It takes a biological man and a biological woman to be fruitful, to increase the number of humans on earth. This is how God, on page 1 of the Bible, chooses to define "male" and "female." God himself stamped our gender on our chromosomes, hormones, and bodies. And he looked at all that he had made, and God himself said, "That's good."

In modern times, many have tried to turn sex and gender into two separate categories, one biological and fixed and the other more personal and fluid. But that approach is not what we find in the pages of Scripture. Not in the beginning. Not anywhere else.

Our language throughout millennia has supported this assumption. Notice how the word *gender* is similar to the words *genetics* and *genitals*, which give us the ability to "generate" new "generations" of our "progeny." This is how God designed us, and his design was declared very good.

But why, then, doesn't it always feel good? If God is good and his male/female design is good, then why don't some of us feel good when we look in the mirror? Why do we feel the dysphoria, the disconnect, the discomfort? Why do some of us want to crawl out of our skin instead of live in it? Why are some people born with altered chromosomes, as intersex people, or with a desire to change their gender?

These are essential questions. And the Bible, just a few pages later, offers us God's explanation. Because in Genesis 3, after the man and the woman fell into sin, everything fell apart. Everything. Our bodies, our brains, our world. Every good and perfect connection was strained if not outright destroyed. The fall came with catastrophic consequences.

In Genesis 1 and 2, Adam and Eve loved God. In Genesis 3, they ran from him. In Genesis 1 and 2, Adam and Eve loved each other. In Genesis 3, they blamed each other. In Genesis 1 and 2, Adam and Eve were naked and absolutely unashamed. In Genesis 3, they covered their own bodies with fig leaves. Where the Father had created unity, the father of lies ripped it apart.

Look at how honestly the apostle Paul describes the results of sin: "The whole creation has been groaning as in the pains of childbirth right up to the present time. Not only so, but we ourselves, who have the firstfruits of the Spirit, groan inwardly as we wait eagerly for our adoption to sonship, the redemption of our bodies" (Romans 8:22,23). Since it all fell apart, we suffer like a woman in labor. Even if we have the Holy Spirit, even if we are truly Christians, life on this planet, in these bodies, is enough to make us groan as in the pains of labor.

You don't need gender dysphoria to know that. Have you ever battled anxiety, when your mind worries about anything and everything? Or depression, when a chemical imbalance in your brain robs you of the euphoria you crave? Or addictive behavior, when your mind is like a magnet toward the substances that will make you suffer? Or a heart that suffers from obsessive comparison disorder, when you obsess over how you compare to her looks, his achievements, their family, his house, her job, their everything? Or anorexia, when the way you feel about your body is so disconnected from the reality of what it is? Why is that so natural for us? Why are we born that way? Because when humanity fell into sin, everything fell apart. Everything broke, even the harmony between our brains and bodies. And each of us, in varied ways, bears that burden and feels the weight of that struggle. Something's not right. Something needs to change. We are not yet whole.

WHERE THE FATHER HAD CREATED UNITY, THE FATHER OF LIES RIPPED IT APART.

Given the cultural place we are in, this is a theological point that you must not miss. As biblical Christians, we don't trust our brains. We don't trust our hearts. We don't assume that what we feel or think is good. We don't allow our instincts or desires to define what is morally right or wrong. Before Genesis 3, Adam and Eve could have done all those things, since everything about them was good, but Paul's words remind us that the world has changed. We have changed. This does not deny the reality of our feelings or the pain of our dysphoria. But this does say that what we feel is not the basis of our faith.

Thankfully, however, Paul didn't fill Romans 8 to the brim with brokenness. He found his hope in Jesus. "We ourselves, who have the firstfruits of the Spirit, groan inwardly as we wait eagerly for our adoption to sonship, the redemption of our bodies" (Romans 8:23).

If you or someone you love deals with gender dysphoria, highlight that phrase, the "redemption of our bodies." Jesus has a future plan for the body that you battle with, plans to redeem it, to change and perfect it. Soon—believe your Savior's promise!—very soon, you will see Jesus' face, and everything about your body will change. Your body won't be broken anymore. You won't feel things that aren't factual. You won't want to crawl out of your skin. You won't have to battle the voices that scream in your head. You will be glorious when Jesus comes back.

Until that day comes, you have a Savior who not only walks by your side but knows what it is like to have a body that doesn't quite fit. Have you ever thought of that? Jesus, as the Son of God, lived in eternal euphoria. Forever and ever, with his Father and the Holy Spirit, Jesus existed in a place where everything is whole. But two thousand years ago, he took on flesh, and his existence drastically changed. He chose to limit himself, to contain all his divine power. In other words, Jesus chose to take on a body that could be broken.

Look how Paul puts it in Philippians: "He made himself nothing by taking the very nature of a servant, being made in human likeness. And being found in appearance as a man, he humbled himself by becoming obedient to death—even death on a cross!" (2:7,8). The God who saw our broken bodies got a body so he could be broken and we could be whole.

Every time you see a cross, know that Jesus gets it. Even better, through that same cross (and the glorious bodily resurrection that followed), Jesus will get you through it, all the way to that day when your dysphoria will be dead and gone.

As I wrap up part two, let's pause for a quick review. Up to this point, we have learned that God gives us a gender, either male or female, which is based on our genetics/genitals. When, due to the effects of our sinful world, we experience a disconnect, God does not want us to "trans" our gender but instead, like Paul, to faithfully wait until Jesus comes to restore our bodies and our souls. Yet we do not wait alone but rather with the Savior who understands our human pain and is full of the compassion and strength we need to trust him day by day.

THE GOD WHO SAW OUR BROKEN BODIES GOT A BODY SO HE COULD BE BROKEN AND WE COULD BE WHOLE.

That brings us to our final question—What now? As people who follow Jesus, depend on his forgiveness, and want to do his will even if it means denying our own desires, what do we do now?

Actually, the answer is pretty simple—do life together. I'm absolutely convinced that the best thing for us is to do life together as brothers and sisters in Christ in these temporarily broken bodies. We don't need secret groups for transgender people and adulterers and porn addicts and worriers. We just need to do life together. To talk about our struggles as a church. To join with fellow sinner-saints and be honest, because everyone in that room is groaning too, wishing that their struggle didn't feel so natural, didn't feel so good. To pray for each other. To encourage each other. To forgive each other in Jesus' name. Just like the author of Hebrews told suffering believers to live their lives "encouraging one another—and all the more as you see the Day approaching" (10:25).

Personally, I've never experienced gender dysphoria, but I do know the sunup-to-sundown struggle of living with this sinful nature and in a broken body. Better yet, I know Jesus. I believe in the worthiness of Jesus for being so patient, kind, forgiving, so merciful to me, a sinner who struggles in so many ways. Maybe you've been jealous in your heart. Perhaps you've shared secrets behind closed doors. Maybe you've worn underwear of the opposite sex beneath your clothes. We all have something. Something to repent of. Something to bring to Jesus. Something to lay at the foot of the cross.

Our struggles with sin and our love for Jesus are the common denominators that let us do life together. Because in the gathering of God's saints are people who love you and love Jesus. People who are ready to pray, ready to hug, to forgive, to walk with you, all the while needing you to walk with them. Would you do that?

I pray to God that you and I would, because it is so good when we do. Just ask her. Remember that sister in Christ whom I mentioned at the start of this chapter? I wasn't the first person she told. No, her first confession was to her Life Group. The Holy Spirit was compelling her to disclose her dysphoria instead of struggling alone with that secret. So she did. To a group of people who, perhaps, had never been through it and could not truly understand it.

And do you know what happened? They loved her. They hugged her. They prayed for her. They kept talking to her. And when she told me that, I was so proud of God's people. So proud. Because that is how God gets us through it. God is in the sustaining and transforming business, and he does it through us. Through our honest confessions. Through the love of Jesus, our Savior who is coming back to make all things new, even you.

STUDY QUESTIONS

1. What has been your experience with gender dysphoria? Based on this chapter, did you balance God's grace and God's truth well?

2. Why is understanding the two separate comings of Jesus so crucial to a hopeful view of sexuality?

3. What does Proverbs 3:5,6 have to say to a believer who is battling gender dysphoria?

PART 3

MARRIAGE, ADULTERY, AND DIVORCE

Chapter 12

LIVING TOGETHER BEFORE MARRIAGE —AN OPTION FOR CHRISTIANS?

I once forced a room full of pastors and ministry leaders to take a theological stand on one of the more personal issues of modern times. I began, "On the count of three, I want you to vote for option 1 or 2, and those are your only two options. Option 1—Living together before marriage is wrong no matter what. No matter what a couple does or doesn't do under the same roof, sharing an address before marriage is sinful. Option 2—Living together before marriage isn't essentially wrong. You may or may not do wrong things while living together, but the very act of sharing an address is okay with Jesus. Ready to vote? Three, two, one, go!"

The answers that followed were interesting. The debate that followed the answers was even more so.

But no matter the vote, we all realized that living together before marriage is something we needed to figure out, because it has become, in just a few generations, the new normal, even in the church. And that debate—Is it wrong? Is it right? Does it depend?—is happening all the time among families, friends, and fellow Christians.

I am not sure about you, but the longer I live and the more couples I see, both healthy and dysfunctional, the more I realize why living together is such an emotionally charged issue. Marriage is meant to be forever, so it's important to know, as best you can, if you are meant to share a marriage. How will you do sharing a house, a bathroom, a budget? Divorces happen every day because of money, sexual compatibility, and day-to-day doing life together. So, many would claim, it only makes sense to spend some days living together before taking those sacred vows.

Add to that all the failed marriages many of us have seen, often up close and painfully personal. Grandma might scold you for "shacking up" with your boyfriend, but after watching your parents argue for years until their separation, you are terrified to jump into marriage and end up in the same sad situation.

Add to that the crazy cost of rent, the inconvenience of driving back to your apartment every night, and the simple fact that you love each other and love being with each other, and you see why, in so many ways, living together seems to make sense.

No wonder a 2019 study of eighteen- to forty-nine-year-olds revealed that for every one person who thinks that living together is bad, five to six believe that it is good.[1] I wouldn't be surprised if you were persuaded to join that majority because of the reasons listed previously.

But if you are in love and love God, there are two questions you need to answer in regard to this issue. First, will living together make us happy? Second, does God see living together as holy? If your goal is to have a happy, holy home, you need to know the Bible's answers to those crucial questions, so let's explore them here.

Part 1—Does living together make couples happy? Does living together make us better, stronger, and happier as a couple? Is it good for relationships? Good for children?

I mentioned the pros, but what about the big picture? Wise people aren't persuaded by one side of an argument, so what speaks against the wisdom of moving in before marriage?

One of the helpful parts about living in the 2020s is that we have a truckload of in-depth studies on this issue, and the data, surprisingly, is quite one-sided. According to the latest research, couples who marry *without living together* trust each other more, serve each other more, are more satisfied with household chores, and more satisfied with their sex lives.[2]

Those who marry without living together first are more likely to be faithful to each other and more likely to raise healthy children—two outcomes that are on the top of our list of relationship goals.

If you or someone you love is living with their partner pre-vows, I encourage you to take a second to reread the last two paragraphs. Without assuming you will be the exception to the rule, honestly ask yourself if that is the kind of relationship you prefer. Is the risk worth saving a few thousand in rent or a few hours of travel each week?

As you compare the pros and the cons, I encourage you to wonder why. Why would living together first and getting to know each other better lead to a less satisfying life? That almost feels illogical, doesn't it?

But there is a logical, biblical explanation. Living together might look a lot like an unofficial marriage, but it is missing the most important part—the vow. When you live together, you have not taken a vow. You have not made a promise to your partner. You have not bound yourself to better behavior. In fact, you might be doing just the opposite.

LIVING TOGETHER MIGHT LOOK A LOT LIKE AN UNOFFICIAL MARRIAGE, BUT IT IS MISSING THE MOST IMPORTANT PART—THE VOW.

When you live together before marriage, you are teaching yourself to see your relationship in a way that violates the essence of marriage. Like a basketball player who practices with bad form and then hopes to jump into a real game, cohabitation is not a paperless version of marriage but a dangerous distortion of it.

What do I mean? Here's what God says about marriage: "Each one of you also must love his wife as he loves himself, and the wife must respect her husband" (Ephesians 5:33). Notice what word isn't in this verse—*If*. Marriage isn't, "I love you, but if I'm not happy, then I'm moving out." It's not, "I love you, but if you don't do enough for me, I'm packing up my stuff." No. The vow of marriage is not, "I will if," but simply, "I will." I will love you (period). If you deserve my love, I will love you. If you don't deserve my love, I will love you. Or, as the classic vow states, I will love you "for better or for worse." Marriage is unconditional love with no ifs or asterisks, a vow to be together until death do us part.

But that's not living together. Living together comes with a thousand "ifs" and zero vows. Living together leaves the door unlocked, giving you a chance to leave whenever you want. And that trains you to treat marriage like a contract and not a covenant.

No wonder couples who cohabitate end up divorced more often. They have hundreds, perhaps thousands, of days of practicing the thought, "I can leave if I am unhappy." That's why the wisdom of the church has urged couples over the years, "Wait! If you want to be happy, wait." While it won't be convenient, the wait is worth it.

In chapter 6 of this book, I mentioned a guest to one of my middle school Bible classes when I was a younger pastor. Remember him—Keandre? If not, here's what he said again about sex and marriage after I opened the Scriptures and tried to faithfully teach God's view on such issues.

"Pastor, the world would be better if everyone did that. There would be no families who don't have dads around and no people having kids before they're ready."

Wow. He wasn't talking about biblical morality. He was just talking about being happy. He was talking about family and stability. This young man hadn't read all the studies about the pros and cons of cohabitation.

Instead, he just reacted based on his own experiences and said, "God's way seems way better."

Does doing our own thing with sex and marriage make us long-term happier? No. The risks outweigh the rewards. Thus, studies and scriptural wisdom says, "If you want to be happy, wait until you're married."

But what about the holy? That's the second question we need to cover here. Because if you are wired at all like I am, you know the difference between a probability and a prohibition. If I was living together with my girlfriend and taking this message to heart, I might push back: "Okay, I hear what you're saying. We are more likely to have issues if we live together, but answer this question—Is it wrong? Is there a passage where God says it is sin? If we try to remember what you said about the vows and 'no ifs and asterisks,' can we live under the same roof and still love God?" Those are fair questions. Can Christians say that Scripture forbids cohabitation?

I'll be straight with you. In the entire Bible, there isn't a verse that says, "You shall not live together."

But there is a verse that deserves our full consideration: "Marriage should be honored by all, and the marriage bed kept pure, for God will judge the adulterer and all the sexually immoral" (Hebrews 13:4). Let's break that down and see how it applies to our questions.

"Marriage should be honored by all." Who should honor marriage? All of us. If your parents were happily married or bitterly divorced, if you have been divorced, if you two are still in school and living off ramen and water, if you two are older and living off Social Security benefits, you should honor marriage. Marriage should be honored by *all*.

Every so often, I hear someone say, "Marriage is just a piece of paper." Hebrews 13:4 forbids such a view. Marriage is not a piece of paper but rather one of God's first ideas. It shows up on page one of the Bible and is a frequent theme in the teaching of Jesus himself. The Bible honors marriage. We all should too.

"And the marriage bed kept pure." Not only did God give us marriage; he gave us the marriage bed. Sex was God's idea! And God, who loves every person he has ever created, has put a sign on the bedroom door—Reserved for marriage. In God's eyes, sex is a marriage thing. Sexual pleasure is a marriage thing. The joy, creativity, and pleasure that make sex good is for a husband and wife to explore together under the protective roof of their lifelong vows.

THE BIBLE HONORS MARRIAGE. WE ALL SHOULD TOO.

If you wonder why God reserves sex strictly for marriage, check out the first three chapters in part 2 of this book, which explore the wisdom of being both excited and strict about sexual morality. But, for now, note the clear words of Hebrews 13: the marriage bed (a.k.a. sex) should be kept pure.

"For God will judge the adulterer and all the sexually immoral." Apparently, the marriage bed is not a joke to God. He doesn't laugh when singles sneak into that reserved room. He doesn't wink when one thing leads to another with vowless couples. If you're sleeping together, let that sink in. God will judge all the sexually immoral. Not might. He will. Sex before marriage is sin, as serious to God as racism or child abuse is to you.

If you just shrug and say, "Whatever," if you go back to that same bed and do those same things, if you pressure her into moving into your house or seduce him into climbing into your bed, if you stay sexually active without any remorse or repentance, God will judge you.

That is my concern. If you live together, you won't be holy. If you share the same bed, you won't keep it pure. I doubt I'm wrong. I didn't live with Kim until after our wedding night, but we still struggled to honor God's boundaries for our bodies. When you love someone in every way and are physically attracted to them every day, who can resist? Be real with me right now. Can you share the same bed, bedroom, and bathroom and remain pure? Can you be right there when he gets out of the shower or she puts on her bra and yet remain self-controlled and holy?

No, there is no passage that bluntly says, "Thou shall not cohabitate," but there is this: "God will judge the sexually immoral."

I imagine some of you are mad right now because I'm messing with your plan. You planned to live together and save money so you could have your dream wedding, and now I'm throwing a holy wrench right into your spokes. I bet, for some, this is going to cause a fight if you bring it up. You feel convicted, but he doesn't care. You know, deep down, that you are disobeying God, but she isn't bothered by these words. This message might mess with your relationship. But listen—I would rather mess with your sexuality in this life than lose your soul in the life to come.

Some of you have a decision to make. Maybe that means moving out because you love God more than the money or the convenience. Maybe it means getting married sooner rather than later, even if the wedding isn't what you dreamed about as a little girl. Maybe you get married now and have a big party in two years, something that my church does with couples all the time. I'm not sure what step you will take, but I am sure you should wait. That's what people who are pursuing holiness do.

Back to Keandre from my Bible class. After I got done teaching about sex, marriage, and living together, he raised his hand again, this time not with his perspective but instead with a direct question. "Pastor Mike, do you keep all these commandments? Loving your wife, waiting for marriage, not lusting with your eyes, all the stuff you just taught us. Do you do all that?"

Ugh. Some of you know from other messages that my sexual history has not been spotless. Kim and I were both virgins until our wedding night, but there are other ways to be sexually immoral, and I was. Hebrews claimed that God will judge "all" the sexually immoral, which includes men like me. So, what do I do? What do we do?

Answer—We run to Jesus. We run to Jesus in repentance. We cling to the cross and make our confession: "We sinned. Jesus, we sinned so many times. We are sorry." Like the prodigal son in Jesus' story, we say to our partner, "I have sinned against heaven and against you" (Luke 15:21). We confess that we loved convenience more than Jesus, money more than our Maker, our wants more than God's will. No blaming it on our parents' ugly divorce. No excusing it on our tight budget. We simply own it. We repent.

And (this is my favorite part) Jesus forgives us. He opens his arms to us, to all of us who come to him broken and remorseful. Your situation might be as sinful as the prostitutes who gathered around Jesus or the woman caught in the act of adultery or the countless sinners who cried out to Jesus for mercy. But Jesus' reaction to you is the same as it was toward them. He loved, cleansed, and saved them.

HE OPENS HIS ARMS TO US, TO ALL OF US WHO COME TO HIM BROKEN AND REMORSEFUL.

Just like the father loved his prodigal son. When that sexually sinful kid finally came home with nothing to offer his father but his confession, the father saw him (because he was waiting for him), ran to him, hugged and kissed him, forgave, clothed, and cleansed him, wrapped his arms around him, and threw a party in his honor. That's what our God is like to sexual sinners who come back to him.

You might be living with your girlfriend right now and finally realizing your sin. Or perhaps you're thinking back to how your marriage began—out of order and far from holy. But Hebrews 13 tells us that the Jesus who forgave sinners two thousand years ago is still at it today: "Jesus Christ is the same yesterday and today and forever" (verse 8). Jesus has not changed. The same Savior who opened his arms to messy souls is opening them to you and me. The cross of Jesus doesn't have an expiration date! We run to him again and again, and the blood that he shed makes us clean. It makes us pure. It makes us enough for God. This is why we love God. This is why we trust God.

The five pastors at my church, in our 100 total years of ministry, have probably officiated a thousand weddings. Church weddings, barn and beach weddings, all the weddings. We've heard more "I dos" and eaten more fried chicken than you can imagine. But do you know the weddings we've loved the most? Not the one with the designer dress (although a beaming bride is beautiful) or the late-night pizza bar (although I do adore that recent invention). No, the weddings we love most are the weddings where God is loved most. Where a man and his wife love each other a lot but love Jesus even more. Where their lives say, "Father, not our will but yours be done."

So, if you are living together or thinking about living together or know someone who is living together, remember this: a couple that puts Jesus first, no matter how hard that choice may be, creates the happiest, holiest home.

STUDY QUESTIONS

1. Go back to God's creation of marriage in Genesis 2:18-25. What does verse 24 have to say about the beauty of intimacy and the commitment of marriage?

2. Agree/Disagree: Christian friends should say something to Christian friends who are living together.

3. "Where sin increased, grace increased all the more" (Romans 5:20). Why is this verse so important as many of us think about our personal history with relationships?

Chapter 13

WHAT MAKES MARRIAGE WORK (AND WONDERFUL)

When an older friend told me about his epic anniversary party, I knew I needed to hear the whole story. He and his wife decided to go big after being together for fifty years, so they threw a multigenerational marriage celebration. They spent an entire week together—eating, talking, swimming, hiking—and toasted five decades of love. At the same time, their children celebrated twenty-five, twenty-three, twenty, and ten years of marriage, a total of 128 years of commitment. But even better was that at the start and end of every day of their celebration was Jesus. Every morning, one of their sons led their entire family in worship. Every evening, one of the grandchildren led them in praying to that same Savior.

#relationshipgoals! Isn't that incredible? This isn't some made-up story. My friend would tell you (emphatically) that he is a sinner, that he and his wife are far from perfect, but I bet you would agree with me they seem to be a happy, holy family.

Isn't that what we all want? Whether we are married, hope to be married, or just love people who are married, we all want happy homes. We want to get as close to happily ever after as possible. And for those of us who follow Jesus, we want to be holy too. We want to follow God's plan for relationships, doing what he says is good for our souls.

Sadly, my friend's story is not normal. So many relationships are less happy and holy and more sad and sinful. Maybe your parents' relationship was like that or you are currently in a relationship like that. You might not be happily married, and you don't know how to get unstuck.

Maybe you hope to be married but are scared that something will go wrong. Maybe you're living with your partner, and Grandma is freaking out, but you need to know if you're compatible before you say, "I do."

Maybe you're one of the many couples from my church who is trying to heal from infidelity, to rebuild what sin wrecked, something even better than before. Or maybe you just know people in those situations, and you aren't sure how to help them.

Regardless, I bet you want a relationship that is happy and holy.

That's why in this chapter, I want to address people who are married or one day will be. What should you do (or not do) to have a happy, holy home?

Let's start with the guys. I recently typed "husbands" and "married" and "marriage" into a Bible search engine, and what I discovered was golden. This passage seemed like a helpful summary: "A married man is concerned about the affairs of this world—how he can please his wife" (1 Corinthians 7:33).

A married Christian man is not just concerned about Christ in heaven but also about his wife on earth. Specifically—don't miss this phrase—how he can "please his wife." What is pleasing to her? What puts a smile on her face? A holy husband cares about that. To use Paul's language, a holy husband is "devoted" to that. His passion is pleasing his wife.

In those "husband" passages, I found what I'm calling Seven Commandments for Husbands. Write these down or highlight them right in this book:

- Be considerate.
- Don't be harsh.
- Treat with respect.
- Love. Love. Love. Love. Ha!

Dudes must depend on repetition! Love her. Do what makes her feel loved, consider what's loving in her eyes, and respect the way she receives love. That's the holy work that will help create a happy home.

Here's the most famous example: "Husbands, love your wives, just as Christ loved the church and gave himself up for her" (Ephesians 5:25). Just like Jesus, love will cost you. If she's wired differently than you, your love will have to be intentional, and if she wants it differently than you, your love will likely be inconvenient. But this is how you can please your wife—love, love, love, love her.

I am aware a man should never claim to know what a woman wants, but I recently took a chance and posted what I knew was a stereotype but true to my own experience. The paragraph that follows is the first piece of viral content I have ever produced. It was viewed more than 1,000,000 times in less than three weeks on Instagram alone and shared tens of thousands of times. Apparently, couples found this advice to be true and essential to marital happiness. Ready for it?

The best husbands act without being asked.

Most modern women do so much and carry more stress than we realize. They go to work and then come home to work—the cooking, cleaning, emails, and scheduling. (If you have kids, multiply the weight of that last sentence by 17!) Thus, few things mean more than when a husband who loves his wife sees her stress and tries to solve it without being asked. If she asks for help and you give it, you are a good husband. If she doesn't even have to ask and it gets done, you are a great one.

You might object: "I can't read her mind!" Maybe not. But think of it this way: Marriage is like running your fantasy football team—(1) you examine the data you have in order to (2) make this week the best it can be. You listen to a podcast or check a website to find out who is playing whom, who is injured, who is playing well, and who is not. You use that information to make specific decisions that give you the greatest chance of success.

What if you did that with marriage? What if you simply (1) examined the data you have to (2) make this week the best it can be? Ask her about her week, listen to her answers, note what stresses her, peek at her to-do list, and then act! Without being asked, react to her emotions. I guarantee she will be stunned. And grateful. And find you very attractive.

Guys, God has called us to be the head of our households, to be the first to love like Jesus, so act without being asked. That's what leads you to a happy, holy home.

In 2021, archaeologists in northern China discovered the skeletons of a couple inside a 1,500-year-old grave. They were not side by side but with arms wrapped around each other. The archaeologists, upon examining the remains, suggested that this couple had found "eternal love." I like that. Guys, we want something eternal, don't we? Love that lasts. And God is helping us with a clear and direct call to action. Don't wait until you feel respected; just do what makes her feel loved. Be devoted to pleasing your wife, and you'll lead the way to a happy, holy home.

BE DEVOTED TO PLEASING YOUR WIFE, AND YOU'LL LEAD THE WAY TO A HAPPY, HOLY HOME.

All right, ladies, your turn. What does your Father in heaven say to you about your marriage here on earth? Kind of the same thing: "A married woman is concerned about the affairs of this world—how she can please her husband" (1 Corinthians 7:34). Every wife must constantly ask herself, "What's pleasing to my husband?" Ladies, if that question never slips down your list of priorities, if you never push pause on that question because of your job or your kids or your screens, you will be blessed. If, to steal Paul's word again, your "devotion" is to that question—How can I please my husband?—your home is highly likely to be very happy and very holy.

In my study of those same passages on marriage, I discovered the Seven Commandments for Wives. God, in his Word, commands seven specific things to his beloved daughters. Write these down or highlight them:

- Respect.
- Love.
- Be subject to.
- Submit. Submit. Submit. Submit.

Interesting. And perhaps a bit uncomfortable. But before you check out on me, let's remember that this is God's list. This isn't the Patriarchy Club saying, "Yeah. Let's put *submit* down four times just to keep them in their place!" No, this is God speaking. This is the God of love whom you pray to, the Jesus who saved you, and Lord whom you trust.

AT THE HEART OF SUBMISSION IS A YOU-FIRST HEART.

Second, let's remember what *submit* means. It's what Jesus did when he put the Father first and said, "Not as I will, but as you will" (Matthew 26:39). Submitting doesn't mean you're inferior or unintelligent any more than Jesus was inferior or unintelligent. It simply means that when there's a difference, you put him first. When you can't do it your way and his way, you humbly submit to his way instead of forcing him to submit to yours. At the heart of submission is a you-first heart.

Ladies, this is a stereotype that isn't always true but one I hear all the time from men in struggling marriages. I'll try to summarize it. Ready? Here goes—Sex.

I know that sex can be complicated for many reasons, but statistically 75 percent of husbands have a higher desire for sex than their wives. You might not be as interested as often, and that's okay, but that difference is your chance to show him love. When you care as much about this as you do your kids' education, your career, or your favorite show, that makes a man feel so respected. When you respond to his advances, he feels like a man. When you initiate the advances, he feels like *the* man. Honestly, most guys I know would rather wear dirty clothes and eat ramen seven days in a row if their wives were passionate about passion (and all the married men said, "Amen!").

Set this book down and put your fingers up (hold up two index fingers a few inches apart). Every day, spouses make choices that either draw them closer or push them apart. Be considerate about her needs (move closer). Respect his wants (move closer). Care more about work (move away). Give all your energy to the kids (move away). Love, submit, love, submit, love, submit, love, submit (move closer and closer and closer). God knows that selfless love and you-first submission that imitates Jesus is what makes a happy, holy home.

Most of the passages I shared with you in this chapter came from the writings of the apostle Paul, and they had something in common—they were written later in his ministry. All those "husbands, love" and "wives, submit" commands come in the middle, if not the very end, of what Paul wrote to various churches. Want to guess what Paul always said first? Jesus.

Before 1 Corinthians 7 said to "be concerned" about your spouse, 1 Corinthians 1 said, "Christ Jesus . . . is our righteousness, holiness and redemption" (verse 30). Because Jesus loved you, you are right with God. You are holy in his sight, even if you've done some unholy things in your relationship. You are redeemed, bought with the price that he paid at the cross.

Before Colossians 3 said, "Submit . . . love," Colossians 1 said, "[God] has reconciled you by Christ's physical body through death to present you holy in his sight, without blemish and free from accusation" (verse 22). Because Jesus submitted to his Father, you are reconciled to the Father, completely one with God. You are holy in his sight, forgiven for everything you've done wrong, with no sin left to make God accuse you.

Before Ephesians 5 said, "Submit . . . love," Ephesians 1 said, "Praise be to the God and Father of our Lord Jesus Christ, who has blessed us in the heavenly realms with every spiritual blessing in Christ" (verse 3). Every spiritual blessing! If you have Jesus, you are forgiven, loved, saved, guarded, kept, chosen, precious, invited, included, accepted, and bound for the most blessed life with God.

Do you see? Marriage starts with Jesus. It always starts with Jesus. What makes us so happy and completely holy is Jesus, who, like a perfect husband, loved us by giving up everything and who, like a perfect wife, submitted to the plan the Father had to save us. That love is so foundational, so transformational, that when we get married, there is only one way to live—like Jesus.

MARRIAGE STARTS WITH JESUS.

Husbands, love like Jesus. Wives, submit like Jesus. It isn't easy. But it is the path to a happy, holy home.

My friend gets that. Remember my buddy and his fifty-year anniversary party? When I emailed him about the party, I asked for some details about his marriage and family. He responded with a section that contained 310 words (I counted). And guess how many of those words were about Jesus? (I also counted.) Let me quote some of what he wrote: *"Blessings, blessing, God, grace, forgiveness, prayer, Lord, bless, God, pray, pray, Lord, grace, faith, bless, God, God, forgiving, grace, blessings, forgiveness, prayers, prayers, Savior, Lord, blessed, blessings, blessed, Jesus, Jesus, God bless."* Out of 310 words, 32 were about Jesus! In the midst of all the differences and disagreements, all the sin and stress, was Jesus.

I'll let my friend have the last word here: *"Both my wife and I had parents who were blessed with over 60 years. We both remember talking with our parents about how foolish it is for people to think that there would never be rough spots or bumpy roads. We are all sinners. We need Jesus, and we all have Jesus."*

We all need Jesus. Through faith, we all can have Jesus. No matter how many people live under your roof, Jesus is the heart of a happy and holy home.

STUDY QUESTIONS

1. Whether you are single, married, dating, or divorced, take ten minutes today to pray for the married couples you know. Ask our Father to guide them to put this chapter into practice.

2. Study Ephesians 5:22-33, one of the longest sections in the Bible about marriage. Which words/phrases grab your attention? Why?

3. Agree/Disagree: "Act without being asked" is a way for couples to divorce-proof their marriage.

Chapter 14

ADULTERY: HOW TO AVOID IT AND WHAT TO DO AFTER IT

A while back, my church family, sadly, had a series of unfaithful marriages. As I tried to help this couple and that couple, three things struck me—them and me and you.

Them—They were not once-in-a-while church people whom I barely knew but every-Sunday, Bible-reading, deeply rooted Christians. And yet adultery happened to them, and when it did, they struggled to know what to do, even how to function.

Me—Despite all my knowledge of the Bible, I didn't know exactly how to help. Since I had never experienced it, I didn't really get it. The things some people said confused me. The way some people felt didn't make sense to me. My advice too often seemed shallow and unrealistic.

You—People like you were affected too. Friends were pulled into complex relational dynamics that challenged their friendships. They took a step away, not knowing quite what to do. Others got overly involved. They didn't have a script to follow, which explained the confusion and frustration.

After thinking about *them* and *me* and *you*, I realized that I needed to address another tough topic—adultery.

Few things are as common, catastrophic, and complex as adultery. In a culture where one out of five husbands and one out of eight wives will be unfaithful, adultery, sooner or later, will be part of your life or the lives of loved ones.

Maybe that's you right now. Maybe you too are on this ultramarathon of rebuilding trust, moving past the pain, and finally feeling the tiniest bit of hope. Or maybe you are still stuck in the shame and the pain, and you don't know how to move on or forgive or feel what you used to feel. You're on autopilot, numb, just trying to survive. Or maybe you haven't cheated, but honestly, you're close. Things are stale at home, you don't feel like his priority, but there's that guy from work or that girl online who has your attention and attraction. Or maybe you love someone whose love has been rocked by a broken vow. Your friend just came clean. Your sister admitted an affair. And now you're trying to figure out what to do, say, and how to help, and people are picking sides, blaming, suggesting, gossiping, giving up. It's a mess, and you don't know how to help them heal.

FEW THINGS ARE AS COMMON, CATASTROPHIC, AND COMPLEX AS ADULTERY.

For those reasons, I have written the next two chapters on adultery. We won't be able to cover everything, but in this chapter, I want to share five biblical truths about adultery.

Ready for truth #1? *Don't!* Write that down. When it comes to adultery, God says, "Don't!" In fact, of the fifty-five uses of the word *adultery* in the Bible, the very first one that shows up is this: "You shall not commit adultery" (Exodus 20:14). You shall not. Why not? Because adultery butchers God's blessings. It takes the "one flesh" of marriage and rips it in two. Committing adultery, as one author says, is like hosting a picnic with the people you love . . . on an interstate. Eventually, your sin will smash into your life like a cement truck, and the carnage will be your fault.

Have you ever considered the consequences of adultery? Like the loss of trust. The half-truths and the total lies will take away one of marriage's most important gifts—trust. If you cheat, he won't trust you to look at your phone, go out with friends, travel for work, be on the computer, come home late, or run a quick errand after work. Every hour of every day, she will wonder where you are and with whom and what you might be doing.

And then there are the triggers. Everything connected with the affair will trigger your wife. The device you used to DM her. The job where you worked with her. The date you confessed to her. The church where you worshiped with her. People, places, and things will now be traumatizing for your wife in a way you never thought about. You should fear adultery more than you fear fentanyl. The Bible says that road leads to death. It's like starting a campfire in your lap. It can ruin you, and you must run from it.

In 1941, a woman from the Soviet Union was put in a Nazi concentration camp where she witnessed murders, lost family members, and endured Hitler's horrors. But she survived, got married, and, sadly, was cheated on. And this Holocaust survivor said, "The affair was the most painful experience of my life."[1] Don't.

Truth #2—*Don't come close!* Picture it this way: imagine me standing at the edge of a stage. On the stage is a faithful marriage, and down below the stage is an affair. Few people, if any, think they would ever cheat, but what happens is that they get close and then slip. That's how affairs happen. We get too close.

Every act of adultery is unique, but there is a fairly predictable pattern. Highlight this:

Step 1—It starts with deprivation. When one spouse feels deprived of attention or affection or someone who will listen, they can get desperate.

Desperate for someone who notices them, who compliments and flirts, who initiates physical touch, who makes them feel like they matter.

Step 2—Attraction. You notice her. You start to think of him. She's your type. He gives you the butterflies. It could be her looks or his personality, but you feel something different with them.

Step 3—Intention. You do something with the intention of connecting with the person of your attraction. You go out of your way to stop by her office. You do your hair for the Zoom call because he's going to be in that little square.

Step 4—Emotion. You open up about emotional stuff, about hurts and hopes and dreams, and—don't miss this—about your struggles with your spouse when you're not with your spouse. When your confidant is your crush, you are so close. In fact, if your biggest emotional connection is with them, you are already having an emotional affair.

Step 5—Connection. A physical connection. Once you touch someone who has touched your heart, your toes are over the edge. One author admitted, "*I offered [her] a friendly shoulder. That offer of comfort became much more within seconds. Falling was much easier than I'd ever believed possible.*"[2]

Those are the steps that lead you over the edge.

Maybe you see yourself in one of those steps, but you never would step over the edge. Listen! No one thinks they will. So, before you fall, take a step back. Even if it's awkward. Even if she's confused by your behavior. Even if your friends think you're being a prude. Some people call these guardrails, personal habits that keep us from getting too close to a catastrophic fall. It's why I will never meet privately with a woman at church if no one is around. It's why some women won't text a married friend unless his wife is on the thread. It's why others share their passwords with their spouses, so there are no places for secrets. It's why the smartest spouses ask each other often, "How are we doing? How can I love you better?" There's little room for deprivation when you're that devoted to each other.

If you think this is all a bit dramatic, listen to what Jesus said about it. In his famous teaching on adultery and lust, he said, "If your right eye causes you to stumble, gouge it out and throw it away. It is better for you to lose one part of your body than for your whole body to be thrown into hell" (Matthew 5:29). The point? It's better to take a drastic step than end up with a devastating ending.

This brings us to truth #3, perhaps the most essential thing I have learned from all my studies. Highlight this: *Healing = Time × Work × Work*. Couples who commit adultery can heal. They can. They have. They will. Some, by the pure grace of Jesus, end up with stronger marriages than they had before. You might not believe that yet, but it is true. God can heal your marriage. And here's how God heals marriages—Time, Work, and Work.

First, time. You know the saying, right? Time heals . . . all wounds. This wound is a big one. Adultery is like a bus hitting a pedestrian, and there is no shortcut to getting back on your feet by Friday. You can work, she can work—work with a counselor, a pastor, on yourselves, together. But if time equals almost 0, your healing will be minimal. It takes time.

How much time? Since every couple is different, I'm reluctant to suggest an answer, but many authors say about two years after the last secret is out is when many couples mutually feel like they're going to make it. You need time to talk about everything, and then time to talk about everything again and again. Time for him to play detective, to ask every question, for her to "have an affair with the affair," obsessing over everything. I wish it was faster, but it isn't. Healing takes time.

And work. The one who cheated must work. Two years can pass, but if you multiply 2 x 0, the healing is 0. I won't lie to you. If you stepped over that edge, you have so much work to do. In four thousand different ways, you will have to be humble. Like telling the whole truth. You cannot—please hear me!—you cannot trickle out the truth. I know you're scared the whole story will make them leave you, but you cannot, must not, please do not lie to them again. Do the necessary work of telling them the truth. And then the real work begins.

You will have to talk when he wants to talk. You will have to give her the right to your phone whenever she wants. You will have to accept her absolute disgust with sex for the time being. You will have to resist the temptation to yell, “I already answered that question!” No, instead, you must do the holy work of humility. You-first is always important in marriage, but never more important than after an affair. If that’s you, then make “work” the biggest number it can be. Because Healing = Time × Work.

Times work. This is probably the hardest thing I’m going to write here, but if Healing = Time × Work × Work, then the one cheated on must work too. If you don’t work, this won’t work.

Years ago, I tried patiently to help a couple heal from a devastating affair. Lots of time had passed, and the husband, who had cheated, had done so much work. One day, I asked his wife, “What are you doing to serve him these days?” And she said, “Letting him live in our house.” I smiled. She smiled. We laughed. Then she said, “That sounds bad, doesn’t it?” (She said I could share that story with you.)

I get it. You are the one who was betrayed. You are the one who can’t sleep. You are the one whose life got turned upside down. That’s true. The Bible doesn’t command you to stay after an affair, but if you do stay, then you still have a vow to keep, and you don’t get a free pass to sin. There is good work for you to do on yourself. Because, even before this happened, you were a sinner. In fact, you were a sinful spouse. You had stuff to work on then. You still do now.

A fellow pastor likes to ask couples these questions: Before the affair, were you happy? Were you two close? Did you feel emotionally connected? Did you feel loved? Did you feel respected? Was your marriage, communication, and sex life a bigger priority than work or the kids or the screens? If not, what good and holy work might God be calling both of you to do today?

I know that work, for both of you, feels overwhelming. So let's bring God into it. I invite you to pray the Lord's Prayer, but this time think of what it means for couples dealing with adultery. Ready? "Our Father in heaven, hallowed be your name. Your kingdom come. Your will be done on earth as it is in heaven. Give us today our daily bread. Forgive us our sins, as we forgive those who sin against us. Lead us not into temptation, but deliver us from evil. For yours is the kingdom, the power, and the glory, now and forever. Amen."

Truth #4 is quick, because it's what the next chapter is about—*Run to them.* You will need them. Friends. Family. A counselor. A pastor. A network of people who know you, love your marriage, and want to help you with the healing equation. Your mind will be a mess, and every lie will be so easy to believe. You'll need help. You'll grow impatient with the process or think you have the right to sin now. You'll need help. And that's what Christian friends are for. This is complicated and messy, so we'll spend the next chapter on the details. But for now, believe Paul's words: "Carry each other's burdens, and in this way, you will fulfill the law of Christ" (Galatians 6:2).

Truth #5—*Run to Him.* Run to God. Whether you cheated or were cheated on, run to God. If you cheated, here's what you need to know about God. He forgives people just like you. King David was just like you. He was married, and he was attracted to Bathsheba even though she was married. He had an affair and covered it up for an entire year. But when God sent the prophet Nathan to expose him, David repented, and God forgave him. Even for his adultery. David later sang, "Then I acknowledged my sin to you and did not cover up my iniquity. I said, 'I will confess my transgressions to the Lord.' And you forgave the guilt of my sin" (Psalm 32:5).

That is true for you too. Confess to God. He will forgive the guilt. He will forgive the sin. That's what Jesus did. Before you crossed that line, our Lord knew it. Ever thought about that? Two thousand years ago, when Jesus was on a cross, he knew all about this. He knew her name. He knew your secret. And Jesus loved you so much—you!—that he took that massive weight on his shoulders and bore it on a cross. Jesus didn't just die for some sins. Jesus died for all sins. So that no matter what happens to your marriage, you would know what happens with your God. Hear me, all you who have cheated. Because of Jesus, God likes you. You might hate yourself, but God refuses to hate you. He won't. He never will.

And if you've been cheated on, run to God too. You might have wondered a million times what's wrong with you, why you're not good enough, why he chose her, why she didn't choose you. You might be appalled at all the bitterness and hate that are coming out of you. The best thing I can say is that God chooses you. Because of Jesus, you are always, today and forever, enough for God. He always has time for you. He is never tired of you. You can't run out of prayer minutes. You can't make Jesus sigh and roll his eyes. God is love. And he loves you. He chooses you today. And that choice, because of Christ, will never change. Your marriage may heal, or it may not. It may be better after the affair, or it may be worse. But at the end of every day, your relationship with God is perfect. Jesus made it that way. Nothing to fix. No trust to rebuild. No holding your breath. Jesus made it perfect. You have a spot in the happiest, holiest home of all, in heaven itself. And Jesus made sure that nothing will change that.

YOU MIGHT HATE YOURSELF, BUT GOD REFUSES TO HATE YOU. HE WON'T. HE NEVER WILL.

"There is hope." That's what a local Christian counselor told me when I shared this chapter with him. "Things will be different, but they can be better than ever before." That's what a fellow pastor told me about his own experiences with couples who committed to do the work and wait on the Lord. He had many testimonies of couples who ended up better than before. And it's what I heard from some couples I interviewed who had been there and made it to the other side, not just back to where they were but better than before.

I will leave you with one word—*hope*. Maybe not today, maybe not tomorrow, but you will be better than before. Work and wait until the Lord restores what sin has broken. He will do it, either in this life or the next. But if you have Jesus, you have hope. Believe that.

STUDY QUESTIONS

1. Which of the five truths impacted you the most while you read this chapter?

2. Read Galatians 6:1-10 and find at least three connections you see between Paul's words and the topic of infidelity.

3. Whom did you think of as you read this chapter? Share this message with them and pray that God would use it to give them hope.

Chapter 15

ADULTERY: WHEN FRIENDS CHEAT

One of the hardest times to be a good friend is when adultery happens by or to someone you love. It's hard to know what to do when she is furious or numb or done, obsessed with what must be wrong with her, or unwilling to admit anything is wrong with her. What do you say when he is so ashamed or not ashamed enough, when he is sick with guilt or when he's sick of talking about the same things over and over? What do you do when friends and family members pick sides, point fingers, gossip, or step back altogether? Statistically, sooner or later, adultery will happen in your family, church, or among your friends. What does being a Christian look like in those moments?

It's a complex question with a simple answer—when friends cheat, give them grace and truth. Give them. Him and her. The betrayer and the betrayed. Grace and truth. And. Not one or the other but both. That's what you do. That's how you take God's side and help them rebuild a happy, holy home.

The gospel of John says Jesus Christ was "full of grace and truth" (1:14). I want to help you bring a whole lot of Jesus to the situation—it's what your friends need when they cheat.

This chapter is a bit complicated, just like infidelity is complicated. On the following pages, I will share how you can help him and her with grace and truth. Instead of one big idea, I'm presenting a lot of parts, so you may want to take notes. Ready?

WHEN FRIENDS CHEAT, GIVE THEM GRACE AND TRUTH.

Let's start with the friend who was cheated on—the victim of adultery. What does it mean to show him or her grace? It means, maybe more than ever before, to show up and share Jesus. You don't need to be a professional, just be present. Be there for coffee, when he needs to cry, or she needs to text. Even if you don't have anything profound to share, be there. Proverbs 27:10 says, "Better a neighbor nearby than a relative far away." It's helpful when you just show up.

Sound easy? It's not. In the previous chapter, you learned that many experts suggest it takes up to two years for unfaithful couples to start to heal. That means you're running a marathon without much training. That's the hard part. And because adultery isn't something couples share with the whole world, you might be only one of ten, eight, or six people who know. That's the even harder part. And because adultery is adultery, that weight will weigh about a thousand pounds. That's the hardest part. This chapter of your friendship might feel pretty one-sided, like you're listening and listening and not getting a lot in return. Most friendships are fueled by fun experiences, but dealing with adultery isn't fun. Which is why most friends fade away.

But grace shows up. Not all the time. You're not God, and you're not a 24/7 counselor who has no life besides being a friend to this one person. You are, however, called to be faithful. To shoulder that burden with them. So, pray for the strength to be there. Commit yourself to giving more for the next year. "God, you put me here for such a time as this, to be here during his time of greatest need."

And while you're showing up, share Jesus. He's the best grace of all. When God's chosen ones get cheated on, they tend to think about the cheating and not on the choosing. Your calling is to direct that person to the Rock they can stand on. Remind her that her identity, the deepest definition of who she is, isn't being the cute couple or the perfect family. No, her identity is as a child of God, and that hasn't changed. You get to bring this kind of grace to your hurting friend: that nothing will separate him from the love of God that is in Christ Jesus (Romans 8:38,39). "You may feel separated from your spouse. But there is nothing in the world, not even this, that can separate you from Jesus' love." In her trauma, those words won't sink in, so keep saying them. "God chooses you. God is here with you. God loves you." Show up and share Jesus. That's grace.

Next, give him or her the truth. Here's a truth your friend needs to know. I wrote about it in the last chapter: Healing = Time × Work × Work. In the midst of the emotions, she'll forget that truth all the time, so encourage her: "You're doing the work. He's doing the work. You're talking. He's listening. You're going to counseling. It just takes time. I remember three months ago you couldn't even smile, but I saw you smile today."

Or maybe he needs to hear some hard truth. I once asked a woman, "When you were trying to heal, did you need more of the gospel or the law? Did you need someone to remind you that you were loved, chosen, and beautiful to God? Or did you need someone to tell you, 'Stop sinning!'?" Her answer was immediate: the law. As she wrestled with vengeance, hatred, and pride, she needed her closest friends to say, "We love you, but you need to stop that." This same woman encouraged people to ask for permission. "If I ever see you sabotaging your own healing, can I say something?" That's good truth.

Picture grace/truth like a dumbbell. Ever done a shoulder raise? It's really hard to lift a lot of weight because the deltoid in the shoulder is relatively small, and this exercise isolates the muscle. In other words, the deltoid doesn't get a ton of help from the biceps, pecs, or quads. Being cheated on is like doing deltoid raises with heavy weights. You can't do this alone. That's where friends show up. With grace and truth, we help them remember Jesus and do the work of Jesus. Grace and truth. That's how you help a friend who has been cheated on.

And—ready for the next part?—grace and truth are also how you help the one who cheated. What does grace look like in those conversations? Show up and share Jesus. Sound familiar? It is. Sound easy? It isn't.

Adultery is so painful and brutal that many people will keep their distance. "How can I be friends with you after what you did? If I hang out with you, people might conclude that I'm okay with what you did. If you went after his wife, how do I know you won't go after mine?" Most people don't show up. But grace shows up.

Isn't that what Jesus did? Luke 15:1,2: "Now the tax collectors and sinners were all gathering around to hear Jesus. But the Pharisees and the teachers of the law muttered, 'This man welcomes sinners and eats with them.'" They muttered because Jesus showed up. He hated sin, but he loved sinners. And you can hate adultery but still love an adulterer. Put on your running shoes and jump into the marathon of healing by showing up.

And while you're showing up, share Jesus. I once knew a married man who, unfortunately, crossed some emotional and physical lines with another woman. Fortunately, he was wrecked by his sin and repentant. He was sorry. But that sorrow made it hard for him to see the cross. His shame came in waves, especially as he realized all the consequences of his actions. So, I made him a promise: "For the next month, I will text you a passage about God's grace every day, about forgiveness for all sin, for your sin." And I did, and he said it really helped. Could you do that too? You might not know the Bible as I do, but you can Google "best passages on forgiveness" and send them to your friend. Share Jesus. The grace of Jesus is what that friend needs.

And truth. Remember this? Tell your friend: "Healing = Time x Work x Work. It's your opportunity to do things a different way, to start over at square one, to talk about everything, to build your marriage on God's foundation. None of us would choose it, but God can use it. He can use this to help you prioritize each other, to communicate about everything, to listen without shutting down or blowing up. This is going to be harder than anything you've ever been through. This is going to make you humbler than anything you've ever been through. And this can make you holier and happier than anything you've ever been through.

"But the truth is you'll have to work. One day at a time, God will call you to do good work; like owning the wreckage and accepting that the consequences are your fault. He's obsessing, and you did that. She cries in the middle of making love, and you did that. A year later, he still wonders what you were doing during work, and you did that too. You have to own all that."

Say to your friend: "I know this sucks. But you reap what you sow, bro. So how can I help you get through this? Maybe the work is doing something nice, no matter what your spouse is doing for you. Put a note in her lunch with five things you respect about her. If he lets you, put your hand on his leg while he drives. Find a babysitter, take a walk, and agree to talk about something besides the affair, something good from your week, just for one hour. Go back to the basics—love and respect—think of your spouse and do it." As a friend, help him set a short-term goal and hold him to it. Applaud her if she makes it. He or she will need the encouragement.

This passage summarizes that work so well: "Do nothing out of selfish ambition or vain conceit. Rather, in humility value others above yourselves, not looking to your own interests but each of you to the interests of the others" (Philippians 2:3,4). That's the work. You-first matters more than ever after adultery, and your friend will need encouragement to put their spouse first.

That's what friends do. Grace and truth. That's how you choose God's side and help people heal.

YOU-FIRST MATTERS MORE THAN EVER AFTER ADULTERY.

I want to wrap up this discussion on adultery in an obvious way—banana bread. I love banana bread. Chocolate-chip banana bread that is barely visible because of all the butter might be as close to heaven as you can get on this earth. My daughter Maya makes banana bread, and it rarely lasts forty-eight hours once the hungry vultures of our family descend upon it. Do you know the primary ingredient in banana bread? Bad bananas. Overripe, smushy, too-nasty-to-eat bananas are what end up in banana bread. I don't quite know how that's possible, but it is true.

And adultery is like that too. God takes something bad, something sinful, and he adds in time, work, and friends who gave grace and truth to her and him. He covers the whole thing with Jesus, and, somehow, he brings out a blessing. A restored marriage. Or healing even if divorce happens. A family that makes it. Or friends who help friends make it through.

We can't guarantee a happy ending for every family, but when friends show up full of grace and truth, there is always a blessing.

I'd like to end this with a blessing, one spoken by Jesus' own brother Jude. Whether you are healing or helping, may these words comfort you: "Be merciful to those who doubt; save others by snatching them from the fire; to others show mercy, mixed with fear—hating even the clothing stained by corrupted flesh. To him who is able to keep you from stumbling and to present you before his glorious presence without fault and with great joy—to the only God our Savior be glory, majesty, power and authority, through Jesus Christ our Lord, before all ages, now and forevermore! Amen" (Jude 1:22-24).

STUDY QUESTIONS

1. Close your eyes and try to remember the main points from this chapter. Can you recall them? Could you summarize them to a friend? If not, study your notes until God's truth is stored in your heart.

2. Proverbs 11:13 says, "A gossip betrays a confidence, but a trustworthy person keeps a secret." Why is being trustworthy a vital quality to helping friends after an affair?

3. Read Psalm 23. How might these words comfort a friend whose marriage didn't make it after adultery?

Chapter 16

GOD'S CRASH COURSE ON DIVORCE

A friend of mine once preached a forty-nine-minute sermon on divorce. When I asked if there was anything he would do differently, he answered, "Preach longer." I get it. I've studied Scripture and interviewed people who've been divorced, and forty-nine minutes barely scratches the surface. There are so many issues, so many deeply personal situations, so many questions, like . . .

Is divorce ever okay with God? What if you are profoundly unhappy? Or if the kids are hurting? Does God want you to live sadly ever after? What if she cheats? If he leaves? If she drinks? If he belittles? If she's emotionally abusive? If he's physically abusive?

And why do the divorced so often feel second-rate in churches? Like they don't exactly belong? Like everyone is watching, staring, judging?

And what about heaven? Will Jesus forgive you if you get a divorce? Or does divorce equal damnation? And how do we help each other? What do you say if your son already filed for divorce? If your sister wants to remarry after her divorce? What does God say about all this?

I couldn't answer all those questions if we had a week, let alone forty-nine minutes. But I know where to start this needed conversation—with an open Bible. Through Scripture, I want to answer four key questions about divorce:

- What does God think about divorce?
- What are godly reasons to divorce?
- What about life after divorce?
- What does God think about the divorced?

I know that what God says is always good and for our good, so I pray that this chapter, which is admittedly shorter than it should be, brings you and those you love hope and healing.

Question 1: What does God think about divorce?

In the beginning, God made marriage. He made a man, then a woman, and then a marriage. God brought her to the man, and the two became one flesh. "'A man will . . . be united to his wife,'" Jesus said (Mark 10:7). In Greek, the verb literally means "glued" to her. Their relationship would be closer, more intimate, and more vulnerable than any relationship on earth. "Therefore what God has joined together, let no one separate" (Mark 10:9).

If you try to separate two pieces of paper that are glued together, there is no clean break, no simple separation. There are frayed edges, ripped-up hearts, divided children. There's the emotional exhaustion of custody battles and the kids who need two pillows for their two beds. There's the girl who wonders if her heavenly Father will leave her like her dad did. There's the running away from your church, pastor, group, from your God. Divorce rips us apart when God wants us to be together.

One man told me, "I hate divorce. The feelings of absolute failure, rejection, and disappointment are awful." Another woman lamented, "How my kids have been affected. . . . It tears me up." Our Father hates divorce because he hates to see his beloved children suffer the consequences of one being torn into two.

Malachi 2:16 explains, "'The man who hates and divorces his wife,' says the LORD, the God of Israel, 'does violence to the one he should protect.'" God hates divorce because God hates hate. God hates when a man doesn't love his wife—doesn't protect or serve her like Jesus protects and serves. A husband's calling is to be like a rib, a strong, sacrificial servant who protects the "heart" of his marriage. When a man breaks that vow, he assaults the beauty of the institution God created.

Divorce does not just happen. It is too traumatic for anyone to wake up one day and choose it. Instead, divorce is the fruit of some other rotten root. Something is wrong beneath the surface, something has changed since the vows, something sinful started growing in the home, and what it produced was the desire for a divorce.

Maybe you idolized your needs—sex or romance or doing more around the house. You had needs and weren't going to serve or love unless those needs were met. You would work on her list only after she worked on yours. Predictably, your spouse reacted by doing the same, and the destructive cycle of conditional love took root in your marriage.

Or maybe you idolized power. You wanted the promotion, respect, and public image so much that you left your marriage on autopilot. You feared disappointing your boss more than disappointing your spouse. And the sad reality of being second place on your schedule took root in your spouse's heart.

Or maybe you idolized the kids. You filled the calendar with classes and lessons, and there was no time to love him, to flirt, or be with him.

God hates divorce. He has to. Because God loves marriage. Not just being married in general but being married biblically. Loving and serving, not because your spouse deserves it but because you follow the Lord of undeserved love. If God loves love itself, freely and sincerely given, how could he not hate divorce?

I got a fascinating phone call a few months ago from a former church member who is recently divorced. "Can you preach on divorce?" he asked. I replied, "Can you tell me about yours?" He did. He told me about the toxic habit of keeping score. "In marriage," he said, "you divide up the household duties and then keep score. You expect your spouse to serve you because you served them." I am not shocked that such an attitude suffocated that marriage. Love keeps no record of wrongs; neither does it keep a record of all my rights.

IF GOD LOVES LOVE ITSELF, FREELY AND SINCERELY GIVEN, HOW COULD HE NOT HATE DIVORCE?

So, what does God think about divorce? God hates it because he loves unconditional love.

Question 2: What are godly reasons to divorce?

When Jesus was a kid, divorce was fiercely debated by two of the most famous rabbis of all time—Shammai and Hillel. Both spiritual leaders looked carefully at these words from the Torah: "If a man marries a woman who becomes displeasing to him because he finds something indecent about her, and he writes her a certificate of divorce" (Deuteronomy 24:1). Then both men debated what Moses meant by "something indecent." Shammai said *indecent* meant "adultery." Hillel said it meant anything you didn't like, even the way she overcooked last night's dinner. They disagreed on decent reasons or circumstances that would allow God's faithful people to end a marriage.

In the middle of this debate, Jesus became a rabbi and got pulled in:

> Some Pharisees came to him to test him. They asked, "Is it lawful for a man to divorce his wife for any and every reason?"

> "Haven't you read," he replied, "that at the beginning the Creator 'made them male and female,' and said, 'For this reason a man will leave his father and mother and be united to his wife, and the two will become one flesh'? So they are no longer two, but one flesh. Therefore what God has joined together, let no one separate."
>
> "Why then," they asked, "did Moses command that a man give his wife a certificate of divorce and send her away?"
>
> Jesus replied, "Moses permitted you to divorce your wives because your hearts were hard. But it was not this way from the beginning. I tell you that anyone who divorces his wife, except for sexual immorality, and marries another woman commits adultery." (Matthew 19:3-9)

Jesus took a side in this fierce and very personal theological debate. Except for "sexual immorality," you can't separate. You can't divorce. You can't remarry. Shammai was right. If you've been the victim of sexual immorality, you can get a divorce without sinning.

Or, better said, you can make public what your spouse has done in private. This is a point that people in the church too often miss, so please note—filing for divorce does not mean the divorce is your fault. Did you hear that? The fault is in the sinner, the one who broke the marriage.

God hates what first caused the marriage to end, not the first one to go to court. Sometimes the innocent feel guilty while the guilty claim innocence based on who filed the papers. I've known sexually immoral men who throw Malachi 2 at their victimized wives who want a divorce. No, God walks with the innocent to court. So, if your spouse cheated on you, making you the victim of sexual immorality, if you choose, you can go to court and file for a divorce.

The apostle Paul adds a second reason for divorce. In his lengthy chapter on marriage and divorce, he writes:

> A wife must not separate from her husband. But if she does, she must remain unmarried or else be reconciled to her husband. And a husband must not divorce his wife. . . . But if the unbeliever leaves, let it be so. The brother or the sister is not bound in such circumstances; God has called us to live in peace. (1 Corinthians 7:10,11,15)

If he "leaves," you are not bound. You don't have to stay. You don't have to sit there for the next sixty years, rejected but with a ring on your finger. You can divorce. God has called you to live in peace. This is often called the cause of desertion.

But notice something else. Paul says, "In such circumstances." Not "In this circumstance," as if physically leaving were the only form of desertion. There are other circumstances when one person deserts the marriage. He might come home every night, but he has unilaterally, without cause, deserted his spouse.

I am not writing about the common, crazy cycle where two spouses are stuck in a selfish standoff—you don't serve him because he doesn't serve you. She isn't going out of her way to love you, but you aren't putting in the effort to love her—that's heartbreaking, but it isn't the kind of desertion that Paul is speaking of in 1 Corinthians 7.

This desertion is about one person deserting the vows of marriage. Not struggling to love (every spouse does that) but living in sin. It might be deserting for alcohol or the violence of domestic abuse. When you are doing what you can, repenting of your sin, trying to love and respect, striving to keep your vows, but your spouse is an unchanging, manipulative, just-tell-the-pastor-the-right-thing-but-go-home-and-do-the-same-thing kind of person, then you are not bound to that marriage. You can divorce.

Here's a huge question: How do you know if you have God's blessing to get a divorce or if you need to bear your cross and keep working on your relationship? My answer—you will need some loving, biblical, objective assistance. When marriage goes sour, our sinful hearts are not objective. The devil lies on both sides. He convinces some of us that we can divorce when God says we can't, while persuading others that we can't divorce when God says we can. That's why we need each other. We need people who love God, love the Bible, love our marriage, and love us. We need people who comfort us if we're right and confront us if we're wrong. There aren't many reasons to divorce, but there are some. Together we can follow God's path, the one that leads to lasting blessing.

THIS DESERTION IS ABOUT ONE PERSON DESERTING THE VOWS OF MARRIAGE.

But sadly, as you well know, not every marriage makes it. Divorce happens. And there are reasons for you to leave in peace and move forward with God's help.

Question 3: What about life after divorce?

I'll never forget the tears in her eyes. "Pastor, can I marry him?" She was happily engaged to a divorced man but just realized the Bible has something to say about divorced men. I give her immense credit for her question—Can I? If you were listening to Jesus and Paul, you might have wondered about that question. What if you yourself are divorced? What should you do? What if you were cheated on or deserted and ended up divorced? What if you did the cheating and deserting and divorced? What if you just ended the marriage because you both were far from happy? What options do you have that are God-approved?

Let's start with the victim of adultery or desertion. You have three options: remarry, remain single, or reconcile.

First, you could remarry. Paul said that you are not bound in such circumstances (1 Corinthians 7:15). You are free to remarry in the Lord. No stigma. No shame. God will be sitting in the first row, cheering as you say your vows.

Second, you could remain single. First Corinthians 7 is a celebration of singleness and its many benefits. Singles aren't second-rate. You can join Jesus and Paul and worship God with a single life, finding companionship in deep relationships with family and friends.

Third, you could reconcile. If your ex and you want to, your second marriage could be a picture of God's grace. Just like God pursues his cheating bride, you could pursue her despite her infidelity. Just like Jesus takes us back after we've broken our vows yet repented, you could take him back after he sincerely desires to be a different man. Your reconciliation might remind the world of God's desire to reconcile with us.

YOUR RECONCILIATION MIGHT REMIND THE WORLD OF GOD'S DESIRE TO RECONCILE WITH US.

But what if your sin ended the marriage? What if you cheated, deserted, or filed for divorce? If that's you, God gives two commands (not options): repent and repair.

First, God commands you to repent. Hate the sin that God hates. Agree with God that your actions were wicked. Turn your back on your sin, the idol that led to desertion. Turn back to God, the God who loves to forgive wicked people.

Second, God commands you to repair. Repair what you've broken as much as possible. Produce the fruit of repentance, as John the Baptist called it. Just like a thief has to return what he took (he can't just say sorry and keep the cash), the guilty party must repair what he or she has broken. Does your ex want to be married? Then God commands you to go back. I know that might shock you, but that's what repair looks like. Go back and start a new marriage, one drastically different from the dysfunctional version you left, one with God at the center. Make your home a sanctuary, and see what God does differently this time.

Has your ex moved on? Despite your repentance and desire to do things differently, does she have no interest in a future with you? Then God commands you to live in peace even if you won't live together. Own your sin. Admit your guilt. Apologize to your ex and to Jesus. That's the "fruit" of a humble heart that is pleasing to God.

But what if you messed that up too? What if you ignored reconciliation and ran off to remarry someone else? What if, according to Jesus, you married a wrongly divorced woman? What if your wedding day was adultery in the eyes of God?

I won't lie to you—that is quite possible, especially if you didn't have a thorough understanding of the Bible's teaching on divorce and remarriage. You might need to repent today for the sins you committed in your ignorance or your stubbornness.

But here is some refreshing news: God forgives really messed-up stuff. When Jesus shouted, "It is finished!" on the cross, he meant it (John 19:30). That sin, your sin, was on his list. You were on his mind. What you have done in your relationship history, no matter how unbiblical, isn't the unforgivable, you-must-carry-it-around-forever sin. You can breathe. You can go back home to your new spouse and love him or her. God wants you to stay. Even if it had a sinful start, your marriage can have a godly ending.

If you're divorced, those are your options. No matter how challenging those paths might seem, remember the promise of God: "Trust in the LORD with all your heart. . . . In all your ways submit to him, and he will make your paths straight" (Proverbs 3:5,6).

GOD FORGIVES REALLY MESSED-UP STUFF.

Question 4: What does God think about the divorced?

As Jesus walks into Samaria, he spots a deep well outside town, finds a seat, and waits. For her. She shows up in the heat of the day, alone and ashamed, and Jesus asks for a drink. Jesus isn't hitting on her. He's hinting to her—*Your heart is thirsty, and nothing works.*

And then, in an equally cringing and compassionate moment, Jesus brings up the most sensitive part of her story—marriage. "Go, call your husband," Jesus says. "I'm not married," she dodges. "Nope. But you're living with someone. Because the first five marriages ended in divorce, didn't they?" She changes the subject, but Jesus isn't offended. He listens. He answers. He loves. And he stays. For two days, Jesus stays in her town. He stays with her (read John 4:1-26).

What does God think about the divorced? You could ask that woman, the woman at the well, when you get to heaven. Or you could read her story here on earth. "He had to go through Samaria" (John 4:4). Jesus said, "I have to. There is a divorced woman in Samaria who needs me, because she needs grace." And grace is exactly what Jesus gave her.

That's the same grace that Jesus offers us, whether your marriage is a mess or you've been divorced enough times to know the county clerk by name. Christ died so there would be no second-class Christians, no people only partially holy. "For God so loved the world (guess whom that includes?)

that he gave his one and only Son, that whoever (guess whom that includes?) believes in him shall not perish but have eternal life" (John 3:16). Life. Never-ending life with God. Life that starts now. For the divorced. Even those divorced as often as she was.

I know that's hard to believe. If she tore you apart, spewed venom, convinced you that you were worthless. If he left you, told you that you weren't good enough, not pretty enough, not worthy enough. If Dad is gone, and you wonder if God won't do the same. Listen to me. Jesus does not change. He does not vow to stay and then decide to go. He will be with you forever. He will never leave you. Never forsake you. He does not smile when you walk down the aisle and then scowl when you walk into court. His face is shining upon you, looking on you with favor. "As a bridegroom rejoices over his bride, so will your God rejoice over you" (Isaiah 62:5). The expression you saw on that day is the expression on God's face forever. That's what Jesus did. So that you and I—single, divorced, dating, married, and remarried—might be the bride of Christ, the beloved. So be loved. Because that's what God thinks about the divorced.

And if you are happily married, please help your repentant divorced friends not to forget it. The enemy assaults them, makes them misinterpret every sideways glance, convinces them everyone is watching, whispering, judging. So please—please!—be the one who smiles, says hello, speaks forgiveness, sets an extra spot at the dinner table. Our hurting brothers and sisters need a living, breathing reminder that they are not too damaged to be loved, welcomed—to be one with us. Show them what God thinks about the divorced.

In the Old Testament, God told a man named Hosea to pursue an unfaithful, immoral woman as his wife. Why would God do that? So that you and I would remember no matter what we've done, said, thought, or failed to do, we can always come home to God.

I know I haven't answered all your questions, but I deeply hope and passionately pray that God's Word, no matter your relationship status, has filled your heart with truth and grace.

STUDY QUESTIONS

1. Reread Matthew 19:1-12. Find three additional points Jesus made that I did not cover in this chapter.

2. Think of three divorced people you know. How is God calling you to show them love after reading this chapter? Make a plan this week to share truth and show love to someone whose marriage has ended.

PART 4

RACE AND POLITICS

Chapter 17

JESUS

I grew up pretty White. I'm a Caucasian who, for most of his childhood, was surrounded by mostly Caucasians. My high school had 138 teachers and staff and, if my yearbook count is correct, 135 of them were White. Our basketball teams had fifty-three total players—fifty-two White guys and a lone Asian.

But in my 20s, I learned that one way to spell diversity is S-O-C-C-E-R. Soccer exposed me to the world. I've been the token White guy on teams of all Mexicans, all Hondurans, all Argentineans, and all El Salvadorans. Even in my city of Appleton, Wisconsin, which is 88 percent Caucasian, I am a minority on one of my soccer teams. Donning our team's jersey are a Bosnian, a Gambian, two Americans—one with an impressive beard—an Argentinean, a Mexican, a Romanian, a Latvian, a Lebanese man, and me. These men have taught me so much about the world, culture, different people, and places.

I've had other experiences too. In seminary, I once taught a Hebrew class in Spanish to men from Peru, Ecuador, Venezuela, and Colombia. I've been a Spanish court interpreter (that was something!). I've had Mexican, African, and Thai people at my dinner table. In fact, one time, my daughters researched the nation of Gambia and made a personalized place mat for our West African guests.

With all sincerity, I can say that few things make me happier than seeing diversity in my church. The Sundays when Puerto Rican, Pakistani, Brazilian, African American, Caucasian, Hmong, Mexican, Hawaiian, and German Jesus-lovers clap, sing, and praise God together are the services I love the most.

Put all those experiences and more together, and you have my story with race.

What's yours? Think about your family tree. Your friends' ethnicities. Your parents' beliefs. Your pastors' teaching. The authors you've read. The colors of the hands you've shaken and the faces you've befriended. The dinner tables you've dined at. I wonder how all these experiences have shaped your beliefs and behaviors about race.

I bring this up because when I look at our world today, something seems wrong with race relations. As we try to discuss complex issues like poverty and the police force, borders and immigration, social programs and family structures, the judicial system, workplace inclusion, and the generational effects of slavery, something sinful happens.

Sometimes it's a subtle remark that slips out, and sometimes it's a disgusting belief that screams through our screens. Sometimes it just takes the right headline to force something ugly out of our hearts, something that was quietly there the entire time. The names and places in the headlines change (I bet you can list at least one from the past year), but our struggle to love each other remains the same.

And, tragically, that happens in the church too. The issue of race has rarely been easy for God's people. Jesus' friend Peter struggled to love Gentiles as much as he loved Jews. America's Founding Fathers didn't practice the "all men are created equal" that they preached. Dr. Martin Luther King Jr. lamented how church was the most segregated hour in

"Christian America." And even today in a country where 89 percent of people say they believe in God, sin regarding race still rears its ugly head.

Before you assume, "I'm not racist," let's not make racism a black-and-white, yes-or-no issue any more than jealousy, pride, or impatience. Racism, like any sin, is on a spectrum that stretches from pure godlessness to absolute holiness, from Hitler/slave traders on one end to Jesus on the other. The question, therefore, isn't "Am I racist like Hitler?" Instead, it's, "How racist am I these days? How often do I prejudge people from other ethnic backgrounds? Where and when do I show favoritism based on the color of one's skin or the sound of one's accent?"

RACISM, LIKE ANY SIN, IS ON A SPECTRUM THAT STRETCHES FROM PURE GODLESSNESS TO ABSOLUTE HOLINESS.

Your spiritual life, as you follow Jesus, is meant to increase humility and decrease pride, boost kindness, and chip away at impatience. Those virtues are all a process to be more like Jesus. Racism is the same. It starts by admitting you are not like Jesus just yet, which allows you to identify which sins you are committing and address them, repent of your wrongs, find forgiveness at the cross, and make better choices in the days ahead.

That's why I'm glad you're reading this. We may not be in control of every public policy, social media post, or parent's belief, but we are, with God's help, in control of our choices in the way we treat one another, no matter what our color.

The Holy Spirit has always wanted his church to be holy, to be wonderfully different from secular culture, set apart from the sinful world. Our Father has always wanted his family to be equally colorful and compassionate, which is why I want to get us back to a biblical foundation, a return to the New Testament vision that has changed the world in wonderful ways. I want to rewind to the moments that made the early church so diverse and drove Dr. King to keep fighting for a better America. Only that biblical seed of God's unconditional love for the whole world, persistently watered, can produce something better for tomorrow.

That's a big dream. Which is why I want to start with a potentially boring long list of names you probably don't know and definitely can't pronounce. The New Testament begins with the genealogy of Jesus. As we read through the names, I want you to think about Jesus' race—his face—and compare the genealogy of Jesus to . . . my collection of Jesuses . . .

I searched my office and discovered some action figures of Jesus, a painting of Jesus, an icon of Jesus, and some ceramic Jesuses. Every artist and painter had to pick a look for our Lord. A certain color for his complexion. A size for his nose. A shape for his eyes. If you had to pick your Jesus, what would he look like? What shade of skin was bundled up in Bethlehem? What color hands blessed the kids and calmed the storms? How much melanin was in the man who died and was raised to life for our salvation?

"This is the genealogy of Jesus the Messiah the son of David, the son of Abraham: Abraham was the father of Isaac, Isaac the father of Jacob, Jacob the father of Judah and his brothers, Judah the father of Perez and Zerah, whose mother was Tamar, Perez the father of Hezron, Hezron the father of Ram, Ram the father of Amminadab, Amminadab the father of Nahshon, Nahshon the father of Salmon, Salmon the father of Boaz, whose mother was Rahab, Boaz the father of Obed, whose mother was Ruth, Obed the father of Jesse, and Jesse the father of King David" (Matthew 1:1-6).

Do you know the stories behind the names in the genealogy of Jesus? Abraham was from Ur, modern Iraq, but God called him to become an immigrant and move to Canaan, that is, modern Israel. His son Isaac was born in Israel and later married Rebekah, who was from Syria. After some family drama with Jacob's sons, Jesus' ancestors immigrated to Egypt for 450 years before returning to Israel where good ol' Boaz met a Moabite woman named Ruth, who lived in modern Jordan. So, Jesus' story starts with Iraqi, Israeli, Egyptian, and Jordanian people. Are you starting to form a picture of the race and face of Jesus?

The other day I bought one of those 23andMe kits, a popular way to do some DNA testing and discover your ancestry. I knew I had some Bohemian and Czech ancestors but was curious what else was in the mix. If I went back two thousand years, like the gap between Abraham and Jesus, what would I find? Who would be included, and how would that affect my definition of "my people"?

What would we discover if Jesus took the test? What countries and cultures would show up on his results? Would it make you think differently if you knew that "those people" were your Savior's people?

Matthew continues, "David was the father of Solomon, whose mother had been Uriah's wife, Solomon the father of Rehoboam, Rehoboam the father of Abijah, Abijah the father of Asa, Asa the father of Jehoshaphat, Jehoshaphat the father of Jehoram, Jehoram the father of Uzziah, Uzziah the father of Jotham, Jotham the father of Ahaz, Ahaz the father of Hezekiah, Hezekiah the father of Manasseh, Manasseh the father of Amon, Amon the father of Josiah, and Josiah the father of Jeconiah and his brothers at the time of the exile to Babylon" (Matthew 1:6-11).

Here's where it gets even more interesting. These men were all kings in southern Israel who lived from about 1000 to 600 B.C. Their wives are listed in other parts of the Bible; one is from Tyre—modern Lebanon. King Solomon was famous for marrying foreign women and had many mixed-race children who filled the palace and the land of Israel.

In 722 B.C., the Assyrians forced the Jewish people into exile and replaced them with their people, who were from Iran, Iraq, Turkey, and Syria. These cultures mixed and formed the Samaritan culture.

Next, in 586 B.C., the Babylonians forced the remaining Jews into another exile back to Abraham's land, where they spent seventy years surrounded by their Iraqi neighbors.

Then Jesus' diverse family came back to the Promised Land. "After the exile to Babylon: Jeconiah was the father of Shealtiel, Shealtiel the father of Zerubbabel, Zerubbabel the father of Abihud, Abihud the father of Eliakim, Eliakim the father of Azor, Azor the father of Zadok, Zadok the father of Akim, Akim the father of Elihud, Elihud the father of Eleazar, Eleazar the father of Matthan, Matthan the father of Jacob, and Jacob the father of Joseph, the husband of Mary, and Mary was the mother of Jesus who is called the Messiah" (Matthew 1:12-16).

We don't know much about the names that cover the time between the Old and New Testaments, but we do know the history. After the Babylonians came the Persians from Iran. Then the Greeks from Greece, and then the Egyptian Ptolemies fought the Syrian Seleucids until the Jewish Hasmoneans fought back. Finally, the Italian Romans showed up and a little baby was born in Bethlehem—Jesus, the Messiah.

Put all those people, places, countries, and cultures together, and what do you have? You have a multiracial Messiah. You have a very cultured Christ. You have a divine Son with dark skin. Jesus' people are Iraqi, Iranian, Syrian, Jordanian, Egyptian, Turkish, Lebanese, and mostly immigrants. What's more—this list was written by a Jewish man in the Greek language!

Here's how I would summarize the DNA in our Savior's genealogy—Jesus isn't just like you or me or him or her. Jesus is like us. Write it this way—JesUS. You can't even spell our Savior's name without mentioning "us."

If you think I'm reading too much into this genealogy in order to promote some politically correct view of race, know this—Matthew comes back to diversity constantly. In chapter 2 the wise men from Iran show up to worship Jesus. In chapter 5 Jesus tells his disciples they are the light of the world. In chapter 8 Jesus raves about the faith of an Italian soldier. In chapter 15 Jesus tells a Canaanite woman, "You have great faith!" And then in chapter 28, just after he rises from the grave, Jesus gives this mission to his Jewish friends: "Go and make disciples of all nations." The Samaritans. The Romans. The Egyptians. The Ethiopians. The world.

JESUS ISN'T JUST LIKE YOU OR ME OR HIM OR HER. JESUS IS LIKE US.

Aren't you glad he did? "My people," the northern Europeans who made the Novotnys, aren't on this list. But that didn't stop God from getting us the gospel. Maybe your roots don't reach back to Abraham. But Jesus told his friends to go into the world, because his love is for the world. His love is for you! Jesus wants your nation, your tribe, your people to know that his love is for you! His grace is for you! His forgiveness is for you!

Our prejudiced world might prejudge you, but our Jesus was judged for you. He died and rose so that people with skin, hair, and eyes like yours might be part of the body of Christ. He reached out his hand so that your people would never be less than, never inferior or segregated to the back rows of eternity. Jesus gave his life so there would be no shame in being Black, no guilt in being White. Jesus told his friends to go into the world because his love is for the world.

That's what Jesus said back then. And that's what his people do today. We tell the world the good news because the good news is for the world. We love and serve and open our arms because the arms of Jesus are open to the world. We become culturally flexible, becoming all things to all people so that our love is a light for our dark world. We approach differences in culture, language, looks, food, family, time, and traditions with deep humility because our Jesus humbled himself to love us. We love the nations because our Savior is from the nations.

As we will see in the next chapter, it will not be easy. Sin makes us love what's familiar and avoid what's uncomfortable. But Jesus has overcome sin. So much has changed in the last 100 years, but there is still so far to go. Thankfully, our God is still at work. Peter and Paul never expected the early church to be so diverse, but God worked a miracle. And God can work miracles again. I know that because I watched the members of my congregation.

OUR PREJUDICED WORLD MIGHT PREJUDGE YOU, BUT OUR JESUS WAS JUDGED FOR YOU.

A few weeks ago, a biracial couple sat right in the front row, but people didn't whisper, stare, or shake their heads. And then that couple came up on stage, but people didn't gasp, frown, or walk out the door. No, instead they saw an Asian woman being baptized by a Caucasian man. Church members smiled as the name of our Father, Savior, and Spirit was placed upon her heart as water flowed over her head. And when she embraced me in joy, people wept. They clapped louder and longer than ever before. They refused to let race play any role in undermining their rejoicing over someone's salvation. They are proof that God is changing us, that God is showing us there are so many races but just one Jesus. The Jesus who is for us. The Jesus who is from us. The Jesus who is with us.

STUDY QUESTIONS

1. Write out your own history with race. Consider your family, friends, classmates, etc. Which people from your past best embodied God's love for all people of all cultures?

2. In your mind, what does Jesus look like? Did this chapter change your mental image of our Savior?

3. Read Matthew 28:18-20. What does the Great Commission that Jesus gave to his followers mean for Christians' views of races and cultures?

Chapter 18

THE "REASON" FOR RACISM

A few years ago, I tried to explain racism to my kids, including the ugly history of kidnapping, plantations, and White people treating Black people like their personal property. With disturbed, innocent eyes, my girls asked, "Daddy, why? Why would people do that? How could people believe that?"

It's a good question. How? After we have come so far and learned so much, how can racism still exist today? Racism, by definition, is the belief that one race is better than another. It's not just that you and I are different, but that one of us is better. How does that keep happening?

Given all the biblical truth we have heard over the years, how do we still have churchgoing friends going off about "those people" in crass or subtle-but-still-sinful ways? How do we have parents still saying cringeworthy stuff about other races while at the same time claiming to believe John 3:16? Or maybe it's you? Be honest. Do you struggle with loving and not prejudging certain ethnicities? If so, how does that struggle still exist?

I have thought about the issue of racism for a long time, and I have two theories. My first is that sin doesn't make sense. Our hearts don't need a logical reason to hate, judge, feel superior, mock, assume the worst, etc. After the tragic fall into sin, we were born with hearts that don't need a reasonable reason to be bad. They just are.

My second theory: racism still exists because *they* are not like *us*. Sometimes different types of people (ages, genders, personality types, races, cultures) sin in ways that "your people" do not. And when you see someone sin in that "strange" way, you think, "They are not like us. The way that we behave is better than the way they behave." And when you start to believe that your people are better than "those people," that is when race can quickly turn into racism.

To further explain requires that I paint with a very broad brush. I ask for grace as I use stereotypes in a way that seems true for a culture but is not true for every individual within that culture. I realize we are all individuals who behave individually, but I'm hopeful this example will help explain how racism can exist within the Christian church.

Think about people like me—White, middle-class, middle-aged, American men. What sins do "my people" regularly commit that might cause people from other communities and cultures to say, "That's bad. Our way is better"?

One answer might be the self-centeredness of my materialistic, individualistic culture. In many Asian cultures, there is a massive value placed on honoring and caring for your family, no matter how much time or money it costs. That level of sacrifice is uncommon in my culture, where my hopes and dreams drive most of my decisions. In Middle Eastern culture, few things matter more than hospitality, but in my culture, unexpected guests are more of an interruption than an opportunity to serve.

Thus, it would not be absurd if Christians from other cultures looked at my culture's behavior and said, "They are not like us. They do not value hospitality, community, generosity, and family like we do. There is a difference, and it appears that difference has moral implications."

But it isn't just middle-class, American men. As a Spanish speaker and lover of Latino culture, I have seen the reality of machismo up close, and it is biblically concerning. As a lifelong fan of hip-hop music, I have listened to the sexual ethic of many popular Black artists, and it is not biblical but rather a factor in the sad, statistical realities of the average Black home. Like the apostle Paul when he saw and addressed the idols of the Athenians, we can and should be deeply disturbed by the sins that are common in other cultures while uncommon in ours (Acts 17:16).

Since stereotypes can be so dangerous, I repeat: I don't believe all Americans are selfish, all Mexicans are sexist, or all Black people reject God's plan for marriage and children. I do believe that cultures have different strengths and weaknesses, good works and besetting sins, and those differences are what can lead to the sin of racism.

DIFFERENCES ARE WHAT CAN LEAD TO THE SIN OF RACISM.

Our hearts have a way of focusing on *their* sin, ignoring our own, and coming to the conclusion that we are better than they are. The result? We shake our unsympathetic heads when we hear another story about that specific sin happening again. We offer simple solutions to complex problems: "They just need to stop doing that once and for all!" Whether you and I say it out loud or not, we think, "If those people were just like me, life would be better. They would be better. Because I am better."

So how do we escape that temptation? How do we deal with such differences without thinking our people are better? I think you can find the answer in the story of Peter and Cornelius, a Jew and a Gentile.

Before we dive in, let me give a bit of biblical context. We often think of Jewishness as a religion, but originally it was a race. The Jews were all the people descended from a man named Abraham around 2,000 B.C. Everyone who wasn't a Jew was a Gentile. Got it so far?

In the Old Testament, God had this strange but wonderful plan for Abraham's descendants. He told the Jews to be different. He wanted their clothes to be different, their beards, their Saturday plans, and, important for this story, their diet to be different. Read Leviticus 11 and you'll learn all about kosher or "clean" foods that God had put on the menu for the Jewish people. "You can eat this," God said to the Jews, "but not that."

Why would God make this family tree so different? His goal was to make the Jews stand out in obvious ways, to bless them in evident ways, and thus draw all the Gentiles to the gracious, patient, forgiving God of Abraham. God's end goal is to bring the whole world to know his love. The Jews were to be a light that all the surrounding nations would notice and explore. Jesus picked up on this same idea when he told his followers to let their light shine (Matthew 5:16) so that unbelieving people would notice and praise their Father in heaven, the God of Abraham.

But many Jews, even those who followed Jesus, started to believe they weren't just different—they were better. Most Jews, especially the Pharisees, were all too aware of the sins of the pagan nations around them but way too unaware of the sins that still existed within them. Gentile idolatry and sexual immorality were impossible to miss, much more evident than the pride and jealousy that lurked in the dark corners of many Jewish hearts—and that difference led to widespread racism among first-century Jews.

So, God intervened and proved to his people that he was the Lord who loved the whole world.

> At Caesarea there was a man named Cornelius, a centurion in what was known as the Italian Regiment. He and all his family were devout and God-fearing; he gave generously to those in need and prayed to God regularly. One day at about three in the afternoon he had a vision. He distinctly saw an angel of God, who came to him and said, "Cornelius!"

Cornelius stared at him in fear. "What is it, Lord?" he asked.

The angel answered, "Your prayers and gifts to the poor have come up as a memorial offering before God. Now send men to Joppa to bring back a man named Simon who is called Peter." (Acts 10:1-5)

Meet Cornelius. A God-fearing, devoutly praying, poor-people-helping Gentile. Now meet Peter, a God-fearing, devoutly praying, poor-people-helping Jew who thought that all Gentiles were inferior.

About noon the following day as they were on their journey and approaching the city, Peter went up on the roof to pray. He became hungry and wanted something to eat, and while the meal was being prepared, he fell into a trance. He saw heaven opened and something like a large sheet being let down to earth by its four corners. It contained all kinds of four-footed animals, as well as reptiles and birds. Then a voice told him, "Get up, Peter. Kill and eat."

"Surely not, Lord!" Peter replied. "I have never eaten anything impure or unclean."

The voice spoke to him a second time, "Do not call anything impure that God has made clean."

This happened three times, and immediately the sheet was taken back to heaven.

While Peter was wondering about the meaning of the vision, the men sent by Cornelius found out where Simon's house was and

> stopped at the gate. They called out, asking if Simon who was known as Peter was staying there.
>
> While Peter was still thinking about the vision, the Spirit said to him, "Simon, three men are looking for you. So get up and go downstairs. Do not hesitate to go with them, for I have sent them." (Acts 10:9-20)

If you have read the food laws from back in Leviticus, you understand this argument. "Peter, eat that pig!" God said. But Peter wouldn't. He couldn't.

"That's not kosher, Father!"

But God repeated himself two more times: "Peter, don't call anything bad that I've declared to be good." Huh? What was God trying to tell his Jewish son? Keep reading.

> The following day he arrived in Caesarea. Cornelius was expecting them and had called together his relatives and close friends. . . . Peter went inside and found a large gathering of people. He said to them: "You are well aware that it is against our law for a Jew to associate with or visit a Gentile. But God has shown me that I should not call anyone impure or unclean. . . . I now realize how true it is that God does not show favoritism but accepts from every nation the one who fears him and does what is right." (Acts 10:24,27,28,34,35)

Peter admitted, "You all know we Jews don't do this. It's against our law to step inside a house with people like you. But God has shown me that we were wrong. I now realize how true it is that God does not show favoritism, even if my people do."

God is kind of like Blake Shelton from the TV show *The Voice.* At the beginning of the show, Blake and the other judges purposely face away from the singers. Why? Because they seek to prioritize talent over appearance. They don't want to be biased toward beautiful people. They want to hear the heart, the persona, the Voice.

It's the same with God. Peter learned on that uncomfortable and important day that God does not show favoritism. God's favor is not just for people of a certain color, with that kind of hair, and those shaped eyes. No, he accepts from every nation the one who fears him and does what is right.

HE ACCEPTS FROM EVERY NATION THE ONE WHO FEARS HIM AND DOES WHAT IS RIGHT.

And in that Gentile home, Peter preached Jesus, the Jew who loved Gentiles too. The Jesus who healed all who were under the power of the devil. The Jesus who was condemned by Jews and crucified by Gentiles. The Jesus who rose from the dead and told his friends to preach the good news to the whole world. Here's how his sermon ended:

> "All the prophets testify about [Jesus] that everyone who believes in him receives forgiveness of sins through his name."
>
> While Peter was still speaking these words, the Holy Spirit came on all who heard the message. The circumcised believers who had come with Peter were astonished that the gift of the Holy Spirit had been poured out even on Gentiles. For they heard them speaking in tongues and praising God.

> Then Peter said, "Surely no one can stand in the way of their being baptized with water. They have received the Holy Spirit just as we have." (Acts 10:43-47)

There it is—a light bulb moment for this previously biased, Jewish believer. Don't miss the brilliant truth in those four words—"*just as we have*." "We thought the Gentiles were not like us. We believed they were so different. We thought we were so much better. But God says they are just like us. Same struggle. Same sin. Same Savior. Same Spirit. Same Baptism. Same blessing. Same family. They are just like us." After listening to God and spending time with them, Peter concluded, "I realize they are just like us." Write down that big idea; plant it in your heart—racism's cure is to remember that they are just like us.

I encourage you today, whenever you notice the difference, whenever that culture, that race, or those people do things that frustrate you, whenever your compassion has run out and you think they "just" need to [insert simple solution here], God wants you to know they are just like us. They are just like you.

To be clear, I am not excusing cultural sins or eliminating the need for repentance. God does not want us to conform to the pattern of this world (Romans 12:2), which includes the patterns of our biological family and ethnic culture. Jesus never once shrugs at destructive patterns but instead says, "Repent and believe the good news!" (Mark 1:15).

Believers who struggle and sin in different ways are not inferior to you. As Paul went to great lengths to prove in Romans 1-3, "All have sinned and fall short of the glory of God" (Romans 3:23).

When we are zoomed in on a situation, we might think, "I don't do that nor understand why anyone would." But when you zoom out you realize, "Oh, I do that. I get that. All have sinned. They are just like me."

Think of the kid who skips school, sits around, and lives off social programs that others pay for. You might think, "That's wrong! That's lazy! I would never do that. Those people just need to stop that!"

But let's zoom out. That kid is doing what his closest friends are doing, following their bad example. Do you ever do the bad stuff your friends do? He's perhaps repeating the sins he saw at home growing up. Do you ever sin the same way your parents did? He's choosing the easy path of sin instead of the hard path of sacrifice. Do you ever do what's easy in the moment? Ah, now his sin makes sense. His struggle is your struggle. He is just like us.

BELIEVERS WHO STRUGGLE AND SIN IN DIFFERENT WAYS ARE NOT INFERIOR TO YOU.

Or think of the poor Christian immigrant reading the posts of her rich Christian friend. She might be baffled: "How can she read the same Bible, follow the same Jesus, and have so little compassion for the poor? I would never be so selfish!"

But zoom out. The rich Christian is focusing on one part of the Bible and ignoring other parts in order to live a more comfortable life. She's thinking of herself instead of her neighbor. Do you ever do that? Ah, now her sin makes sense. Picking and choosing passages is a human temptation. She is just like us.

Those key words from Peter's story—*just like us*—they don't just apply to sin. They also apply to grace. Everyone who fears God, cries out for mercy, and believes in Jesus receives the forgiveness of sins. The same Jesus who came into the world for you came into the world for them. The same Messiah who marched his way to the cross, thinking of you, was also thinking of them. The same blood that makes us clean, the same hope of eternal life, the same promise of unconditional love, the same faith, the same grace, the same God. Jesus prevented Peter from making Christianity a closed group but instead threw open the windows of mercy to the north, south, east, and west, to Africa, to Asia, to Europe, to the world!

Aren't you glad he did?

Peter could have looked at Gentiles like us and kept his distance. But he didn't. He and his friends made sure the news crossed borders and reached the ends of the earth, reached you and me, so all the nations could meet Jesus. Just like the Jews.

No matter what our color, we all have a cross within.

That's why you can look at any Christian of any race and say, "They are just like us. Sinners just like us. Saved just like us. Children of God just like us."

STUDY QUESTIONS

1. Read the entire story of Peter and Cornelius in Acts 10:1-48. Note every time the text mentions something that both Jews and Gentiles have in common.

2. Study the reaction of some of Peter's Jewish friends in Acts 11:1-18. What did they think about God's love for the Gentiles? How did Peter change their minds about race?

3. Think of a group of people (another race, gender, age, economic class, etc.) whose behavior frustrates you. Practice "zooming out" until you see what you have in common. Pray for humility as God helps you see our common need for his mercy and grace.

Chapter 19

THE DIVERSITY OF ETERNITY

One of my soccer teams consists of a crew of middle-aged men born on five different continents who gather weekly with a singular goal: to not pull a hamstring. Even more fascinating than the cultures that wear the same jersey is the place where we meet, a sports facility called—I'm not making this up—Soccer Heaven. My most diverse day of the week happens in a place called Heaven!

I need that reminder right now, because this has been a hard month for my soul. I was pretty ignorant about race, a fact that led me to read, interview, watch, listen, and learn. And the truth of our story, our history, the church's complicity, broke my heart. Racism's demonic ability to endure, morph, and adapt post-Civil War, post-Civil Rights, challenged and frustrated me.

Even more frustrating was that I couldn't figure out my own solution. What would I do if I could change the systems, rewrite the laws, and reform the institutions? What would be just, right, and fair? I have some ideas, but I am not confident they would work. That thought messes with my hope.

But during this same research, something else happened. In all the books I read from both White and Black Christian authors, they kept quoting the same verse. As author after author lamented our history, ancient and recent, they kept coming back to the same Scripture. It's a word from the Word that we need to keep trying, keep fighting, keep marching forward toward the finish line of love and justice. It's a word from John, Jesus' closest friend. In the midst of his own suffering, oppression, and injustice, John had a dream of Jesus, a revelation of what is happening right now in heaven. That dream drove John to keep working and pursuing his favorite theme: to love God and to love others in God's name. As we pursue faith and love for every race, let's dream together with John.

This is that oft-quoted Scripture from Revelation 7:9: "After this I looked, and there before me was a great multitude that no one could count, from every nation, tribe, people and language, standing before the throne and before the Lamb. They were wearing white robes and were holding palm branches in their hands."

"Look!" John says, "a massive multitude."

Back in 2016, the Chicago Cubs' World Series victory parade amassed five million people. Three years earlier, a religious pilgrimage in India brought thirty million people together. But the multitude in heaven that John describes is even bigger, so big no one could count them.

IF YOU LOVE DIVERSITY, YOU WILL ADORE ETERNITY.

And look where they are from—every nation, every tribe, every people, every language. Those by Jesus' side are Africans, Americans, Asians, Canadians. They speak English, Arabic, and all the accents you can choose for Alexa. Your people, my people, all people are there. If you love diversity, you will adore eternity. If unrepentant racists were allowed into heaven, they would hate the VIP section. Because in heaven, there is love without hesitation, community without discrimination, worship without segregation.

And they are all wearing white robes. That isn't a nod to white supremacy but to gospel equality. In heaven, no one is stained or dirty. Grace makes everyone so fresh and clean. Like the father of the prodigal son, God says to his angels, "Quick! Bring the best robe and put it on him. On her. On them!"

And they hold palm branches in their hands. In those days, palm branches were symbols of victory. Ancient kings and lawyers would bring them out after victories in war or in the courtroom. That's how all the races and nations feel in heaven, bursting in celebration of their ultimate victory over sin and every form of evil.

What a dream! It reminds you of what Dr. King dreamed, doesn't it? It was August 28, 1963, when Dr. Martin Luther King Jr. stood in front of the Lincoln Memorial in Washington, DC, with 250,000 souls packed around and in front of him. And he thundered words of hope, about a dream he had, about a day when suffering would end, a day when Black and White children would love each other, a day when we would be free at last, thank God Almighty. Watch a clip of Dr. King's speech, and it will stir you to keep fighting for equality and an end to favoritism of every shade. Read about John's dream, and it will do the same for your soul.

Maybe this text can be your quick boost of hope when the headlines make you feel hopeless. When you read of another hate crime or experience any snide comment connected to the color of your skin, remember how our story ends. Remember why Jesus fought to the very end. Then get ready to do the same.

Because John's not done:

> And they cried out in a loud voice: "Salvation belongs to our God, who sits on the throne, and to the Lamb." All the angels were

> standing around the throne and around the elders and the four living creatures. They fell down on their faces before the throne and worshiped God, saying: "Amen! Praise and glory and wisdom and thanks and honor and power and strength be to our God for ever and ever. Amen!" (Revelation 7:10-12)

This is my favorite part. There are two words here that show up often in John's dream, two words that you never see together, except with Jesus.

The first word, used seven times in this text, is the word *throne*. A throne is the place of a king, a place of power, honor, and authority. If you sit on a throne, you get what you want. You have the last word. You live in a palace filled with servants, far from the pain of the streets.

But there's another word here, used four times: *Lamb*. A lamb, in the Bible, is a symbol of gentleness, humility, sacrifice. What sets the multicultural saints off in praise, what inspires even angels to worship, is this combination that only exists in Christianity—our King is also a Lamb!

As the King of kings, Jesus had every right to sit on his throne and be served. Instead, our King came to serve. As the Lord of lords, Jesus could have stayed in the comfort of the palace. Instead, he chose the pain of a cross. As the Son of God, Jesus could have used his authority for his own security. Instead, he chose humility, adversity, tragedy. The King who could have stayed away from the ghetto of this world got down into it. Jesus had nails put into his hands so he could put palms into ours. Jesus' robe was stripped off him so that it could be wrapped around us. Jesus was stained with blood so that we could be washed white. Jesus was our King but chose to become our Lamb.

"Salvation belongs to our God, who sits on the throne, and to the Lamb!" (verse 10). That glorious thought—throne and lamb—brings people together in explosive praise. And the sound is so good.

But John is not done dreaming: "Then one of the elders asked me, 'These in white robes—who are they, and where did they come from?' I answered, 'Sir, you know.' And he said, 'These are they who have come out of the great tribulation; they have washed their robes and made them white in the blood of the Lamb'" (verses 13,14). The elder asks a question when he already knows the answer. Why? Because he needs John to know who these people are. He needs John to know where these people came from. These are they who have come out of the great tribulation.

JESUS WAS OUR KING BUT CHOSE TO BECOME OUR LAMB.

The great tribulation. Sounds funny, doesn't it? *Tribulation* is a word that just means pain or pressure. In the New Testament, giving birth is a great tribulation. Going to jail is a great tribulation. So much of life is a great tribulation.

You've felt that pressure too, haven't you? No matter what your race or class, you know about the great tribulation. There are intense pressures to being rich and to being poor; to being the CEO and the third-shift janitor; to being White, brown, or Black. Back pain doesn't discriminate. Chronic pain couldn't care less about your color. Broken relationships hurt regardless of race. If life has hurt you, if people have hurt you, listen to the elder's answer: "These are they who have come out of the great tribulation." They have come out of it. They are no longer in it. It's part of their past, not their present. And that pain will never show up in their future.

Here's the proof:

> Therefore, "they are before the throne of God and serve him day and night in his temple; and he who sits on the throne will shelter

> them with his presence. 'Never again will they hunger; never again will they thirst. The sun will not beat down on them,' nor any scorching heat. For the Lamb at the center of the throne will be their shepherd; 'he will lead them to springs of living water.' 'And God will wipe away every tear from their eyes.'" (verses 15-17)

Every tear. Tears of fear. Tears of frustration. Tears because you can't change the system that discriminates against you. God will wipe away every tear. Never again. No hunger. No poverty. No prison food. Never again. No more pain, greed, power-hungry people, selfishness. No more sin.

JESUS HIMSELF WILL LEAD YOU TO THE ONLY THING THAT CAN SATISFY YOUR SOUL—GOD.

One day you will stand before the throne of God, enter his temple, and feel the cool shadow of his presence. One day Jesus will bring you to the springs of living, bubbling-up, never-running-out water. The Lamb, the Good Shepherd, Jesus himself will lead you to the only thing that can satisfy your soul—GOD. And that GOD will wipe away every tear from your eyes. That GOD will bubble up and bless you with everything you've always wanted—love, freedom, acceptance, attention, justice, joy. Everything will be yours. Forever. Because you will be with GOD forever.

Oh, John had a dream! A dream with no majority or minority. No unfamiliarity or insensitivity. No negativity or disparity due to diversity. No monstrosity of slavery. No brutality of inequality. Only a glorious community of every ethnicity. Only diversity gathered in flawless unity. Only the beauty and fraternity of final victory. Only humanity and divinity for all eternity. Oh, come quickly, Jesus! We cannot wait for this day!

But if Jesus decides to wait, let's start practicing. On that day, every people and tribe will stand before the throne. On that day, every race and color will love God and love one another. On that day, every nation and voice will join together to worship God. So, God, your will be done on earth as in heaven. May we do here what they are doing there, right now.

Like I saw last summer.

Last summer, I led an interracial wedding. A white guy married an Asian girl. But when I arrived at the church, I saw something else—a number of Black kids running around. *Hmm*, friends of the couple? Then a woman walked in with a gorgeous, dark-haired, half-Mexican baby. *Hmm*, what's the connection there?

I soon learned about the groom's family. His Caucasian parents raised three white kids in Wisconsin. But their family loved diversity. Literally. The oldest brother fell in love and married a woman of African-American heritage. Then the younger sister fell in love and married a man from Mexico. Which led the family to prod the remaining brother, "You should marry an Asian girl!" And he did! That day, as I stood at the front of the church, beneath the cross of Jesus, the wedding party came walking together up the aisle. Black and White, Latino and Asian, the people, the nations.

John's dream is coming true. So, when the headlines discourage you, when the never-ending fight frustrates you, close your eyes and dream like John. Dream of Jesus. He's coming soon. And all things, everything, will be made new.

STUDY QUESTIONS

1. Reread Revelation 7:9 and try to imagine what John saw. What would be the closest equivalent here on earth?

2. What steps could you/your church take to make worship services a preview of the worship service John saw in his vision? How might our earthly diversity get people excited for eternity?

3. Study Revelation 21:1-5. What will God's people, from every race and nation, experience in his presence? List the struggles that will never be endured again once Jesus returns to make everything new.

Chapter 20

POLITICALLY INCORRECT: GOD'S GOALS FOR CHURCH AND STATE

Two weeks ago, my wife and I were browsing a gift shop in San Antonio, Texas, searching for trinkets to pacify our present-loving daughters. Back in the corner of the gift shop, we found some military crosses. Stars, stripes, and bullet casings shaped like Jesus' cross. Two of the strongest symbols we know—God and country—mixed into one.

A week later, I came across a yard sign back home in Appleton, Wisconsin. "Jesus for Savior" it read, with the red, white, and blue billowing in the background. God and country, mixed into one. But we're used to that. In God We [Americans] Trust. One Nation Under God. God Bless America. There's this undefined connection, this unspoken expectation between church and state, between God and this government.

Is that good? Bad? Is the connection too much? Not enough? Some say God's people are too political, that the religious right implies religious people must be Republican. They say that the Moral Majority backfired, and now Christians are becoming an American minority.

Others say God's people aren't political enough. Our country is losing the Christian values that the Founding Fathers had faith in, a loss of beliefs exhibited in a heartbreaking increase in sinful behavior. It's clear we need more Jesus, prayer, and Scripture in our public schools, congressional halls, and presidential speeches.

There's a debate. How much Bible should be involved in American democracy rages on cable news, social media, and at family dinner tables, often so heated that we either raise our voices or tune out.

If I asked you how spiritual the government should be, what would you say? And why would you say it? What chapter and verse from the Bible led you to your beliefs about church and state?

Much more important, what does God expect of the governments of the earth that he created? And what does God expect of us as citizens of one of those governments? Tough questions, right? That's why I'd like you to open a Bible so we can tackle the toughest questions about politics and religion—so God himself can make us politically correct.

Out of the 1,189 chapters in the Bible, Romans 13 is, in my opinion, the best section on God and government. Here's how the apostle Paul, a first-century Christian, starts: "Let everyone be subject to the governing authorities, for there is no authority except that which God has established. The authorities that exist have been established by God. Consequently, whoever rebels against the authority is rebelling against what God has instituted" (verses 1,2). If repetition means anything, Paul wants us to know the government has authority. Authority means the right to get the last word, to make and enforce decisions. Those in authority might be people just like you and me, but they are not in the same position as you and me. There is a hierarchy of authority.

That's a good thing. Can you imagine a world without authority? A society without rules and consequences? Imagine parenting without authority. "Sweetie, I would suggest you not eat ice cream for breakfast, but who am I to tell you what you have to do?" Imagine middle school without authority. "Biff, you really shouldn't push Billy's head into the toilet, but that's just my opinion, and you can make your own decisions." Imagine driving in

Chicago without authority. "Sir, I don't advise driving 90 mph in a school zone. But you are a free citizen, so do whatever you want." We know what would happen without authority, without laws and consequences, without the threat of fines and jail time. Selfishness would devour us. The strong would oppress the weak. Survival of the fittest, strongest, and richest would determine the law of the land. For the sake of justice and peace, God himself instituted authority.

FOR THE SAKE OF JUSTICE AND PEACE, GOD HIMSELF INSTITUTED AUTHORITY.

So, what should that authority do? What should judges, cops, and lawmakers do? Paul continues:

> Rulers hold no terror for those who do right, but for those who do wrong. Do you want to be free from fear of the one in authority? Then do what is right and you will be commended. For the one in authority is God's servant for your good. But if you do wrong, be afraid, for rulers do not bear the sword for no reason. They are God's servants, agents of wrath to bring punishment on the wrongdoer. (verses 3,4)

What should authority do? Punish the bad and praise the good. Authorities should terrify wrongdoers and inspire rightdoers. Those who are breaking the law should be afraid of the God-given authorities whose job is to catch them and make them regret their transgressions. Those who are keeping the law should not be afraid since the God-given authorities are there to protect them from injustice.

This is an incredible responsibility (and one of the hardest things in the world). Just ask parents. Moms and dads, how hard is it to punish bad choices and reward good ones consistently? If your kid flips out in the store, acting like an emotional terrorist because you won't buy her that bright, shiny toy, and then you bribe her just to end the embarrassment—"Honey, I'll take you to McDonald's if you stop crying"—that's bad authority. If I forget how to count to three and instead say, "1, 2, 2.5, 2.75, 2.99," giving my child more chances to be stubborn and disobedient, that's bad authority. Why? I have let the guilty go undisciplined. I have taught my child that she can rebel without consequence. My job as a dad is to teach her that choices have consequences, good or bad. That's the hard calling of being in authority.

Look at how the apostle Peter puts it: "Submit yourselves for the Lord's sake to every human authority: whether to the emperor, as the supreme authority, or to governors, who are sent by him to punish those who do wrong and to commend those who do right" (1 Peter 2:13,14). Punish the wrong. Commend the right. Just like Paul told the Romans. Because when that happens, when God-given authority upholds justice and people respect their authority, life is good.

Paul describes this good life under good authority to his friend Timothy: "I urge, then, first of all, that petitions, prayers, intercession and thanksgiving be made for all people—for kings and all those in authority, that we may live peaceful and quiet lives in all godliness and holiness" (1 Timothy 2:1,2). Peaceful and quiet lives. That's what good government gives. The president doesn't have to preach the gospel or lead the nation in prayer. Just give us peaceful lives, and we will be happy. We don't need a theocracy, a government that is run according to our Holy Book. We just need justice. Punish the bad. Commend the good. And we Christians will thank God for our government.

Compare and contrast Peter and Paul's "job description" for the state with that of the church. What's the goal of the government? Peace on earth. What's the goal of the church? Peace with God. What does the government use to get peace? Threats. The sword (as Paul says) includes any painful punishment that dissuades people from breaking the law. What does the church use to get peace with God? The Word, the sword of the Spirit (as Paul says). The sermon, devotion, and Baptism in Jesus' name. What does the government care about? Outward actions. You can hate paying your taxes as long as you pay them. You can really want to drive 60 mph as long as you stick around the posted limit. But what does the church care about? Inward motivations. Love, humility, selflessness. The law-keeping, self-righteous, I'm-better-than-you Pharisee needs to be confronted, not commended. Both God and the government care about murder, stealing, lying, etc., but only God cares about worship, prayer, idolatry, etc.

We might say God cares about all Ten Commandments, about what gods you worship, what you covet in your heart. But the government cares only about the commandments in the middle of God's top ten list—murder, stealing, and false testimony. The government cares about how you treat your neighbor. The church cares about loving your neighbor and loving our God. In other words, God cares about much more than the laws written in the government's books. He cares about worship, faith, and the heart and not just about outward action.

A local cop said it best. Recently, a police officer who attends our church let me ride in his patrol car for some sermon research. We parked the car by a notoriously ignored stop sign and got ready to commend good drivers and terrify bad ones. When I saw a guy who didn't quite come to a complete stop, I yelled, "Get 'em!" (because people only obey the laws that are enforced). My favorite moment, however, was when the officer said, "Pastor, we both try to help people. You use your words and a Bible. I use my words and a gun." Amen. Both authorities serve people, but we have different goals and different tools.

When we forget this distinction, we end up politically incorrect and with a massive mess for both the church and the state. Study the Holy Roman Empire when kings and popes tried to tell each other what to do. Summary: the gospel was quickly lost. Research how Catholic explorers from Spain and Portugal sailed across the Atlantic to modern-day Mexico and South America where they threatened the locals, "Be baptized or die!" Look at the state church in Sweden where 85 percent of church *members* say they do not believe in Jesus.[1] Imagine the early American colonies where church attendance was a law on the books. Because nothing honors God like forcing someone to sit in church!

No legislation can do what the Bible values most: changing the human heart. And the heart is what God wants. As much as we love Christian values, what Christ values is true worship, the soul that loves and trusts in God. And no law can make that happen. Only the gospel can. That is not Congress' calling. It's mine. And yours. So give me a government that keeps our churches safe from vandalism and theft, and I will praise God. Leave the teaching about marriage, prayer, God, and his commandments to those of us who follow Christ. That's church and state as God intended. Jesus, Peter, and Paul taught in days when the government was anything but godly, but their focus was not on legislation. It was on proclaiming the love of Jesus.

If you understand that distinction, you are ready to move on to a second key question that applies to every Christian on the earth: How should you treat the authorities that govern you? What is your responsibility toward the police officer, the president, and the current government?

Paul has an answer: "Therefore, it is necessary to submit to the authorities, not only because of possible punishment but also as a matter of conscience. This is also why you pay taxes, for the authorities are God's servants, who give their full time to governing. Give to everyone what you owe them: If you owe taxes, pay taxes; if revenue, then revenue; if respect, then respect; if honor, then honor" (Romans 13:5-7). In the next chapter, we will talk about times when we might need to speak against injustice, but the overall picture is clear. Christians are called to submit to authority.

Submission, in the Bible, applies to both the hands and the heart. We pray, pay, and obey. We pay taxes. We don't take cash under the table. We don't try to get away with anything. We are honest citizens who obey the laws. We don't lie about insurance. We drive the speed limit. We don't drink and drive. With our hearts, we pray for the authorities, for justice, humility, our country, law and order, and peaceful and quiet lives. Every disrespected parent, exhausted teacher, depressed cop, and hated vice principal knows that being the one to enforce consequences is a thankless job. The authorities need our support. They need our prayers. We need them, and they need us.

Years ago, I asked the four pastors at my church, "Do you know of any members who are staunch Republicans who honored President Obama?" One pastor immediately burst out laughing. Another agreed, "Um, no." Sadly, the lack of honoring our leaders has become a new normal in America. But God's not laughing. It is nothing like what he described in Romans 13, 1 Peter 2, and 1 Timothy 2.

You might be so political you end up incorrect. Unchristian. You might be so passionate about immigration policy, the budget deficit, health care, or the size of government that honor, respect, patience, protecting reputations, assuming the best, being grateful, not being a critic, and not giving into fear are out the window for you. You might think that unless the authorities are the people you want, you can say whatever you want. (Imagine if every kid applied that same thinking to their parents.)

Let me be biblical and blunt—That is sin. That is rebellion. That is insulting not only the authorities but the God who gave them. And before you push back and lament the current people who hold office, search the internet for the Roman rulers of Paul and Peter's day. They were worse. They worshiped false gods. Yet the apostles still commanded Christians, "Honor them!"

You might be like me, so sick of the unchristian bickering that you don't do what Paul says. You and I don't pray. We don't appreciate the hard work of governing. We don't see what a gift even flawed rulers are to our country and families. We naively think that if all the politicians disappeared, America would be better. But it wouldn't. It would be a nightmare. It would be a jungle where the gang with the greatest firepower would rule the streets and rape our sisters. Being ungrateful is no better than being too political.

We need God's help, don't we? Our culture is not helping us develop a biblical theology of authority. And our hearts aren't either. But there is help. Specifically, the twelve chapters before Romans 13, where Paul teaches time and again about grace. About unearned love. Only when you realize that you can't earn God's love, that he chose to love because he is love, do you find the strength to love people you don't agree with.

Do you love grace? Me too. Paul writes in Romans 3:23,24, "All have sinned and fall short of the glory of God, and all are justified freely by his grace." And in 4:8: "Blessed is the one whose sin the Lord will never count against them." And in 5:8: "While we were still sinners, Christ died for us." And in 6:23, "For the wages of sin is death, but the gift of God is eternal life in Christ Jesus our Lord." And in 7:24,25: "What a wretched man I am! Who will rescue me from this body that is subject to death? Thanks be to God, who delivers me through Jesus Christ our Lord!" You get the point? We didn't deserve it. We sinned. We earned death. We were wretched and couldn't rescue ourselves. But God didn't let it stop him. Jesus died for us. He delivered us. He loves us so much that he will never count our sins against us. That's grace. It's amazing, and it's grace. And it changes us.

Paul starts Romans 12 with "Therefore." Therefore, since you know grace and love grace, show grace. Submit to the authorities. They might not deserve it, but neither did we. Pay taxes. Obey the laws. Honor the office.

Be a blessing to those who are in authority over you—make your mom, dad, teachers, referees, coaches, pastors, governors, and presidents blessed. And pray. Pray that God blesses their hard work. When it's hard, when it seems impossible not to disrespect, not to share the story, not to yell, not to give up on government altogether, just think of the God whom you worship because he doesn't treat people as their sins deserve.

SINCE YOU KNOW GRACE
AND LOVE GRACE, SHOW GRACE.

I've heard a hundred ugly rumors about Donald Trump and Barack Obama and Joe Biden. They might all be true. I doubt it. But what I do know without a doubt are one hundred thousand sins about myself. They are not rumors. They are sad but true. Yet my King didn't let that stop his love. My Jesus didn't let that stop him from submitting to God's plan to save me. So maybe with God's help, you can love because he first loved you. Love the God who saved you. And love the authorities who protect you.

STUDY QUESTIONS

1. How do Peter's and Paul's words (1 Peter 2:13-17; Romans 13:1-7; 1 Timothy 2:1,2) compare to your previous understanding of the role of government? How did their teaching affect your point of view?

2. Paul writes in Romans 13:5 that submission to the government is necessary "not only because of possible punishment but also because of conscience." What does that mean?

3. What injustices might you need to speak up against this week? What love might you need to show to unjust authority this week?

Chapter 21

POLITICALLY INCORRECT: LOVE ACROSS THE AISLE

It was a chilly day in March as thousands of people lined College Avenue in downtown Appleton, Wisconsin, hoping to catch a glimpse of Donald Trump. I wandered over from church, curious. Being naive about the political temperament, I wasn't expecting what I experienced.

"Get a job!" one Republican bellowed at the liberal protestors from a local college. The angry man turned to those of us in line and remarked, "It's the middle of the day. Why aren't they working?" I didn't answer while suddenly wondering why he wasn't working. My thoughts were interrupted by the series of snarky insults that people muttered under their breath or shouted for all to hear. The smoldering rage was stoked by the vendors who sold partisan trinkets like the best-selling buttons that read, "Hillary for prison."

The Democrats weren't any nicer. That same night I had a meeting at a downtown coffee shop. The same protestors I had seen earlier in the day walked in with their signs, desperate for caffeine after an exhausting day. An older woman saw their signs about Trump and suggested, "That's not very nice." And their reaction wasn't any nicer. One protestor instantly spewed aggressive words as her friend held her back from physically going after a woman who was old enough to be her grandmother. That day people on both sides of the aisle behaved badly. This wasn't Washington, DC. This was the family-friendly community that I knew and loved.

But that's what politics has devolved into in America. Divisive. Aggressive. Assuming. Interrupting. I recently read a book by one of America's favorite conservative bloggers. It opened, "The first liberal was named Lucifer." Pages later, the author (in all seriousness) lumped Hillary Clinton with Judas, Nero, and Hitler.[1]

America, it seems, has gone from a democracy to democrazy. That crazy constitutional right to wrong you because you are wrong and I am right. We see the madness on social media, where fake news is forwarded just because it makes the other party look stupid. Or on cable news, where interruptions are rewarded and the reddest faces of rage are given prime-time promotions. Or at Mother's Day brunch, when the health care debate is literally bad for our health. Try to talk about immigration, race, abortion, or an election, and it's likely to get crazy.

AMERICA, IT SEEMS, HAS GONE FROM A DEMOCRACY TO DEMOCRAZY.

Sadly, it's not just the world who practices democrazy; that same behavior has seeped into the church. Accurate or not, it has become part of our reputation. When asked why they don't trust Christians, non-Christians quickly say, "They're too political, hypocritical, and judgmental." Jesus said the world would know we are his disciples by our love, but that's not what the world knows us for (John 13:35). So, what should we do?

The answer is, of course, in the Bible. The first century had so much in common with the twenty-first. Jesus and the apostles lived in a world of political and religious factions that had little love for one another. The Pharisees were the moral conservatives. The Sadducees were more liberal and political. The Herodians loved Big Government. The Zealots hated it. And the Essenes said, "Y'all so crazy that we're going to live in the desert."

How did those early Christians live in a world like that? What drove them together instead of apart? There are four key passages on God and government that answer those questions. Romans 13, 1 Timothy 2, 1 Peter 2, and Matthew 22 tell us how to live in a world that tries to pull us to angry extremes. Christians now, just like Christians throughout history, have desperately needed these words to get them grounded in a world gone mad.

Let's start with Romans 13. In verses 1-7, Paul tells us that God instituted authority to punish the bad and praise the good, one of many reasons that citizens should submit, pay taxes, and honor the authorities. Then, in verse 8, Paul continues, "Let no debt remain outstanding, except the continuing debt to love one another." You may be financially debt free, but you are still called to make a never-ending payment to love your neighbor.

And who is my neighbor? Jesus said, "Everyone." The old guy with the MAGA hat. The liberal woman whose bumper stickers about sexuality, feminism, and nature worship stretch from taillight to taillight. The gay couple in the apartment next door. The Republican uncle whose emails always start with "Forward." The cousin who voted for the candidate who makes your blood boil. We have a continuing debt to love them. We have a continuing debt to love all people.

Love simply means to treat others as you'd want to be treated. To be quick to listen, slow to speak, and slow to become angry. You want people to understand and be kind to you, even if they disagree with you, right? You like it when people prove they've been listening, trying to grasp the why behind what you believe. Do that, Paul says, and you'll be biblically correct.

One of the fellow pastors at my church recently posed the issue this way, "Is the goal to defend my position or to win over their souls?" The former excuses all kinds of bad behavior. The latter leads you to think about love, humility, and the grace of Jesus. If my goal is to get you right with God, then I'm going to love, respect, and dialogue with you. I'll take no pleasure in making you look dumb, because I care about tomorrow's conversation and not just today's. When it comes to politics, remember the continuing debt to love one another.

That brings us to text #2. In 1 Timothy 2, Paul tells us to pray for all those in authority so we can live peaceful and quiet lives. Just verses later, Paul adds, "I want the men everywhere to pray, lifting up holy hands without anger or disputing" (verse 8). Paul has a word for the fellas. "Guys, I want you to pray, lift up your hands, and thank God, confess to God, ask God for help, but do so without anger or disputing. Don't be that guy who raises the volume in the room. That guy who argues about everything. The guy who knows he's right and everyone else is wrong." That takes a godly humility, a willingness to admit life is more complicated than our arguments often admit.

For example, think of the issues that intersect with the hot-button issue of immigration. Some come because drug dealers are decapitating their neighbors. Some come because they are making as much in a year as you make in a week. Immigration poses major stresses on our national budget, yet immigrants are a major part of the national economy. Some people get angry when discussing these tensions, but Paul tells us to rid ourselves of anger and disputing.

About 250 years ago, Pastor John Wesley, the founder of the Methodist church, spoke in the midst of a crazy political election. He gave his fellow believers this advice: "I met those of our society who had votes in the ensuing election and advised them, 1. To vote, without fee or reward, for the person they judged most worthy; 2. To speak no evil of the person they voted against; and, 3. To take care their spirits were not sharpened against those that voted on the other side."[2] That sounds perfectly in line with what Paul told Timothy.

Which takes us to text #3 from 1 Peter 2. Peter tells us to submit to the governing authorities to such an extreme that we even love those who persecute us. Notice what comes before and after his words about politics: “Live such good lives among the pagans that, though they accuse you of doing wrong, they may see your good deeds and glorify God on the day he visits us. . . . But do this with gentleness and respect, keeping a clear conscience, so that those who speak maliciously against your good behavior in Christ may be ashamed of their slander” (1 Peter 2:12; 3:15,16). Shame them, not with bad words but with good works. Live such good lives and speak with such respect that they feel bad for the bad things they say about you. They might not agree with you, might not believe like you, but when others trash people like you, their consciences will preach, “But she’s a good person.”

PAUL TELLS US TO RID OURSELVES OF ANGER AND DISPUTING.

In a world that expects black-and-white politics, where we only love “our people,” that kind of respect stands out. A few years ago, a campaigner stopped by my home to ask about the upcoming election. “I haven’t thought much about it just yet,” I admitted.

“Well, are there any issues you are passionate about?”

I replied, “Abortion is a big one for me.”

“Oh,” she sighed, “well, thanks for your time.”

“Wait,” I said. “We can still talk if you’d like. Do you want something to drink?”

And she stopped dead on my sidewalk, stunned. “Seriously?” she gasped. “The opposition offered me something to drink?” She said, “I’m going to talk about this at our debrief tonight." And then she left. I stood there, stunned. A glass of water moved her that much? It made me wonder about her experiences at the doors of others. . . .

What if you and I loved those with whom we disagreed? What if we loved political friends and foes? What doors might open for a real conversation? What drama might be avoided if we came to know each other better?

That takes us to our final text from Matthew 22. Jesus preaches that tweetable line, "Give back to Caesar what is Caesar's, and to God what is God's" (verse 21). Pay taxes. Praise God. Those are your goals.

Do you know who was there to hear Jesus' words? A group of guys that included Matthew and Simon the Zealot. Don't miss this: when Jesus called Matthew to follow him, he was working as a tax collector, meaning he was on the government's payroll. And when Jesus called Simon to follow him, he was a Zealot, a member of an anti-government group that was known for random acts of terrorism and sedition against the state. This was Big Government vs. "Boo! Government!" But Jesus chose them both.

What does that teach us? Perhaps that Jesus' love reaches across the aisles, inviting all to be saved and, at the same time, all to be changed. Matthew would need to repent of his greed and extortion and Simon of his rebellion and violence. But Jesus didn't wait until they got everything right. He loved them first. And his love would change their behavior next.

That's a valuable lesson. Years ago, a Christian told me, "Pastor, a woman came to church, and she was wearing an Obama button!" Oh boy! Call the ushers! More recently, during the fierce debate about COVID restrictions, an older gentleman came to worship with a piece of duct tape over his mouth in protest. Written over the tape—"F*** Biden!"

Reread the four key texts from today, and you will find that God is calling us to a higher standard, namely, to imitate the love of Jesus. If Matthew and Simon teach us anything, it's that Jesus loves all kinds of people. The

Son, sent from the Father, is proof that God loves the whole world. Maybe there should be a passage about that. . . .

Get the point? Jesus, Peter, and Paul were all telling the church the same thing. Be patient with people. Respect people. Include people. Love people. All people.

It is easier to block, unfollow, and avoid people whom you disagree with, so why would you put in the effort to do otherwise? The answer is found in these same four passages—the gospel. Check it out:

"I urge you, brothers and sisters, in view of God's mercy . . . do not conform to the pattern of this world" (Romans 12:1,2). Why not conform? Because of God's mercy. Because God did right for us when we were wrong. He didn't lock us up in hell but set us free to enjoy heaven. Jesus endured the injustice of the cross so that you and I can experience everlasting joy.

JESUS' LOVE REACHES ACROSS THE AISLES, INVITING ALL TO BE SAVED AND, AT THE SAME TIME, ALL TO BE CHANGED.

"[God] wants all people to be saved and to come to a knowledge of the truth. For there is one God and one mediator between God and mankind, the man Christ Jesus, who gave himself as a ransom for all people" (1 Timothy 2:4-6). Why live at peace with your political enemies? Because God made peace with you. He died as a ransom, a price paid to bring you back to God. That's what God wants for all people. That's what God wanted for you.

"'[Jesus] himself bore our sins' in his body on the cross, so that we might die to sins and live for righteousness; 'by his wounds you have been healed'" (1 Peter 2:24). Why live for righteousness? Why not get revenge? Because

Jesus didn't. He took our sins. He was wounded for us. He healed us of all our incorrectness.

And Matthew 22 was spoken on Tuesday, which came just three days before that famous Friday. When Jesus, upon a cross, looked down at Pharisees, Sadducees, Herodians, Romans, you, and me, and cried, "Father, forgive them, they know not what they do." And he did. God forgave us. For the posts, words, disputing, for everything. That's grace. Unearned love. And once that gets in you, you're ready to undo the democrazy. You're ready to love because you know how much he first loved you.

YOU'RE READY TO LOVE BECAUSE YOU KNOW HOW MUCH HE FIRST LOVED YOU.

Legend says Matthew was stabbed in the back, martyred in Ethiopia as an immigrant who preached against injustice and stood up for grace. Simon wouldn't stop talking about Jesus, so he was crucified. A tax collector and a Zealot on the same team.

How? They met the same Jesus. They experienced the same grace.

STUDY QUESTIONS

1. Evaluate this statement: Showing grace to your political opponents implies that political divisions are not that serious.

2. Study Revelation 19:11-21. What comfort would this passage have given Christians in the first century who were being persecuted by Rome? What comfort does it give the persecuted church today?

3. What makes you most afraid for the future of the United States? Write down your answer and then read Ephesians 1:22. What words/phrases help deal with your fears?

PART 5

ALCOHOL AND PORNOGRAPHY

Chapter 22

JESUS AND DRINKING

Jamie could smell the musty odor even before she opened the storage room door, a scent that triggered her regret. She should have called a professional when water seeped into her basement during a summer storm, but she didn't. She should have called a friend to move the soaked cardboard boxes, but instead, she shut the door and ignored the problem. She should have bought a dehumidifier and dedicated a day to dealing with the mess, but she managed to talk herself out of it a dozen different times. So there, in that dark space that her friends never saw, something unpleasant festered and spread.

That's how mold works, and that's how secrets work too. Keep a secret behind closed doors, locked where no one sees, where no one knows, and it will grow. Try to act like it doesn't exist or ignore it, and it will only spread. Your secret will grow into a habit, your habit will become your addiction, and your addiction will lead to your destruction.

If that is true, why do we keep secrets? Why don't we just fling open the door and tell people the truth? Why don't we confess the details and deal with our reality?

"I drink. A lot. Most days, to be honest. Most of the bottle, to be candid. I need help."

"I turn to pills. When I'm stressed, angry, on edge, or just bored, I uncap the bottle and self-medicate."

"I've been looking at porn for longer than I can remember. My search history is embarrassing. But I don't know how to stop."

"I cope with pain through food and my phone. I binge, and I scroll. That's not healthy, but right now, that is me."

If our struggles with the internet and alcohol and substances and devices will only fester in the dark, why not bring them into the light?

That's easy to answer: because no one talks about them. And if they don't talk, we don't talk. Their silence says it all—that issue is off-limits. So, we keep the secret, and the secret grows. And with it our level of shame.

Sadly, some of the best soil for secrets is in the church. Maybe because it is the place where we call upon sinners to change their ways. Or maybe because no one else confesses the gritty stuff that they do. Or maybe because we fear the unknown, the expression on their faces, if we confess what we have been hiding behind closed doors. Shame, sadly, is alive and well in the church.

SHAME, SADLY, IS ALIVE AND WELL IN THE CHURCH.

But I refuse to let you live with your shame and secrets. The Bible says, "Whoever conceals their sins will not prosper, but the one who confesses and renounces them finds mercy" (Proverbs 28:13). That is my goal and my hope for myself and the members of my church. I long for our church to be a prosperous place, not financially but spiritually, a gathering of God's people where we can confess anything, talk about everything, and enjoy Jesus' unending mercy. It might be uncomfortable, but on the other side of those awkward confessions are some of God's best blessings—true community, freedom, and grace. No one will talk about it unless we talk about it, so let's talk about it.

To start, let's talk about alcohol. In Wisconsin, where I live, alcohol is a part of our culture. If drinking were an Olympic sport, we would dominate the podium. Recently, Green Bay, Wisconsin, was rated the drunkest city in all of America. Appleton, my current home, came in third. Nine of the fifteen drunkest cities were in Wisconsin. Korbel, a liquor company from California, says that although Wisconsin only makes up 1.8 percent of the US population, people there drink 33 percent of the nation's brandy.[1] Or perhaps you've seen those popular shirts that say, "Drink Wisconsibly." Or how about the sign I saw at a local grocery store the other day, the one that read, "Wisconsin's 5 Food Groups—Pilsner, Porter, IPA, Stout, Lager," my state's version of a liquid diet. In fact, my state's Major League Baseball team is called the Brewers, whose original logo from 1970 to 1977 was a half-man, half-beer barrel hybrid!

And alcohol, if I am being entirely open, is part of my church culture too. We drink at the church golf outing. We drink at confirmation parties. We bring Bibles and half barrels to pastoral conferences. Some of my members started a brewery. Preschool parents buy my wife wine as a thank-you for teaching their kids. Lutherans were some of the staunchest opponents of Prohibition. And we still carry the banner today. We love to drink.

But alcohol has affected us. "My dad lost his job," the daughter of an alcoholic recently told me.

"I went from okay to hiding bottles of liquor in eighteen months," another confessed.

"I was supposed to be the responsible one in the family," a Christian admitted, lamenting what alcohol had done.

"Pastor, how can she post about getting drunk and claim to be a Christian?"

My church is filled with stories of addiction, divorce, DUIs, and young Christians who don't mature because they drink more than they pray. So, we have to ask, "What does God think about all this? Is it okay to drink? If so, how much? How often? What would Jesus say about our culture, state, or church?"

After having studied every passage in the Bible that mentions fermented beverages, here is a surprising summary of what I found from the gospels: Jesus drank. Jesus served drinks. Jesus wants us to drink. And we will drink with Jesus. Surprised? I was too!

In Luke 7, Jesus said, "The Son of Man [that's Jesus] came eating and drinking, and you say, 'Here is a glutton and a drunkard, a friend of tax collectors and sinners'" (verse 34). Jesus apparently drank so often his enemies exaggerated and called him a drunkard.

In John 2, Jesus went to a wedding where he revealed his glory as the Son of God:

> Nearby stood six stone water jars, the kind used by the Jews for ceremonial washing, each holding from twenty to thirty gallons. Jesus said to the servants, "Fill the jars with water"; so they filled them to the brim. Then he told them, "Now draw some out and take it to the master of the banquet." They did so, and the master of the banquet tasted the water that had been turned into wine. (verses 6-9)

Jesus' first miracle was to supernaturally uncork 150 gallons of wine!

Three years later, Jesus instituted the Lord's Supper, where he took a cup of wine—one of many that would have been served at the Jewish Passover meal—and commanded, "Drink it, in remembrance of me" (1 Corinthians 11:25).

And when Isaiah wanted to describe what the glory of eternity was like, he predicted, "On this mountain the LORD Almighty will prepare a feast of rich food for all peoples, a banquet of aged wine—the best of meats and the finest of wines" (Isaiah 25:6).

Clearly, based on these verses, Jesus affirms the goodness of alcohol. He made it. He multiplied it. Thus, we can enjoy it. Alcohol is not inherently evil or even unwise. Like sex or smartphones, it can be misused and abused, but it is still God's idea, invention, and gift.

Our family has a tradition whenever a birthday happens in our home. All the other family members make personalized posters for the bedroom door of the birthday boy or girl, mostly humorous reminders that they are known and loved (and that their loved ones are bad at art!). Two years ago, my daughters made me a poster that included alcohol. It included a stick-figure daddy who was hanging out on the couch watching *The Walking Dead* (their zombies were priceless). On the nearby table were two items: a Bible and a bottle. Apparently, my girls have noticed that Daddy often reaches for his Bible and that Daddy sometimes reaches for a bottle.

If that makes you uneasy, remember that Jesus did too. He wasn't ashamed to be around a few glasses of wine. He didn't just come eating the food that his Father created but also drinking the fermented fruit too. That doesn't mean that every Christian has to drink like Christ did, but it does mean there is no shame in doing so. This is why my wife and I talk about alcohol in our home—what it is, how it tastes, how it works.

But I also want to teach my daughters what too much will do. Because while drinking isn't biblically forbidden, drunkenness is. The apostle Paul writes, "The acts of the flesh are obvious: sexual immorality, impurity and debauchery; idolatry and witchcraft; hatred, discord, jealousy, fits of rage, selfish ambition, dissensions, factions and envy; drunkenness, orgies, and the like. I warn you, as I did before, that those who live like this will not inherit the kingdom of God" (Galatians 5:19-21). Idols, witches, orgies, and drunks are all on the same list of forbidden, fleshly, sinful things. Just as clearly as God approves of drinking, he hates drunkenness.

Type "drunk" into a Bible search engine, and you will see just how much God hates overindulgence. Paul said that unrepentant drunks cannot be part of God's family (1 Corinthians 5:11; 6:10). He forbids those who are "given to drunkenness" from serving as pastors (1 Timothy 3:3). Peter adds that drunkenness is what pagans do (1 Peter 4:3). In Revelation, the soon-to-be-destroyed enemies of God are described as "drunk" (17:6; 18:3). Take these words to heart. God does not think that getting drunk is "having a good time." He thinks it's sin.

God is not against you feeling good. God is against you feeling bad. Our Father is not trying to keep something from us. He's trying to keep us from something, namely, the consequences of drunkenness. That's what good dads do.

Most of the passages about drunkenness make that same point. Proverbs, a book about wise living, reminds us where getting drunk gets us: "Wine is a mocker and beer a brawler; whoever is led astray by them is not wise" (20:1). Ever met a mocker? Someone who has a lot to say once wine loosens her tongue? Ever met a brawler? A guy who fights with fists and words at a house party? Alcohol is the storm that strips us of the fruit of the Spirit, especially the fruit of self-control (Galatians 5:23).

Proverbs 31 adds, "It is not for kings to drink wine, not for rulers to crave beer, lest they drink and forget what has been decreed" (verses 4,5). You can forget to be gentle when you're drunk. You can forget your wife wants you to get up early and help with the kids. You can forget to read your Bible when you pass out or forget to wake up and work out. It's not just what you do when you're drunk. It's what you forget to do.

Proverbs 23 offers a vivid description:

> Who has woe? Who has sorrow? Who has strife? Who has complaints? Who has needless bruises? Who has bloodshot eyes? Those who linger over wine, who go to sample bowls of mixed wine. Do not

> gaze at wine when it is red, when it sparkles in the cup, when it goes down smoothly! In the end it bites like a snake and poisons like a viper. (verses 29-32)

Wine sparkles with the promise of relief, joy, and laughter. But then it bites. It poisons. Ask any alcoholic—woe, sorrow, strife, complaints, bruises, bloodshot eyes. Sound fun to you? Noah passed out naked when he was drunk. Lot got his daughters pregnant when he was drunk. Xerxes ruined his marriage when he was drunk. Bad stuff happens when you get drunk.

Simply put, drunks sin more. They insult God by running to a buzz instead of their Bible. They replace God by ignoring prayer as they pay attention to another pour. They lose track of time, stay up too late, skip church, or stumble into a pew with a dehydrated brain that is far from ready to focus on the Word of the Lord. They lie to their parents to go to a party. They lie to the cops who ask if they've been drinking. They give in to gossip, slander, crude behavior, lewd humor, lust, and sexual immorality. A good time? Not according to our good God. That's why our Father affirms alcohol, but he draws the line at getting drunk.

So, what now? What should you do if this chapter has opened your eyes to a problem you didn't see before? Let me close with a few concrete suggestions:

First, count them. Count how much you drink. Be honest. How many do you have in a month? Is that one shot in your rum and coke or three? Is that a 5 oz. glass of wine or a drink and a half? Is that IPA 8 percent ABV, and how many have you had? In order to avoid addressing a potential problem, sinners often say things like, "We had some drinks" or, "We went out for a few beers." Don't. Be honest about your behavior. Count how much you drink.

Second, confess. If you are overindulging, confess your sin to God. Reread the passages referenced previously and realize that what you have done is morally serious to our Father in heaven. Like idolaters and adulterers, you have sinned (reread 1 Corinthians 6:9,10). Confess to God. With a broken heart, humbly approach your heavenly Father and admit what you have done. "If we confess our sins, he is faithful and just and will forgive us our sins and purify us from all unrighteousness" (1 John 1:9).

While you're confessing, don't forget to confess to a fellow Christian. James says, "Confess your sins to each other and pray for each other so that you may be healed" (James 5:16). Healing comes when you confess, so confess to the kind of people who will pray for you and preach Jesus to you. You will slowly get worse if you try to hide this. You will get much better if you don't. Confess it to God and to them.

CONFESS IT TO GOD AND TO THEM.

Third, curb it. If you choose to enjoy alcohol, pick a predetermined amount you will drink. Few people make their best decisions after a few drinks. So, pick a safe number that keeps you a few steps from the line. "I'm one and done." "Two and I'm through." When you drive up a mountain road with a steep cliff on one side, you don't put your wheels on the very last inch of solid ground. You play it safe. Do the same with alcohol. If it takes a person of your gender and weight four drinks to get drunk, stick with two. Stay far from the line. That's how you curb it.

Fourth, cling to him. Cling to Jesus, because Jesus gives you a new identity. Do you know what happens to drunk drivers in the state of Tennessee? They have to do three eight-hour shifts of community service. During those twenty-four hours, they have to wear a blazing orange vest that declares, "I

AM A DRUNK DRIVER." The philosophy, I imagine, is that the embarrassment will keep people from drinking and driving.

But Jesus has something better. Paul writes:

> Do not be deceived: Neither . . . drunkards nor slanderers nor swindlers will inherit the kingdom of God. And that is what some of you were. But you were washed, you were sanctified, you were justified in the name of the Lord Jesus Christ and by the Spirit of our God. (1 Corinthians 6:9-11)

Drunks cannot go to heaven, but that is not what you are. Perhaps you were, but then you turned to Jesus. You were washed in Baptism. You were sanctified and made holy by the Holy Spirit. You were justified, declared not guilty, in the name of the Lord Jesus Christ.

That is who Christians are. Despite all our stupid choices and our addictions to short-term pleasure, God sent his Son for us. Jesus gave up everything for us. So, to God, we are not drunks. We are his kids. The kids he loves. And he is a Father who has forgiven us all our sins, overindulgence included, in the name of his one and only Son.

HE IS A FATHER WHO HAS FORGIVEN US ALL OUR SINS, OVERINDULGENCE INCLUDED.

One summer during college, I threw up in front of my dad. I didn't drink until I was twenty-one, so when I went out with some friends soon after my birthday, I wasn't ready for the two Long Island ice teas that I ordered. I felt it as my friends drove me home. And when I tried to walk calmly past my dad, who was sitting in the living room, the carpet started swirling. I made it upstairs, but then the bathroom started spinning. And I puked. A lot. Unfortunately—sorry for oversharing here—I am the loudest puker in the history of pukers. My dad was only a few feet outside the door, an audio witness of the consequences of my sin.

The next morning, I woke up sick but even more, ashamed. I made it to breakfast and avoided eye contact with my father. But my dad only said one sentence about the previous evening—"Had too much, huh?" He never brought it up again. He still loved me. He knew I was sorry. That's what good dads do.

That's what our Father does too. Maybe your weekends are a mashup of sin and church services. Maybe you dragged an addiction into church last Sunday. Maybe alcohol has made you forget the reason God put you on this earth. But our Father wants to talk. He wants to talk about your sin. But even more, he wants to talk about the love of his Son.

STUDY QUESTIONS

1. Before reading this chapter, what was your view of drinking alcohol? How did God's Word change your thinking?

2. First Corinthians 6:9-11 is a powerful passage about many taboo subjects. Name two or three powerful points Paul is trying to make about the sins we often avoid discussing.

3. What subjects have been taboo among your Christian friends? What sins and struggles are God urging you to confess so that you can find help and healing?

Chapter 23

PORN AMONG GOD'S PEOPLE

A few years ago, I got fed up with the plugged drain in our shower. Maybe it's just me, but I believe that a long, hot shower is one of the greatest gifts God has ever given to mankind. But that blessing disappeared once our drain was plugged. For days I stood in a lukewarm puddle that would rise up to my ankles, a murky mix of water, shampoo, and whatever had been stuck to my body.

Finally, I decided to fix it. I unscrewed the plug and prepared to face the monster burrowed beneath. Have you ever cleaned a shower drain? A sopping wet and stringy hair ferret from all the people who've ever used the shower awaits you. Nasty. But unless you want to miss out on one of God's greatest gifts, you have to deal with this discomfort.

That's some good imagery for this chapter. Because there is something plugging the drain of the church. Something nasty and uncomfortable. Something we wish would go away all by itself. That something is pornography. In every church, God-fearing, Jesus-loving, church-attending people are living with the consequences of plugged-up purity.

I've seen the shame as he avoids eye contact. I've witnessed their struggle to rebuild trust after discovering the search history. I've read emails about her silent struggle. In my time at my church, I've done more counseling for porn than I have for any other topic.

According to Covenant Eyes, a leading Christian website on the topic, 64 percent of Christian men and 15 percent of Christian women admit to watching porn at least once a month,[1] a stat that, sooner or later, will affect you and those you love. Porn is a pandemic that is teaching our children heresy about sexuality, rewiring our brains with unrealistic expectations, wrecking our self-control, stressing our marriages, trashing our integrity, enslaving our bodies, and dirtying our souls. Whether this is your personal struggle or not, it is ours. Porn plugs up the blessings that God wants to shower on the people whom he loves and the people whom you love.

PORN PLUGS UP THE BLESSINGS THAT GOD WANTS TO SHOWER ON THE PEOPLE WHOM HE LOVES AND THE PEOPLE WHOM YOU LOVE.

Dream with me for a moment of the blessings of being part of a porn-free family. No hiding. No shame. No dodging the question, "What were you up to last night?" Just honesty, transparency, and love. No son walking in on his dad and seeing what he cannot unsee. No couples struggling to trust each other or feeling the pressure of competing with a million images from professional actresses. Just closeness and connection as God intended. No time wasted scrolling, clicking, sinfully looking. Just days devoted to Jesus and nights from which you don't wake up with regret. There are so many good gifts our good God wants to give when it comes to sexual purity.

That is why I want to help you clean out the drain, as uneasy as that may make you feel. For the sake of our consciences, relationships, bodies, and souls, I'm going to write clearly and biblically about porn. And I'm going to start with one of the most intense and graphic stories in the entire Bible.

Let me take you back to around 1400 B.C. to the Moabite cities of Peor and Shittim, just east of the Jordan River. Because there they are, the people of Israel. Two million men, women, and children are finishing their long march to the Promised Land. Foreign armies have tried to stop them and failed. Kings aligned forces and fought against them and failed. The pagan nations called upon Baal and Chemosh, their gods, and failed. With the true God on their side, Israel seems unstoppable until the people of Moab try a less savage, more sensual attack. The Moabite women wonder, "What if we seduce them?"

Numbers 25 says, "While Israel was staying in Shittim, the men began to indulge in sexual immorality with Moabite women, who invited them to the sacrifices to their gods. The people ate the sacrificial meal and bowed down before these gods. So Israel yoked themselves to the Baal of Peor" (verses 1-3). One of the twisted beliefs of the Moabite culture was a "sex for rain" exchange. The Moabites believed that Baal, the storm god, would only send rain after being intimate with the goddess Asherah. But Baal, they believed, could only get in the mood when he peeped down on his people and watched them . . . well . . . you know. This "peeping Baal" belief drove their perverted behavior.

Shrines filled the land of Moab, and shrine prostitutes found eager worshipers to get the gods in the mood. Give up your body, the Moabites believed, and Baal will bless us all with rain, crops, food, and life.

And Israel, tragically, bought it. Despite the First Commandment's "You shall have no other gods," the Israelite men bowed down to Baal and gave up the true God just to get a little extra sexual pleasure.

God was not pleased. "And the LORD's anger burned against them. The LORD said to Moses, 'Take all the leaders of these people, kill them and expose them in broad daylight before the LORD, so that the LORD's fierce anger may turn away from Israel.' So Moses said to Israel's judges, 'Each of you must put to death those of your people who have yoked themselves to the Baal of Peor'" (Numbers 25:3-5). God shocks us here, doesn't he? Sometimes his love shocks us as we hear what and how he forgives and how often and whom he forgives, and we think, "No one forgives like that!" As humans, we're not used to forgiveness like that.

But at other times, God's holiness shocks us. We see how he hates sin, how his anger burns against it, and how he must avenge it. And we think, "No one hates sin that much!" As humans, we're not used to holiness like that. But the way we feel about rape and child abuse is the way God feels about all sin.

This is one of those times. God's sense of justice needed to be satisfied. His fierce anger needed to be turned away. And there was only one way to do it. And it's graphic. "Kill and expose them in broad daylight! Then my anger will turn away from Israel." God commanded a graphic sacrifice to deal with their dirty minds and defiled bodies.

But right in the middle of this moral horror, an Israelite man named Zimri and his girl Kozbi showed up. While Moses was gnashing his teeth at the sensual debacle, Zimri walked past, giving Kozbi enough PDA to make Baal blush. Zimri winked at Moses as he rushed his girl into his tent, just feet from the tent of meeting, the church where the Israelites met with their holy God.

The text says, "Then an Israelite man brought into the camp a Midianite woman right before the eyes of Moses and the whole assembly of Israel while they were weeping at the entrance to the tent of meeting" (Numbers 25:6).

What!? Imagine that I am preaching about the sinfulness of pornography, and my church is weeping in repentance when some dude comes strolling up with a stack of *Playboys* and pins a pinup to the cross, loud and proud of his sexual sin. That's what was happening in the camp of Israel.

And Phinehas couldn't stand it. Phinehas was Moses' great-nephew, and he hated sin almost as much as God did. When he saw Zimri's lustful eyes and hard heart, Phinehas' lips tightened. His nostrils flared, and his eyes scowled. Next to his tent, he spotted a spear stuck in the ground. Pushing a few Israelites aside, he grabbed the spear and marched toward Zimri's tent.

"When Phinehas son of Eleazar, the son of Aaron, the priest, saw this, he left the assembly, took a spear in his hand and followed the Israelite into the tent. He drove the spear into both of them, right through the Israelite man and into the woman's stomach. Then the plague against the Israelites was stopped; but those who died in the plague numbered 24,000" (Numbers 25:7-9). Once the spear plunged through their bodies, God's anger turned away. The plague of Israel's pornographic behavior could only be stopped with blood, with pierced bodies, with graphic death.

The end. That is a story not included in most children's Bibles. But what does that have to do with us a few millennia later?

Well, let's start with our culture. While we don't have shrine prostitutes like the Moabites, it should be obvious our culture views sex as a god. If you drive down the interstate just south of my city of Appleton, Wisconsin, you'll see two Christian billboards, one of which asks, "What would Jesus say about pornography?" They are surrounded, however, by six brightly colored billboards for porn superstores. It appears Jesus is outnumbered.

But it's not just that highway. Sex sells, and the love of money moves many to sexualize everything for the sake of more dollars and more followers. Few things get you more internet attention than bodies stripped down for the world to see, meaning you don't have to search "porn" on your computer. Just have a computer, and porn, likely, will find you. Internet pornography makes billions every year, a depressing statistic given that the vast majority of it is absolutely free. Moab and America have much in common.

And like Baal, porn's offer is seductive. Baal promised rain for impurity; porn promises us much more. Do you want pleasure? Porn can give it. Are you stressed? Porn provides an escape. Are you bored? Porn has thousands of brain-stimulating videos. Does your wife have a headache? The girls of porn don't. Is your sex life bland? Porn can spice it up. Are you curious about sex? Porn's class is always in session. Porn has always been tempting because, like Baal, it promises us so much.

PORN HAS ALWAYS BEEN TEMPTING BECAUSE, LIKE BAAL, IT PROMISES US SO MUCH.

But porn kills. Here are five of countless examples of that truth:

First, *porn kills marriages*. I would need two hands to count the number of wives I've counseled who have used the exact same line: "I can't compete with that." Stumbling upon an unerased search history, they found a digital harem and instantly knew they couldn't be thin and curvy, Black and White, shy and aggressive all at the same time. A wife is to be loved, but there is no love in porn. A husband is to be respected, but what man feels respected when she's looking at another man? Porn kills closeness, intimacy, love, and respect. Porn kills marriages.

Second, *porn kills expectations*. Over a decade of marriage has taught me that porn is a fantasy. In porn, all it takes is a look, and everyone is ready to go. But real life in the real world is filled with to-do lists, swimming lessons, mandatory overtime, headaches, PMS, ED, busy weeks, and weekend guests. In real marriage, sex is the culmination of love, of a dozen sweet words and chores done and choices made. But that script is too long for porn. Instead, it teaches us to expect passion to be easy. Porn kills expectations.

Third, *porn kills brains*. Did you know that porn causes your brain to release the same chemicals as crack cocaine? Dopamine floods your brain, bringing intense pleasure and an intense craving to repeat the experience. Oxytocin causes you to relax in the middle of a stressful day. Epinephrine burns the images in your mind, reminding you what caused such a sensation. That's why some people can't just walk away. They're hooked. Their brains are stuck. They need to go through detox. There is no such thing as an innocent look when our brains are involved. Because porn kills our brains.

Fourth, *porn kills consciences*. You might know the feeling of a Baal-over, a sexual hangover, the morning after binging on Baal and his empty promises. The regret. The shame. The feeling you're a huge hypocrite. Recently, a man confessed his sexual sin to me, and I said, "You know God loves you, right?" But he wasn't so sure. Because porn kills your conscience.

Finally, *porn kills souls*. Hebrews 13:4 says, "God will judge the adulterer and all the sexually immoral." Porn makes God angry. When porn pollutes our purity, defiles our dignity, degrades his daughters, enslaves his sons, violates our vows, and profanes our point of view, God gets mad. He hated porn back in Moab, and he hates it still today. His anger must be appeased. His wrath must be turned away.

But how? Should the pure among us pull a Phinehas and find a spear? Should Christ come down and pierce every sexual sinner? What will turn away God's anger so the plague of his punishment doesn't kill us all? The answer is another graphic act that the Bible records.

Isaiah says, "[Jesus] was pierced for our transgressions" (53:5). Instead of driving nails into us, Jesus opened up his holy hands so nails could be driven into him. In fact, on the cross, a soldier took a spear and drove it into his body because Jesus was willing to stand in for sexual sinners.

Not only that, but Christ was killed and exposed in broad daylight. Crucified in public, his body was exposed like the dirty Israelites in Moab so our sin wouldn't be exposed, so we wouldn't be dirty to God.

And Christ took away God's anger. Jesus' sacrifice turns away his wrath by taking away our sins. Porn plagues us, but Jesus' graphic death stopped it. Porn infuriates our Father, but Jesus' graphic death changes God's expression. There is nothing sexy about it, but there is love all around it. Grace, expressed best at a blood-stained cross, is graphic. But only something graphic will be enough to satisfy the demands of justice.

If you are a sexual sinner, any kind of sinner, run to Jesus with a repentant heart. Take hold of his hands that were pierced for you and hear his words that seem too good to be true—"I don't condemn you." He doesn't. Your condemnation happened when he took your place that Friday two millennia ago.

Even though your porn may have killed a thousand things, Jesus does not condemn you. Even if there are a thousand horizontal consequences, there is not one ounce of vertical condemnation. Because God is not waiting until you cleanse your body before he cleanses your soul. That's what Jesus' graphic grace did.

What now? Should I give you a list of fifty-two ways to porn-proof your life, your home, your kids? Not here. In the next chapter, I plan to share the best way that I know for you to escape sexual sin. But here, I simply want you to stare at the graphic gospel that is your Jesus on a cross. Stare at it like it's the most alluring thing you've ever seen. Because it is.

That's what Kim found out. When Kim agreed to go to a Christian concert with her friend Matt, she wasn't sure what to expect. But she didn't expect the rose. The speaker at the concert was trying to warn the crowd about the consequences of sexual sin, so he dramatically took out a freshly cut, beautiful red rose. After smelling it, he passed it to the crowd to hold, to smell, and to see up close. After being passed through hundreds of hands, the rose made it back onstage, broken and nearly petal-less. Taking the dirty rose in his hands, the speaker said, "Now, who would want this?" His point about the promiscuous was clear.

On the car ride home, Kim was quiet. Matt knew she had a less-than-holy past and wondered what she thought of the rose sermon. Soon after, Kim didn't show up for class and didn't return Matt's calls, making him wonder if she had gone back to her old ways.

But then Matt got the phone call. Kim had been in an accident, which had left her with a fractured skull. Matt rushed to the hospital to visit, and in the middle of his questions about the accident, Kim asked a blunt question: "Matt, do you think I'm a dirty rose?" Matt's heart sank because the speaker at the concert had forgotten to say one vitally important thing to Kim: Jesus wants the dirty rose. Jesus died for the dirty rose. Jesus rose for the dirty rose.

If you, like Kim, have dirtied your body and soul with sexual sin, if your conscience screams, "Why would God want you?" remember Jesus. Remember his love, his graphic grace, his cross. Remember porn kills, but Jesus saves.

STUDY QUESTIONS

1. Add at least four more items to the list of things that porn kills.

2. Read 1 Corinthians 6:9-20 and highlight the two or three most powerful things a sexual sinner needs to hear from those verses.

3. Look at how Jesus dealt with an adulterous woman in John 8:1-11. Connect this story to our struggles with sexual purity today.

Chapter 24

THE SECOND-BEST WAY TO QUIT PORN

Porn kills. Jesus saves. That's what we learned in the last chapter. Porn graphically kills marital intimacy, sexual expectations, your brain's self-control, a clean conscience, and your very soul. Porn makes God mad because it kills so many blessings he wants to shower on his people. Porn kills.

But Jesus saves. Jesus was pierced, exposed, and killed for porn users. He was stripped so we could be covered in his love. He endured God's anger so we could enjoy God's favor. The cross wasn't sexy, but it did save us. Porn kills, but Jesus saves.

Now I want to wrestle with a frequently asked question about addiction: When it comes to choosing whether to go back to porn, can people change? If you've been clicking for far too long, can you change your online habits? If you love someone whose brain is wired to crave porn, will they—can they—ever quit?

To be straightforward with you, conquering sin is never simple. The Scriptures describe it as a battle that believers must fight today and then tomorrow and then again and again until our final breath. Some days, we resist temptation. On other days, we give in. In Jesus, the final victory will be ours, but until he comes again, we will need to fight the unmerciful assaults of the devil, the world, and our own sinful nature.

That being said, there are powerful ways to change sinful patterns in your life, even with battles as fierce as sexual purity. I would like to share the second-best way to quit sinning.

The first and best way, in case you are curious, was what we covered in the last chapter. The love of Jesus not only cleanses us from our sins but also compels us to leave our sins behind. Some call this "gospel motivation," which Paul teaches in Titus 2: "For the grace of God has appeared that offers salvation to all people. It teaches us to say 'No' to ungodliness and worldly passions, and to live self-controlled, upright and godly lives in this present age" (verses 11,12). Focus on the love of Christ, and the Spirit will change you from the inside out, creating a greater passion for him than your previous passion for sin. Nothing motivates us to change quite like love, which is why the love of God is our greatest motivation to change.

The Bible doesn't end there, however. Our Father motivates us in multiple ways, which is why I want to share the second-best way to quit sin, specifically the sin of lust. Ready for it? Here goes: keep confessing. That is an essential key to life change! Keep confessing your struggles to others. To your small group, your pastor, parents, friends, boyfriend, wife, whoever loves God and loves you. Instead of hiding in the darkness of your secrets where porn grows like a fungus, drag it out into the light and keep it there. In other words, if you sin, say it. And if you sin again, say it again. Be honest. Stop faking it in front of others. Be real. Keep confessing.

James, the half brother of Jesus, wrote, "Therefore confess your sins to each other and pray for each other so that you may be healed. The prayer of a righteous person is powerful and effective" (5:16). If you want a powerful weapon against your personal weakness, confess your sins to others. They can pray, and those prayers will be effective in your fight against porn.

In fact, in the original Greek of James' words, it literally says, "Keep confessing your sins to each other." More than a one-time, swallow-hard-and-blurt-it-out moment, James is encouraging you to develop a lifestyle of confession. Confessing your sins to others is meant to be your habit. Why? So that "you may be healed."

But that step is easier said than done. Over many years of leading a ministry that helps people fight sexual sin, I've received multiple messages like these:

"Can you give advice about finding someone who can accept this as a part of your past without being disgusted by you?"

"I know confiding in my roommate would be a powerful step to finally kicking my porn habit, but he doesn't seem to have any kind of problem with porn, and I fear he might look down on me if I confessed."

Thus, we live within this tension. We want to quit looking at pornography, but one of the keys to quitting is, frankly, terrifying. So, what do we do?

STOP FAKING IT IN FRONT OF OTHERS. BE REAL. KEEP CONFESSING.

Paul has some answers to that question. Two thousand years ago, the apostle Paul wrote a bunch of letters to a bunch of churches where *a bunch* of the members had sexual purity problems. Most of the churches of the first century were a mix of Jews and Gentiles—Jews who had grown up with conservative sexual ethics and Gentiles who had grown up with temple prostitution, orgies, and promiscuity of a thousand kinds, which explains the common sins that Paul lists in 1 Corinthians 6, Galatians 5, etc. This doesn't mean that Jews didn't struggle with sexual sin. It simply means that sexual sin was much more common among the Gentiles.

Therefore, when Jews and Gentiles came to faith in Jesus and joined the same local churches, there were noticeable differences in their behavior. It would have been easy for the Jews to be disgusted with those Gentiles and just as easy for the Gentiles to hide those habits from the Jews. But Paul knew the power of confessing sins to one another, so near the end of his letter to the Galatians, he wrote these words: "Brothers and sisters, if someone is caught in a sin" (6:1).

Paul knew that even within the church of Jesus, the followers of Jesus sometimes get caught in sin. We get stuck. We think we can handle it, push it away, but like a guy attempting too much weight on a bench press, temptation bears down, and our trembling muscles don't have the strength to push back.

Sooner or later, you will find yourself in such a situation. You will be on a bench press getting crushed by some temptation and unable to resist it by yourself. Or someone you love will be in that desperate predicament.

What should we do? Paul continues, "Brothers and sisters, if someone is caught in a sin, you who live by the Spirit should restore that person gently" (6:1). The word *restore* is a medical term from the ancient world. Doctors and therapists would "restore" bodies by building up the muscles and restoring the original strength and range of motion.

Think of your friend's knee after his ACL surgery. What's easy for you—bending your knee to a 90-degree angle—is not easy for him. He needs restoration, someone to help him get back his strength. He can't do it on his own. He needs help to be "restored."

That's what Paul is calling the church to do. If someone is caught in pornography, they need the help of brothers and sisters in Christ to be restored. The answer might seem simple to you—Just don't! Don't click! Don't look! Just stop!—but Paul is advocating for more than a wagging finger and a lecture on personal self-control. He wants us to help each other. He wants the church to be God's means of restoration for sinners who don't seem to have the strength to say no.

"But watch yourselves," Paul continues, "or you also may be tempted" (6:1). When you have spiritual muscles others don't, the tempter will tempt you too.

He will tempt you with pride: "How could you look at stuff like that? I would never, ever do something like that. You're a Christian! You have children! You make me so sad."

He will tempt you with impatience: "You did it again? We talked about this! You told me you were going to fight this. If you knew that God hated this, why would you do it again?"

He will tempt you with gossip: "Don't tell him I told you this, but he has a serious problem. It's porn."

He will even tempt you with lust: "He mentioned a website he struggles to stay away from. I wonder what's on it . . ."

Watch yourselves, or you may be tempted too. Helping real sinners conquer real sin is really tempting, so be really careful.

Instead, Paul continues, "Carry each other's burdens, and in this way you will fulfill the law of Christ. Let us not become weary in doing good, for at the proper time we will reap a harvest if we do not give up. Therefore, as we have opportunity, let us do good to all people, especially to those who belong to the family of believers" (6:2,9,10). Let's do good to our spiritual family. Let's not get tired of this community restoration project. Let's carry each other's burdens. Let's help them lift the weight. Because this is the law of Christ, to love one another in the same way that Christ first loved us.

If we do, Paul promises, we will reap a harvest. Our confessions and attempts at restoration are like little seeds that can grow into something big and beautiful. Our fellowship will be closer, our habits holier, our lives will look a little more like Jesus' life. This is the second-best way to quit sin.

Paul's words make me think of the gym. While my body may be more ribs than ripped, I do know a fair bit about weight lifting. For example, I know that if you want to get stronger, you need a spotter. A spotter is a person who stands incredibly close to you, within the normal range of personal space, and helps you lift the weight when you can't. A spotter makes sure you don't get stuck. He restores you when 100+ pounds are inching down toward your chest and you can't push back.

It takes humility to ask for a spotter, because you are admitting that you aren't the all-powerful god of the weight room. You might be too weak for this weight. But what makes you a stronger lifter is the presence of a spotter.

**RESTORE THEM GENTLY. LIFT THEIR BURDEN.
DO NOT BECOME WEARY.**

For many of our brothers and sisters in Christ, porn is a weight they can't handle. Lots of our fellow Christians—including some of our best friends, significant others, and our own children—are stuck underneath the bar of impurity and don't know what to do. They can't seem to push back, but they are embarrassed to cry out for help. Paul knows that they need a spotter. They need you. Restore them gently. Lift their burden. Do not become weary.

How blessed would your church be if every believer embraced Galatians 6? If we stopped caring about impressing each other and instead cared about helping each other? If we confessed our sins, inviting others to bear our burdens, and had the mutual love to do the same for them?

Be the brother in Christ who smiles and says, "I've got you. I'm praying for you. Text me if you're tempted. I'll talk you out of it." Be the spiritual sister who texts, "You sinned, but you're getting stronger. You haven't gone five days without it in a long time." Be the small group who encourages each other with, "Thanks for being honest, man. You're not the only one. How can we help?"

We need to be the roommate who's not disgusted even though porn is disgusting. We need to be the wife, fiancé, and boyfriend who's not going to blow up but instead draw near in prayer. We need every muscle in the body of Christ. To push back against the heavy weight of porn, we need each other.

We need to remind one another of the strength we so often forget: God loves sexual sinners. When we fall and fail, when we're embarrassed and exposed, we need to remind one another that our true strength is found in Christ.

Jesus once invited, "Come to me, all you who are weary and burdened, and I will give you rest" (Matthew 11:28). Jesus lifted our burden by lugging the weight of our weakness up the hill called Calvary. Jesus shoulder-pressed the shame off your shoulders and onto his cross. Our Savior is strong enough to bear the burden of any story, addiction, or sin.

That's what Christian spotters do. We carry the burden by reminding one another of the Burden Carrier, Jesus Christ. We restore sinners by reminding one another of the Redeemer who paid the price so that every impurity would be washed away in his blood. We strengthen the weak by pointing to the One who was strong for every second of his entire life, the life he lived in our place. As often as they keep confessing sin, we keep confessing the Savior of sexual sinners.

So where do we go from here? Let me leave you a simple next step: Please ask for a spotter. If you're struggling with sexual sin—porn, random hookups, prostitution, sleeping with your girlfriend—would you confess so God's people can restore you? Would you stop trying to bench press that weight and cry out for help? God wants to help you. And the way he helps you is through others.

My prayer is that your story ends up like Jeremy's. Jeremy was caught in porn. He couldn't trust himself with an internet connection and an empty house, which is why he listened to James and decided to confess. He told me. He told his girlfriend. And, by the grace of God and the power of his Spirit, something changed.

Here's how Jeremy described it: "When I look back at the transformation in my life, I am blown away. A year ago, I couldn't be alone in my house without falling into temptation. Now I've been home alone more than I can count and have never even been tempted to fall back to where I had been. It's amazing what happens when you open up and tell someone. I had just accepted it as part of my life, and it doesn't have to be that way. It doesn't have to be something you constantly fall back into and feel ashamed. . . . Telling [my girlfriend] was BY FAR the most difficult conversation we have had . . . but it was definitely a turning point in our relationship."

Jeremy changed in ways he could barely believe or describe, ways that didn't even seem possible when he was caught in his sin—a reminder that with God, all things are possible!

When Jeremy slipped and fell back into sin, he confessed to me. I told him to keep confessing to others. After taking my advice, he wrote back, "I talked to my fiancée about what happened. It was not an easy conversation, but she was very forgiving and much more understanding of the struggle than the first time she found out." And then most recently, his email was short and sweet: "It's been such a blessing to be more free over the past 18 months than I ever have been."

How do we conquer our sinful habits? We keep confessing our sins to one another. We keep lifting the burden together. We keep asking, "Spot me?" and keep offering, "I'll spot you." And, as our spiritual muscles slowly grow, our actions will reflect what we already are—more than conquerors through Jesus Christ.

Do people change? Ask Jeremy.

STUDY QUESTIONS

1. Proverbs 28:13 and James 5:16 are scriptural encouragements to battle temptation with the help of fellow believers. Take ten minutes to study these two passages, examining every word that they contain.

2. Jesus asked his friends for help when he was overwhelmed and sorrowful (Matthew 26:38). How does that prove that asking for help is not a sign of weakness but one of strength?

3. Reach out to a friend and admit what you're struggling with. That's the whole point of this chapter!

PART 6

ABUSE AND ABORTION

Chapter 25

GOD'S WORD TO THE ABUSED

When my church (The CORE) first opened in an old movie theater, the congregation decided to put three massive words on the side of the building: *Real. Relevant. Relational.* Those words were more than a trendy tagline; they were our hope and prayer, what we wanted in our DNA.

We wanted the church to be real. Even if "real" was raw, messy, complicated, and uncomfortable. We wanted to talk about real life, issues, and struggles. Because "real" is relevant. All of us do and deal with stuff that isn't neat, tidy, and churchy, stuff that we need help with and forgiveness for. And we wanted it to be relational, a church where you wouldn't have to fake or hide it but could confess and deal with it together.

When I became the main speaker for *Time of Grace*, I wanted to be sure to be real, relevant, and relational to that audience as well as my home congregation. That's why we had a sermon series about homosexuality and God, and another on race and God, and another on God and gender. Another series covered depression, suicide, and drinking. Another covered porn, and still another, dating and divorce. But there's something I've barely mentioned in all these years . . . abuse.

Honestly, the complexity of addressing abuse scares me. I'm scared that if I stay silent, you will continue to get hurt, or you won't heal. And I'm scared that if I break the silence, you will get hurt, or my words might trigger old trauma. I'm scared of being so generic you don't see the many forms abuse takes. Talking about abuse is like walking a tightrope, especially for an average pastor like me. So, I just want to say that if I slip up, when I slip up, when the words aren't just right, when I miss the mark, I want you to know my heart is to help. I want to be real, because so many can relate and need a relationship with God and with one another to move forward. I know this is not easy, but it is good for us to talk about abuse.

So what exactly is abuse? According to the National Domestic Violence Hotline, "Domestic violence is a pattern of behaviors used by one partner to maintain power and control over another partner in an intimate relationship."[1] This isn't one-time name-calling but a pattern of behavior. It's not just physical force but also psychological fear—an assault on your mental well-being. And the abuser's goal is to control. Abusers want to get their own way, so they do whatever it takes to get it. He slaps a face, punches a wall, kicks a pet, and controls the cash. She degrades with insults, isolates from friends, and touches without consent. They blow up, blow off a blowup, blame you for a blowup, threaten to take the kids, threaten to hurt themselves. Abusers even twist Scripture—"You have to submit to me"; "You have to forgive me"; "Love keeps no record of wrongs, so you can't call the cops"; "If you honored your father, you wouldn't; if you loved your mother, you'd never." Abusers do whatever it takes to make you do what they want.

And it happens a lot. According to the Centers for Disease Control and Prevention, one in three women and one in four men have experienced severe physical violence from an intimate partner in their lives.[2] That's just physical. And that means abuse affects you and me—men and women, brothers and sisters, us. If 300 people come to my church on Sunday, 150 men and 150 women, 87 of them have endured/will endure severe physical violence. On an average Sunday, by those same odds, 87,000 people watching *Time of Grace* have been through it too. 87,000! Abuse is real, relevant, and affects our relationships.

Given the complexity of it all, I want to spend the next three chapters talking to three specific groups of people. In this first chapter, I want to speak to people who have been abused. Next, to the abusers themselves. Finally, to everyone who knows one or the other. I know those overlap, that the abused can become abusive, which is why I hope you will read all three chapters. Our precious souls need to heal. Let's start by looking into God's Word and addressing those who have experienced abuse.

ABUSE IS REAL, RELEVANT, AND AFFECTS OUR RELATIONSHIPS.

One of my most vivid memories of dealing with abuse is from a few years ago. A man came to our church and was excited about growing in his faith. But one day he confessed to me that he had hurt his girlfriend. He was wrecked by his angry behavior, weeping and sorry for what he had done. (After our conversation, I called a cop from church and asked what I should do with such information, but he said lamentably that the woman needed first to make a charge.) Before the abuser left my office, however, I told him what I would tell any sinner who was truly sorry. I told him that Jesus died for us; that Jesus died even for this; that even though there would be earthly consequences, Jesus could save him from condemnation. I even texted him a Bible passage afterward about God's grace.

Later, however, I would come to regret that text. Weeks later, the woman showed up at my office and told me the rest of the story. She gave me the details of how physical the abuse was, details that broke my heart, and then she revealed what her boyfriend had done with my text. "See?" He shoved his phone in her face. "The pastor is on my side. God is on my side." I have never felt so angry and so sorry at the same time. That experience helped me see abuse up close—how muddied a manipulator can make things. That's why I want to open the Bible and be perfectly clear about what God thinks of abuse.

GOD HATES IT WHEN ANYONE USES THEIR SIZE AND STRENGTH AND THEIR AUTHORITY OR POSITION TO HURT A CHILD.

Let's start with this: *God hates abuse.* Highlight that and remember it. In this broken world, we often wonder why God doesn't just stop the bad stuff from happening. His timing and his plans confuse us and make us question what he thinks about our pain. But this much is clear—God hates abuse. Here are three passages to prove it: "So God said to Noah, 'I am going to put an end to all people, for the earth is filled with violence because of them'" (Genesis 6:13). Remember Noah and the ark and the flood? Why did God do that? Because of abuse. Because violent force replaced humble faith, and God could not stand it. And neither could Jesus: "If anyone causes one of these little ones—those who believe in me—to stumble, it would be better for them to have a large millstone hung around their neck and to be drowned in the depths of the sea" (Matthew 18:6). If you mislead a child; damage, use, and confuse a child; cause them to stumble and struggle for your own power and pleasure, it would be better to have a large millstone—not even a regular one but a large one!—hung around your neck to drown you. Because God hates abuse. God hates it when anyone uses their size and strength and their authority or position to hurt a child. But maybe this psalm says it best: "The LORD examines the righteous, but the wicked, those who love violence, he hates with a passion" (11:5). God doesn't just hate violence. He hates those who love violence. And he doesn't just hate them. He hates them with a passion.

If you have or are abusing someone, you need to keep reading and also read the next chapter (there is hope for you too!), but if you have been abused, let these words cut through all the garbage your abuser piled up to hide the truth. God hates abuse. Every time. God never minimizes it or justifies it. God never, ever says it's okay because he was drunk or because she was stressed. He doesn't blame it on you. It's not your fault. You are not responsible, no matter what they say. Please hear me. It breaks our Father's heart when abuse happens.

Second, *God loves the abused.* A few years back, a wise pastor told me about the funny way our minds do math. He had just read a study that said when one person says something to you ten times and ten people say something to you one time, your brain feels about the same. 1×10 = 1+1+1+1+1+1+1+1+1+1. In other words, it only takes one constant critic or one abusive voice to overwhelm your mind. So, if your mom or boyfriend says, "You're so dumb, an idiot, useless, fat, stupid, and worthless," your brain finds it very hard to remember that only one person said that. Only one. Out of all the people you know, out of 7.7 billion humans on earth, it was just one. But it feels like the truth.

I wonder if that's why the one true God calls you so many names. There are so many names God has for Christians in the New Testament. I counted, trying to note how often Christians were called weak or sinful by Jesus or the apostles and how often they were called holy, pure, beloved, and chosen. I counted 682 total names in the New Testament. Guess how many were positive? 610! What?! 610. A nine-to-one ratio. There's still some hard truth—we are still sinners—but he overwhelms us with the truth of our identity in Jesus. Christian survivors of abuse are saints. They are not damaged. They are a delight to God. It's almost as if God knew how many names we would be called. So he put on every page of the Bible the reality of what the life, death, and resurrection of Jesus did for us.

If you're not a Christian today, this is what Jesus is offering you. Right now. Let the Holy Spirit lead you to Jesus, call out to Jesus, trust in Jesus, and you will be saved from the old labels and so much more. You will get a new name. Lots of new names, actually. Loved. Saved. Treasured. Cherished. Child of God.

At one of Jesus' first-ever sermons, he said that this was his mission: "The Spirit of the Lord is on me, because he has anointed me to proclaim good news to the poor. He has sent me *to proclaim freedom for the prisoners* and recovery of sight for the blind, to *set the oppressed free*" (Luke 4:18, emphasis added). Jesus came with good news. His blood would cleanse us from everything embarrassing and unclean. And his words would set the oppressed, mistreated, and abused free.

I know this might be hard to believe, so I want to offer you a clear next step. After consulting with some counselors and abuse experts, I've put together a short list of places for you to turn. These are websites, books, and organizations that can help you figure this out. Abuse lives on lies, and these places can help you hear the truth, again and again—that God loves the abused. You can find this resource list on page 309 of this book.

But there's one last thing I want you to know—*God was abused*. Did you know that? When you think of Jesus, do you think of an abuse victim? He was. The great Old Testament prophecy said, "He was oppressed and afflicted" (Isaiah 53:7). Jesus was struck, slapped, and stripped of his clothing. He was stricken, smitten, and afflicted. He was assaulted, mocked, and ridiculed in his pain. He ended up all alone with men who used force to control him, to put him on a cross.

That doesn't just mean that Jesus died for you; it also means that God gets it. God gets what you're going through. He knows what it's like. When you pray to him, he nods, because he knows. Every time you see a cross, you see the proof. And just like Jesus' story didn't end in abuse, yours won't either. Easter came after Good Friday, and one day, I pray soon, Jesus will put an end to the hurt and wounds of your abuse.

Last year I was at a farmers' market with my wife, and I ran into her—the woman who had been hurt by her boyfriend. She looked good. She assured me she was good. She got free, and she was healing. She had come to see the truth about that guy and the better truth about God.

I hope you can heal too by putting your hope in Jesus. He is our Refuge, our Rock, our Savior. He came once to save us from our sins. And he will come again to save us from their sins. So, whatever your story, whatever your scars, let's cling to the Savior who gets it.

STUDY QUESTIONS

1. Why do you suppose the church has been so relatively silent on the topic of abuse? Based on what you read in this chapter, list at least three reasons why speaking and writing on a taboo topic like this is necessary for God's people.

2. Think through the suffering that Jesus endured (see John 18 and 19). In what specific ways can he relate to men and women who have been abused? How is Jesus' situation both our comfort in this life and our hope for the life to come?

3. Check out netgrace.org, which examines abuse from a Christian perspective. Let the articles and messages on the site open your eyes to both the reality of abuse and the answers that God provides in his Word and through his devoted people.

Chapter 26

GOD'S WORD TO THE ABUSIVE

Abuse is a pattern of behavior that uses fear or force to maintain power or control. In a country where one in three women and one in four men will be victims of severe physical violence from an intimate partner and many others are victimized by emotional, verbal, sexual, or spiritual abuse, this topic is real and relevant.

In the last chapter, in hopes of helping you heal, I wrote about how God hates abuse, loves the abused, and was abused. Now I want to address those who have been abusive. Since the good news of Jesus draws all kinds of sinners—the proud, impure, gossips, worriers, attention seekers, and addicts—I assume that abusive people may show up at my church or might read this book too. And I want them to show up; I want them to read this.

There's a man who writes me often from prison. He's a guy who now knows Jesus, loves his Savior, and can't wait to finish his time. He's a man who laments his past, is working hard on his faith in the present, and longs for his future to be different. He's a worshiper of Jesus who wants to worship in my church someday.

One day, however, I looked up my pen pal online and saw his legal history. The words *assault of a minor* and *repeated* and *felony* grabbed my attention and broke my heart. Abuse of the worst kind is part of his story. What would

Jesus do if a guy like that was in the crowd and wanted to follow him? And what should I and my church do? If he's released and shows up on Sunday, should we lock the doors? Warn the parents? "Forgive and forget"? Something else? Saying "Everyone is welcome" and "You belong here" is easy, but when people have patterns of behavior of hurting others, what then? In this chapter, I want to address my friend, who I believe watches *Time of Grace* regularly, and I want to speak to you, the reader. Because there are four things every abusive person needs to hear from me and especially from God.

Here's the first thing: *Look at you*.

I want you to take a long look at you. Depending on how you grew up, how your dad treated your mom, how your mom spoke to your dad, or how the adults in your life treated you, you might not even know what abuse looks like. What might seem normal might only be normal because that's what you went through. So here is a list of questions to help you look at you:

I WANT YOU TO TAKE A LONG LOOK AT YOU.

---

1. Do you have a pattern of getting angry when your partner or children don't do what you want?
2. Do you express that anger by name-calling, threatening looks, physical threats, or physical acts like breaking things, hitting pets, grabbing wrists, blocking her from leaving, or pushing him around?
3. Do you blame those moments on alcohol, drugs, or someone else's behavior—you were just drunk or high or having a stressful day; you wouldn't have done it if they hadn't done that?
4. Do you force your partner to spend time with you and forbid them from spending time with friends and family?
5. Do you get jealous or nervous when they do?

6. Do you check their texts, read their personal emails, or control their finances so they have nothing unless you allow it?
7. Do you force them to be intimate with you?
8. Do you ever use the Bible to get what you want, telling him he has to forgive you no matter how much you belittle him, and she has to submit to you because you are the head of the household? Do you believe that "submit" means they have to do what you say? That "forgive" means they have to forget?
9. Have you ever threatened to hurt yourself just so they would stay?
10. Are the people in your life afraid to contradict you? Do they cringe when you're angry? Do they change their plans just to appease you and avoid your anger?

If that's a pattern of your behavior, that's abuse.

And—look—God hates that. David, who was himself threatened and abused by King Saul, wrote, "The LORD examines the righteous, but the wicked, those who love violence, he hates with a passion" (Psalm 11:5). The biggest issue with your anger isn't that it might get you in legal trouble or end your relationship or make your kids hate you when they grow up (as one abuse victim told me). The biggest issue is that it makes God hate you. No one who continues on this path, living in this sin, hurting people God loves, will end up good with God. So, before you have to stand before our Father with a history of hurting his children, look at you. Repent. Confess. Humble yourself. Give up the control, the image, the facade, and get help.

The second thing I want to say to you: *Look at him.*

Look at Jesus. Even if every one of those questions slapped you in the conscience and made you wish you weren't reading this, know this: Jesus is not done with you yet. If you're still alive and breathing, praise the Lord, because Jesus is waiting. Jesus is willing. If you give up control, if you repent, he is willing to call you his friend. Here's some proof. "These are the names of the twelve apostles: first, Simon (who is called Peter) and his brother Andrew; James son of Zebedee, and his brother John; Philip and Bartholomew; Thomas and Matthew the tax collector; James son of Alphaeus, and Thaddaeus; Simon the Zealot and Judas Iscariot, who betrayed him" (Matthew 10:2-4).

IF YOU GIVE UP CONTROL, IF YOU REPENT, HE IS WILLING TO CALL YOU HIS FRIEND.

Did you catch it? Simon the Zealot was a violent man. The Zealots hated that the Romans had control, so they used fear and force to take it back. "Abusers" wouldn't be totally accurate, but they had a past with violence; there were many victims. Yet Jesus invited a guy like that to follow a God like him.

And he wasn't the last. The apostle Paul, the guy who wrote half the New Testament, said this about himself: "Even though I was once a blasphemer and a persecutor and a violent man, I was shown mercy because I acted in ignorance and unbelief. The grace of our Lord was poured out on me abundantly, along with the faith and love that are in Christ Jesus" (1 Timothy 1:13,14).

Paul was violent. People feared his anger and cringed when he showed up at their homes, but he was called by Jesus. He confessed his sins, was baptized, and was transformed by grace and love.

Simon the Zealot and Paul the apostle were forgiven and given salvation—and you can be forgiven too. Remember our Savior hanging on a cross. After being abused, Jesus cried out, "Father, forgive them, for they do not know what they are doing" (Luke 23:34). He still says that. When Jesus hung on that cross, suffering for sins, he suffered for us all. That includes YOU. Abuse is ugly, but Jesus took that ugliness to the cross. Look at him.

Look at Jesus. There will still be consequences, but when you look at Jesus, there is no condemnation (Romans 8:1). So, look at Jesus.

Third, I want you to *look at them*.

Look at the people God has placed in your community who can help you. Now that you know how much God hates abusers and how far Jesus went to forgive abusers, what will you do? How will you change? Here's how: look at them.

It's very possible that the abuse didn't start with you, that you learned to yell and control from your father, your mother, or your mom's boyfriend. Sometimes there are generational sins that families get stuck in, ways they pass on to their children. Maybe that's why the abuse started.

Maybe you don't know what healthy looks like. So, look at them. Look at the professionals whom God has blessed with the wisdom to help you escape the cycle. It's not the job of your significant other or your kids to fix this. I know you'd rather keep it in-house, keep it quiet, hold on to your reputation—but you can't. There is hope, but you need help from the outside. The list on page 309 of this book is filled with resources for you to get help. You might be the first generation in your family in a long time to break the cycle, to break free from the chain. I encourage you to take a step. Call an abuse specialist. Go to anger management.

Fourth and finally, *look at me*.

I'm happy that you're reading this. I've prayed for you to read this. I've begged God that you would keep reading, so thank you. Angels rejoice when sinners repent, and I plan to join them at their party. So let me say this as clearly as I can: you are welcome at my church, at *Time of Grace*, and at every Christian church that loves Jesus and cares about people. Even with a past, you are welcome. Even with a legal record, you are welcome. We have no plans to pick and choose which kinds of sinners can come. Churches aren't country clubs with a minimum morality requirement. Sinners are welcome.

In Jesus' day, the worst people in town were tax collectors and prostitutes, but Jesus called them to repent and follow him. In our day, the categories are different, but the call is the same: sinners can be forgiven and changed as they repent and follow Jesus. That is why, despite all my sins, I am welcome. That's why you are welcome.

SINNERS CAN BE FORGIVEN AND CHANGED AS THEY REPENT AND FOLLOW JESUS.

AND—look at me: As I welcome you with open arms, I also welcome you with wisdom and boundaries that bless the whole congregation. In other words, depending on your story, things might be a bit different for you as part of a church community. We don't let the guy with a gambling addiction be the church treasurer. That's wisdom. We don't tempt alcoholics by having them buy the wine for the Lord's Supper. That's wisdom. And we don't let abusive people alone in situations where abuse can happen. So, yes, we require background checks for our children's ministry. Yes, we will communicate with parole officers and craft a personal plan that meets, if not exceeds, the requirements of the law. Yes, I realize you might not like that. No, I'm not going to change my mind, and neither will many church leaders. Because we care about you. And we care about others.

I imagine that's hard to hear. If you have a history of craving power and control, those rules take all of it away from you. That's actually the point. If sinfully getting control was your issue, then taking away control is your solution. I want you to get better. And this is the path to better. Please don't run or push back. Humble yourself, and God will exalt you.

Because both modern abuse experts and Jesus' apostles agree: When you are truly sorry, you are willing to show it. The apostle Paul wrote, "See what this godly sorrow has produced in you: what earnestness, what eagerness to clear yourselves, what indignation, what alarm, what longing, what concern, what readiness to see justice done" (2 Corinthians 7:11). I hope you are the same. I hope God is producing in you a deep desire to clear yourself, to prove you've changed, to do whatever you can to show that things are different now, that you're giving up control.

It makes me think of a man I met in jail through a member of our church a few years ago. He wondered if he would be welcome at the church after his release. Our church leaders discussed it for a long time, working with his parole officer and pouring over the issue in prayer, thinking of this precious soul craving a Christian community and thinking of our own children and the children at the church we loved. Eventually, we said we'd love to have him, but there would be boundaries, restrictions, and other people who would need to know. And this guy—to his immense credit—said, "The more people who know, the better. The more accountable I will be."

He humbled himself, gave up the power and control, submitted himself to the boundaries we created, and God exalted him. God lifted him up and gave him a church home. Even better, God brought him to a place where he would hear, week after week, something that the world would never tell him: that he was forgiven, saved, and loved through Jesus. He was at my church last Sunday.

The same can happen to you. I pray that it does.

STUDY QUESTIONS

1. What happens when the church is too quick to "forgive and forget" the sin of abuse? What happens when the church has no place for repentant abusers among its members? What would you write about abusers if you were tasked with creating the church policy on addressing abuse?

2. Agree/disagree: If Jesus was known for loving prostitutes, tax collectors, and the worst sinners of his day, faithful Christians should be known for loving the abusive, registered sex offenders, and the worst sinners of our day.

3. Evaluate this statement: God wants my church to tell the abusive to repent/change, offer them the free gift of God's grace, and have unwavering boundaries as a necessary consequence of their past behavior.

Chapter 27

GOD'S WORD TO THE CHURCH ABOUT ABUSE

In the last two chapters, I wrote about abuse, what God says to the abused, and what God says to the abuser. Remember that abuse is a pattern of behavior that uses fear or force to maintain power or control. But what should you do when you're not the victim or the victimizer but rather the friend, family member, or fellow Christian who learns about abuse?

Many years ago, I had to wrestle with that question. A woman came into my office with her children and confessed to me that they did not have a happy home life, that her husband was hurting her and the kids—physically, verbally, and emotionally. What was more, I knew the guy; I was his pastor too. I knew that within days I would sit with him in the same room and address the issue. What would I say to him, to her, to the kids? What should I do?

Given the widespread nature of abuse, we all know, love, and worship next to people who have been impacted by abuse. Therefore, eventually, in some way or another, the truth about that abuse will reach your ears. Your friend shares some concerning details of the fight she had with her boyfriend. While she says, "It was my fault," the bruise on her wrist tells a different story. Your nephew jokes about your brother's parenting in a way that feels . . . off. Your roommate starts dating a girl who belittles him in public and checks his phone in private. He constantly worries he might make her angry. Someone in your Bible study group tells the story of an emotionally abusive mother. Or someone confesses that they have a verbally abusive father. In those moments, what should you and I, as God's people, do?

There is one passage of the Bible that answers that question. It's a tough passage to translate from the original Hebrew, but it gives clear guidance on how to love both the abused and the abuser.

Check out Isaiah 1:17: "Learn to do right; seek justice. Defend the oppressed." God wants us to learn to do the right thing, to seek justice (that means protecting the innocent and punishing the guilty), and to defend the oppressed. My dictionary says that *oppressed* means "ill-treated, tyrannized, or . . . abused." God wants us to defend the abused.

The word *defend* makes me picture an ancient city, like Jerusalem, with its towering walls and strong gates, a place built to keep dangerous people out and those inside, safe. Picture yourself standing on top of the wall with people you love huddled inside, and an abusive person comes riding up toward the city. How do you protect your loved ones? How do you defend the oppressed? Two strategies come to mind.

First, you defend the oppressed with *TRUTH*. Abuse can only exist when lies get the last word, so when you immerse yourself in truth, in what God sees and says, you defend the oppressed. For example, an abuser lies to his victim and says, "This is your fault," even though it isn't. "This isn't abuse," even though it is. "You made me do that," even though he freely chose to do it. Truth turns up the lights, takes off the makeup, and shows things for what they really are.

More truth leads to less abuse. Which is why I want to direct you again to the resource list at the back of this book to help you know the truth. You'll find websites, sermons, books, and qualified counselors who can help, who want to help. There are resources listed that describe what abuse is, how abuse survives, and how you can avoid or survive abuse. The book *Rid of My Disgrace* by Justin and Lindsey Holcomb is the most honest, professional, grace-centered book on sexual abuse that I have ever read. It opened my eyes to see what abuse can look like in a relationship and how Jesus heals, cleanses, and is with people who have endured abuse. Whatever resources you choose, choose truth, because that's how you defend the oppressed.

TRUTH TURNS UP THE LIGHTS, TAKES OFF THE MAKEUP, AND SHOWS THINGS FOR WHAT THEY REALLY ARE.

Second, defend the oppressed with *GRACE*. With undeserved, persistent, enduring love. I once knew a woman who had been badly abused by her significant other (men are sometimes abused by women too, so forgive my one-sided stories here). The details of what she had suffered were heartbreaking and hard to hear . . . and yet, despite calling the cops, she went back to him. And I realized how complicated it all is. There are factors, childhood wounds, generational sins, and decades-long habits that keep us trapped in abuse.

That's why grace is so essential—your willingness to wait, to be there, to love. As your friend fights to believe it really isn't his fault, grace waits. As your sister moves out and then moves back in with him, grace prays. As your daughter goes back to the guy you want to run over with your truck, grace is there when she calls. Abuse is more complicated than you think. You don't just say, "That's bad! Run away!" and it works the first time. Grace is being ready whenever they're ready, like the father of the prodigal son who waited until his boy came home.

And while you wait, grace gives the gospel. If the abused is a Christian, you can say, "You are a child of God. You are so precious to our Father. He loves and delights in you. He doesn't think you're worthless, stupid, or useless. He smiles when he thinks of you."

If the abused isn't a Christian, you can say, "God wants something better for you. He is a Father who doesn't hurt his children. Jesus is a husband who doesn't use the 'head of the household' to get his way but instead loves his bride. Jesus understands what you are going through. He wants you to have hope for a safe place where there is no more crying or tears or abuse." Give the gospel, and you give the grace of our Lord Jesus Christ. God said to defend the oppressed. Defend them with grace and truth.

But what about the oppressor? What do you say to the abuser? Well, this same passage might say something about that too. Isaiah 1:17 says, "Learn to do right; seek justice. Defend the oppressed," but I bet your Bible, like mine, has a little footnote, a little letter to click on in your digital text that says: "Or—here's another valid translation—correct the oppressor." I know that's kind of confusing, but sometimes a sentence can be understood in two ways. This might be saying that we should learn to confront the abuser.

Remember the mom with the kids who told me about her abusive home life? Well, I went on to confront the abuser. I'll never forget that conversation because of how much he cried and how much I didn't. He wept as he told me, swore to me, that he never did any of it. But I didn't believe him. God, forgive me if I was wrong, but I was 99 percent sure he was trying to manipulate me to maintain power and control. So, I said—this is the only time I've ever said this in counseling—"I don't believe you. No, you are lying to me." I straight-faced him because I felt that defending the oppressed meant correcting the oppressor.

Warning—abusive people are, as one expert emailed me, "tough nuts to crack." When lies have been your language for so long, the truth seems strange. When you're used to doing anything to be in control, being asked to confess, submit, and be humble is the hardest thing in the world, especially in churches that value the beauty of a husband's call to lead like Jesus or the power of limitless forgiveness. Abusers can manipulate truth in ways God never intended; they can redefine words in ways offensive to Jesus. Helping an abuser become a safe person who is welcome inside the walls is not for the faint of heart. So, what do you do? You correct the oppressor with *TRUTH*.

Here's the truth: "Abuse is your fault. Abuse is your choice. Yours. Even if he . . . even if she . . . you made the choice to do that, to say that. Okay, you were drunk, but you made the choice to drink. I know you were stressed, but not every stressed person does that. This is on you. This is your issue. God isn't into excuses, so stop making them. Adam tried to blame Eve, but God wasn't hearing it. Own it. Confess it. Because if you hurt one of God's kids, our Father is not going to be happy with you. That power you feel when you rule under your roof—that power will cost you paradise.

"The truth is that you need help, professional counseling. You can't turn off your anger and jealousy and craving for control like a light switch. You need a person or a group of people who can help you. I'll help you. I'll help you find a counselor, meet with the pastor, keep you accountable. But you need help. It's time to humble yourself. Time to give up power. Time to give up control. I'm not running away from you, but I am telling you to leave behind your lies." That's the truth.

But an abuser needs more than truth. They also need *GRACE*. And some of my church members told me I needed to say that. Recently, 159 members of my church completed a survey to help me prepare for this book. One of the themes that came up a lot was not letting the church decide, because of the hurt and messiness, that some people aren't allowed to come. Not letting the church decide that abusers can't come, no matter how sorry they are or how hard they are trying to change. Instead, the church is to offer grace to everyone. Look at what God says next.

The very next verse in Isaiah 1, after exposing the ugliness of oppression and sin, says, "Though your sins are like scarlet, they shall be as white as snow; though they are red as crimson, they shall be like wool" (verse 18). Yes, abuse is a sin that stains us in ways we can't wash out. But God can. Jesus was abused on a cross so even abusers could be saved, so you could come to him with all the consequences and end up with no condemnation, so God himself could look at you and see someone who brings him joy, someone who has been rescued by Jesus.

Grace and truth. For the abused. For the abusive. Truth to see sin as it really is, to see ourselves as we really are. Grace to heal our wounds, to ease our consciences, to get us back to God. It might be messy. It might take time, but grace and truth are how we defend and correct, how we help and love.

IT MIGHT BE MESSY. IT MIGHT TAKE TIME, BUT GRACE AND TRUTH ARE HOW WE DEFEND AND CORRECT, HOW WE HELP AND LOVE.

In those 159 surveys, there was one comment that really grabbed my attention. It's a reminder of what is at stake as I write this and talk about abuse. One person who took the survey admitted they had been abused and then added, "If you can save just one person from the situation they are in, you have done a wonderful thing." I hope that grace and truth, for the abused and the abuser, saves many more than one. Because in God's eyes, that would truly be a wonderful thing.

STUDY QUESTIONS

1. Have you ever tried to help someone who has been abused? If so, what did you do that worked? Having read this chapter, is there anything you wish you would have done differently?

2. Have you ever tried to help someone who has been abusive? If so, what did you do that worked? Having read this chapter, is there anything you wish you would have done differently?

3. Meditate on Isaiah 1:17-20. Find two or three truths in this section that help prepare you to faithfully help the people whom God will place in your path in the days to come.

Chapter 28

ABORTION: THE WOMB

One issue that took me a long time to address in my church is abortion. I was hesitant because I believe some issues are so complex, they take time to teach well.

Teaching on abortion *well* is more than a tweet. I've come to that conclusion, in part, because I've listened to you—your stories, confessions, social media posts, and responses to the surveys I've sent. And I've learned that the church community God has called me to serve—the community where my church is located and our online church—thinks a lot of things about abortion. Different things. Contrasting things.

Some say abortion is an open-and-shut issue: "It's a baby. End of story." For others, however, it's not a baby but a zygote or an embryo or a fetus, a part of a woman's body that belongs to her and not to any court or church council. Some read the black words on the Bible's white pages—"You shall not murder"—and declare, "That settles it!" Others see complicated stories of rape, incest, abusive boyfriends, addicted mothers, severe genetic issues, severe mental illness, and unsupportive families; and the biblical values of compassion, kindness, and wisdom push you to see abortion as a wise and merciful option.

Some have never had, or even been tempted to have, an abortion. Others have been there. You remember the day, the weather, the room, the procedure. Some feel intense regret about their abortion. Others feel it was the best choice at the time, given the complicated factors they were facing.

Some try to represent Jesus by holding graphic antiabortion signs on major street corners. Others think it's wrong to assume that's what Jesus would do. Some have voted one way their entire lives simply because of abortion. Others believe abortion isn't the only issue a Christian should consider during an election. Some think pro-life means doing anything possible to protect a baby in the womb. Others think that "pro-life people" care more about wombs than women, a double standard that strikes you as glaringly hypocritical.

Some believe abortion is too controversial and political to bring up in a place like church. Others believe God demands that churches say something. Some wish this chapter was on a different topic. Others will be hanging on to every word I write.

All of that is why I've waited for some time to talk about abortion. But the time has come. As long as there are unplanned pregnancies in our churches and in our world, abortion, legal or illegal, will be our issue. It will be you or your sister, your daughter or granddaughter, your girlfriend or wife, your roommate or best friend. In a perfect world, every pregnancy would be wanted and planned, but this is not a perfect world. Which means abortion, at the very least, will be a temptation many of us face. So, if you're ready to cover this topic, I am too.

My plan is to write about abortion in the fairest way I know. After reading books from both pro-life advocates and abortion doctors, surveying over 150 Christians about their experiences with abortion, studying 45 stories of women who have had abortions (and are proud of their choices), and meditating on various Bible passages that speak about this issue, I hope to communicate fairly and biblically. No straw man arguments here or worst-case assumptions about the motives from "the other side."

My goal is to help you grasp why certain people feel one way and other people feel another, both on the morality and legality of abortion. Most important, I want to bring you back to God's Word, the place where you and I find truth to guide our lives and grace to forgive all our sins.

Despite their radically different views on abortion, both pro-life and pro-choice people can agree on one thing: people matter. Each individual person matters. Which is why starting our discussion with the womb is so essential. Before we can talk about the reproductive rights of people, the national legislation that affects people, and how best to help people with unplanned pregnancies, we must first ask how many people we are hoping to help.

In the womb is a combination of sperm and egg, but what exactly do sperm and egg combine to make? A part of the mother whom we care about? Or a whole other person within the mother, both of whom we care about? Is that a unique person with the human right to be protected from danger, or does the woman have the right to do what she desires with that unique part of her own body? The more I've read, studied, and wrestled with abortion, the more convinced I am that the first thing we need to figure out with abortion is how many people are involved in the process.

I say that because we all know what to do with a person. Imagine a one-year-old girl, someone whom we would all agree is a person worthy of our love and care. Can you picture a little girl like that, just learning to walk, with her pigtails just long enough to poke out of the top of her head? No matter your religion or political party, we would all agree that she is a person, right?

That adorable (albeit imaginary) girl is our common ground. She's a person.

The fact that she is a person would remain true even if I revealed to you that this little girl had a very complicated story. If we learned that this one-year-old wasn't planned by her father or wasn't really wanted by her mother, would you say that she stops being a person? Do we reclassify her as a thing, an "it" instead of a "she"? While we might lament her parents' lack of love, we would still consider her a person.

What if I told you her father was verbally abusive or her mother was chemically dependent on heroin, that there was no guarantee that her dad would seek help for his controlling behavior, or her mom wouldn't get sober anytime soon? Would those heartbreaking details move that little girl into the category of cells? I don't think so.

What if, God forbid, I whispered to you that she was conceived through assault or incest? Would you consider it merciful to find a doctor who could stop her heart from beating and her lungs from breathing?

What if her parents had plans for work, college, and life that this one-year-old put on hold or changed entirely? We might offer a compassionate word to Mom and lend a hand to Dad, but I don't think their desires would change the little girl's status as one of us, a person worthy of life, liberty, and the pursuit of happiness.

What if the one-year-old had Down syndrome or a genetic issue or a physical abnormality? Or what if the mother didn't want to change the diaper or do the 2:00 A.M. feedings?

My guess is that all the previous situations would elevate your empathy, increase your compassion, and call you to selfless action, but they wouldn't change your answer about who that little girl is. She's still a person.

Do you see the importance of this issue? We all know what to do with people. People come from their mothers, but they are not part of their mothers. They are people. Small people, weak, defenseless, developing people but still people. God says this about such people: "Defend the weak. . . . Uphold the cause of the poor and the oppressed. Rescue the weak and the needy" (Psalm 82:3,4).

So, *the* question that shapes our view of abortion is this: Is that a person in the womb? On the first day or after the first month, or during the second trimester, is that a person? While love urges me to talk to you first about all the circumstances of an unplanned pregnancy (which I will do in the next chapter), logic requires me to start with the essential questions: When does life begin? When do people become people?

THE QUESTION THAT SHAPES OUR VIEW OF ABORTION IS THIS: IS THAT A PERSON IN THE WOMB?

In my research of both pro-life and pro-choice materials, I have found five answers to that question. Before I open my Bible, let's look at what those five are.

First, *some say a person is created at conception*. And, they would add, science proves it. Nearly every cell in a woman's body shares the same genetic code—her lungs and heart and appendix are stamped with almost entirely identical DNA. But when sperm meets egg, something new appears. The DNA is different. At a crime scene, we treasure the uniqueness of genetics, relying on the differences to help us solve cases. Could the same be true for the womb?

Or marvel at how the fingerprints on those tiny developing fingers are unique from the swirls on the tips of the mother's fingers. Or consider that unless a woman has two hearts, four lungs, four legs, and four eyes, there must be a separate person inside of her.

Perhaps such reasons are why numerous medical textbooks on biology and embryology, *TIME*, and the *Rand McNally Atlas of the Body and Mind* all agree with the point the *New Encyclopedia Britannica* makes in saying, "A new individual is created when the elements of a potent sperm merge with those of a fertile egg."[1] In other words, life begins at conception.

Second, *others are convinced that people are created at recognition*. Just watch what is in the womb and see if you don't recognize that as a little person. Look at that little peanut with the beating heart, little nose, and countable toes. Doesn't that look like a human? If we showed the latest ultrasound to a group of preschoolers who had never heard of abortion, what would they say? I haven't run any test trials, but I bet they would recognize that as a yet-to-be-born person.

That's what happened to Abby Johnson. Abby was the Planned Parenthood director who was asked, unexpectedly, to assist with an abortion. The doctor was using an ultrasound during the procedure, which meant Abby was able to see something she recognized. She noticed the tiny vertebrae of the little spine. She gasped as the fetus reacted to the approaching instrument. And she knew it was a person. Recognition shaped, even changed, her views about abortion.

Third, *others say a person is created at viability*. *Viability* is a fancy word that means that you have the ability to live. If you were born, you could survive. Given our modern NICU technology, infants can survive birth long before hitting forty weeks of gestation. The current record is just around twenty-one weeks, a number that would have shocked 99.99 percent of humans who have ever lived on earth. But earlier than that? Dr. Willie Parker is one of the few abortion doctors in the American South, and he makes the viability argument here: "Before 22 weeks, a fetus is not in any way equal to 'a baby' or 'a child.' . . . Every one of the fetal parts—head, body, limbs—like a puzzle that has to be put back together. . . . I place them together, re-creating the fetus in the pan. I have done this so many times that it has become routine: no matter what these parts may look like, this is organic matter that does not add up to anything that can live on its own."[2] This thing in the womb can't live. So that's not life. Not yet.

Fourth, *still others say a person is created by desire. Shout Your Abortion* is a collection of stories from women who are unashamed of their choice to abort. One of the women, Amy, makes the argument about desire when she says, "The simple truth is this: if a sperm and egg come together when a child is desired, a human being is born. But if a sperm and egg come together when a woman knows in her bones that it is not the right time for her to be a mother, then perhaps what is born is her own confident agency over her life."[3] If the time isn't right, if the desire isn't there, then a human being isn't there. That isn't a person. Not until her mother wants it to be so.

Finally, *some say a person is created at birth*. Personhood is obvious then. We can see that this isn't a part of the mother's body but its own unique entity. But until the moment they leave the womb, this is part of the mother, her business, under her wisdom and judgment and authority, since no one can know a woman's body better than the woman herself.

These are the top answers to the key question of personhood—at conception, at recognition, at viability, at desire, or at birth. Have you heard all of those arguments? How about you personally? If I gave you a moment to consider when you personally believe life begins and why, which option would you choose? And what would you say to people who choose the other four?

A bigger issue, an infinitely more important issue—What does God say? If you are a Christian who calls God your Father and Jesus your Savior and the Holy Spirit your Truth-Definer, which of those five options does God agree with? We can talk about the complications of unplanned pregnancy in the next chapter. But for now, let's answer this: What should a Christian believe about the most important issue on abortion, the issue of personhood?

A few Bible passages help us answer that question. First, the story of jumping John and baby Jesus. In Luke 1, Mary is just pregnant with Jesus, and she goes to see her relative Elizabeth, who is six months along with the soon-to-be-named John the Baptist. When Mary shows up and says hi to Elizabeth, John, in the womb, acts like someone just turned on that House of Pain song and starts to jump around.

Scripture says, "When Elizabeth heard Mary's greeting, the baby leaped in her womb" (verse 41). The Greek word originally used here for baby is *brephos*. Okay, but couldn't that mean fetus or something other than baby? Now jump ahead to Luke 2. Mary makes it to Bethlehem, gives birth to Jesus, lays him in a manger, and an angel shows up to the shepherds and says, "This will be a sign to you: You will find a baby wrapped in cloths and lying in a manger" (verse 12).

WHAT SHOULD A CHRISTIAN BELIEVE ABOUT THE MOST IMPORTANT ISSUE ON ABORTION, THE ISSUE OF PERSONHOOD?

Want to guess what Greek word is used for *baby*? *Brephos*. In the Bible's own language, John in the womb is a *brephos* and Jesus outside of it is a *brephos*. A baby. So saying that babies don't exist until birth isn't biblical. And if Elizabeth was only six months along, with the technology of two thousand years ago and not the NICU of today, viability can't be biblical either. Two options down, three others to go.

Is it conception, recognition, or desire? Psalm 139 helps here when King David says to God, "For you created my inmost being; you knit me together in my mother's womb. Your eyes saw my unformed body" (verses 13,16). "Before my body was formed, before you could recognize the little fingers or hear the heartbeat, that was 'my' body; that was 'me.'" David as a person began before he was recognizable. And notice who did it? God. God created that body. God desired to make David. Therefore, the creation of a new person doesn't begin when a mother desires a child but when our heavenly Father does.

This is God's answer to our very human desire to claim authority over what belongs to God. I noticed this theme in *Shout Your Abortion*. One woman said, "My belief is the absolute right to bodily autonomy."[4] Chrissy added, "I deserve to exist in the world as an autonomous and liberated entity."[5] Wendy, a former US senator, preached, "You are the only person who can decide what is right for you."[6] Where many people disagree with God is not just with the womb but with their entire selves. But Christians believe that God made us. He gave us life. We are not our own. We were made and saved, not to be lord and master but to follow the Lord who gave his life for us.

That leaves us with one option—conception. Which is exactly what Psalm 51:5 proves: "Surely I was sinful at birth, sinful from the time my mother conceived me." Here David admits how far back his sin problem went, stretching all the way back to his conception. But *things* aren't sinful. A tree or a chair or a clump of cells isn't good or evil, moral or immoral, godly or sinful. So, if David says that he was sinful from his conception, he is saying his conception created . . . a person.

The saying we sometimes hear, then, is scriptural: *Life begins at CONCEPTION*. Yes, there is lots of developing to do. Yes, that child still needs its mother to survive those first weeks. Yes, we hope every child is a desired child. But our Father has gone on the record in Old Testament and New to tell us that life begins at conception. An abortion, therefore, doesn't scrape off some cells. An abortion ends a life. A choice not to abort, therefore, saves a life whom God loves.

I know you probably have a ton of questions. But what if you're not ready to be a father or if you don't have money to raise a daughter or if you're already depressed or don't want to be bound forever to an abusive man? What will the church do when someone gets pregnant and didn't plan to? How will we love all the lives involved—baby, mother, and father? How can we move into a sacrificial love for complicated families? That will be addressed in the next chapter. But there's one thing I still want to communicate here. Something she needed me to tell you.

Last week I received a lengthy email from a woman who gave me permission to tell you about her abortion. She didn't want one, but her mother, the most God-fearing woman she knew, told her to get one. Then her sisters reasoned it wasn't a person until its first breath, until birth. Feeling completely alone, she agreed. And for years afterward, decades actually, she struggled to believe she could be forgiven.

OUR FATHER HAS GONE ON THE RECORD IN OLD TESTAMENT AND NEW TO TELL US THAT LIFE BEGINS AT CONCEPTION.

Maybe you feel that way too. Maybe long ago or just this week, you ended a pregnancy. Maybe you're the guy who pushed it, who paid for it, or who didn't say anything and just let her do it. Maybe you're the mom or the dad who was embarrassed, the Christian family that didn't want the pregnancy to prove you weren't that perfect after all. Maybe you had some good reasons. Maybe not. But maybe now, with an open Bible, you realize what happened. That a life was ended.

If so, read this: Jesus Christ, the *brephos* born in Bethlehem, came into this world to forgive and save people just like you. Jesus was nicknamed the Son of David, his ancient ancestor, and he wasn't ashamed of the name even though David once committed . . . murder.

And when Jesus took his friends up to a mountaintop and showed them his glory, who appeared at his side? Elijah and Moses, who happened to be . . . a murderer. And when Jesus wanted the good news of his forgiveness for all sinners to go beyond Israel, to whom did he appear? To Saul (a.k.a. Paul), a man with a history of murder. The fact that God chose Moses, David, and Paul to write most of the Bible, despite their pasts, should tell you that Jesus saves us from the worst of it. That through Jesus, you too can be saved.

Listen to Jesus' friend John: "If we confess our sins, he is faithful and just and will forgive us our sins and purify us from all unrighteousness" (1 John 1:9). Jesus is faithful. Jesus will forgive our sins. Jesus will purify us. From what? From *all* unrighteousness. From all of it!

The reason Jesus was conceived of the Holy Spirit and born of the virgin Mary was so that he could suffer under Pontius Pilate, die, and be buried. Why? So that he could rise on the third day and proclaim forgiveness of sins to Paul, to me, to you.

Remember Abby from Planned Parenthood? That day with the ultrasound changed her life, but it couldn't undo her support of abortion or her own two abortions. So she ran to Jesus. And now she says, "Good Friday has never been the same for me since."[7]

The woman who emailed me agrees. She concluded her incredible email with these words: "I'm sharing my story in case YOU are one of my other sisters (or brothers) in Christ, sitting in the pew, hoping no one will discover your past sins. I'm sharing my story in hopes that God may use my story to let you know that you don't have to suffer in silence anymore. That there is no condemnation in Christ Jesus now. That his forgiveness is for YOU. That the water of YOUR baptism washed you clean. That Christ's suffering on the cross was to redeem YOU. He paid for it all. Confess your sins to one another, so you can be healed."

Friends, there is life in the womb. And there is eternal life in the One from heaven.

STUDY QUESTIONS

1. Read and think about 1 John 1:8-10. How would you apply these words to the issue of abortion?

2. If everything in the universe was created by and, therefore, belongs to God, what questions should Christians ask that non-Christians might not consider when addressing an issue like abortion?

3. Evaluate: A good church should be a place where abortion is talked about openly.

Chapter 29

ABORTION: THE WOMAN

Abortion is an issue that eventually affects all of us. In a country where one in four women will have an abortion and many more will consider it, where many men, parents, friends, and churches are involved, abortion is real, relevant, and important for us to talk about.

In the last chapter, we zoomed into the womb and asked, "When does life begin?" We looked at the five main answers to that question—conception, recognition, viability, desire, and birth—and then we opened our Bibles and learned that, according to God, life begins at conception. That makes abortion, unless it's required to save the mother's life, a sin. If abortion is part of your story, please remember Jesus died for every sin so we could come to him and be forgiven, accepted, and saved.

And that's about all I knew as a teenager. If you would have asked a teenage me, the issue of abortion was black and white, short and sweet. During middle school, my church showed me the same passages I shared in the last chapter and showed a video of what happens in a later-term abortion. It was, as you can imagine, graphic. It was an argument from recognition. That looks like a baby. That is a baby. Just like the Bible says. So don't get an abortion. For many years, that's all I knew about the issue.

Since then, I have learned a lot more. Especially from having kids. My daughters are amazing, but raising them is hard. And expensive. And exhausting. (I do love you, girls, really.) And—get this—I have everything in my favor. I am married to a great, godly woman who teaches little kids for a living, for goodness' sake! We have two incomes, money in the bank, and tons of support from our safe and ready-to-help parents. There was no shame or embarrassment in our pregnancies, little to fear besides sleepless nights and blowout diapers. Yet, despite all that, those kids challenged us and changed our lives.

Imagine when the situation is much more complicated, when you barely know each other and there are red flags with the father, when a baby will bind you together forever, when you're depressed or addicted or broke, when your parents are pushing for abortion, when you can't predict your church's reaction.

There's a book that reminded me of these complications. The book is called *Shout Your Abortion*, and it's a collection of dozens of stories of women who got abortions and why. You have likely heard of the heartbreaking cases of assault or incest, two reasons why we get why it would be so tempting to abort. To be fair, even Planned Parenthood admits that such cases are extremely rare—fewer than half of 1 percent of abortions happen for these heartbreaking reasons—but there are other reasons. And compassion requires Christians to consider those reasons, not just what happens during abortion but why abortion happens. And teenage me never went there mentally, never wrestled emotionally with how saying no to abortion means saying yes to an unplanned, complicated, completely changed life.

So, church, what can we do? As followers of Jesus—saved by his love, filled with his Spirit, and on a mission to love God and people—what should we do? Here's the answer I want to unpack—*Be Pro (Every) Life*. Many Christians speak, post, and pray for life inside the womb. God wants to encourage us not to care just about that life but about all the lives involved when someone is pregnant and didn't plan it.

Let's ground ourselves in this incredible description of the early Christian church: "God's grace was so powerfully at work in them all that there were no needy persons among them. For from time to time those who owned land or houses sold them, brought the money from the sales and put it at the apostles' feet, and it was distributed to anyone who had need" (Acts 4:33-35). There were no needy persons among them. The first Christians saw needs and met them. Even if the needs were great, even if the needy were many, they sold their homes. They sold their land to show their love. Because the early church was pro-life. Pro (every) life.

Connect that to an unplanned pregnancy. What are the needs that make abortion so tempting? What fears are people facing that we, as their church family, could ease? I can think of three major needs:

First, there are *spiritual needs*. For some, perhaps many, the need is truth. Planned Parenthood tells us that the number one and number three reasons women have abortions is convenience.[1] "The timing isn't convenient. I got school or work. My kids are grown, and I don't want to do the infant thing again." It's not an abusive father or a personal addiction but a preferred life that they don't want to give up. In that case, we need truth. That's a life within you, a life that God made, that God loves. It would be murder to end that life, a gross injustice, and God won't stand for it. You can't. You must not. You shall not murder.

For others, however, the spiritual need is not truth but love. Sex is a sin that sometimes "shows." Unlike 98.7 percent of sins, an unplanned pregnancy can't be covered up. And that can bring shame. When you're starting to show, you wonder what the church people will say, how they'll look, how they'll judge. Satan loves to make church people judgmental and single moms feel they're being judged even when they aren't. We need love. Lots of love. Evident, obvious, impossible-to-miss love. Smiles. Hellos.

Sit-next-to-me love. You-belong-here love. I'm-glad-you-came love. I'm-glad-you-both-came love. Jesus-forgives, Jesus-welcomes, Jesus-is-pro-me-and-you-by-grace love.

Earlier this year, I met a man who, along with his wife, worked for a pro-life ministry. He told me how they invited a young woman to stay in their guest bedroom while she got on her feet. But the girl liked to party and, one day, found herself pregnant. Since she knew they were church people and since she had grown up with a strict religious father, she assumed her sin meant she was no longer welcome in their home. "I'll leave," she mumbled to the husband abruptly one morning. But this man—thank God—saw her need and met it. He gave her grace. He spoke to her of Jesus' love. "Where sin increased," Paul wrote, "grace increased all the more" (Romans 5:20). The husband met her spiritual needs. And we do too when we apply grace to those who need it most.

But the needs are more than just spiritual. Second, there are *financial needs*. According to a 2004 Planned Parenthood survey, 23 percent of abortions happen for financial reasons.[2] Giving birth isn't a bargain these days. Medical bills, then diapers, formula, and decades of financial needs. The love of money might be a root of all kinds of evil, but the lack of money is a root of all kinds of reasons . . . reasons to get an abortion.

Which is where we come in. Would you sell your cabin to save a kid? Would you drive your car into the ground to convince them to keep their baby girl? Would you put off your retirement, skip a vacation? Would you budget for something like my church's Good Samaritan Fund so our leaders are ready to meet the financial needs within our church family? Would you personally say to a scared friend or a worried niece, "Whatever it costs, we got you"? Could we, like the early Christian church in Jerusalem, create a culture with no needy people, where no one has to starve, shiver, or abort because they're broke?

Jesus' brother James wrote, "Religion that God our Father accepts as pure and faultless is this: to look after orphans and widows in their distress" (1:27). In Jewish culture, orphans and widows had great needs and few resources. In our day, single moms are the same. God loves, accepts, and smiles upon us when we look after those in need. So, before this moment passes, before the marketers tell us all the things we still need, would you take a step, make a gift, meet a financial need?

GOD LOVES, ACCEPTS, AND SMILES UPON US WHEN WE LOOK AFTER THOSE IN NEED.

Finally, there are *relational needs*. If she keeps the baby, she might need help. Moms, she might need to learn how to be a mom because this just happened, unplanned. Guys, that wide-eyed guy might need to learn how to step up, how to grow up, what men do when they put down the controller and pick up a box of wipes.

They might need mentors, babysitters, counselors . . . us. Church, that child will need us to love and accept and affirm. If there's not a dad in the picture, that child will need some men to model the faith for him, to take him under their wing, to remind him who he is and *Whose he is*.

Or, if she chooses adoption (a great option!), she will need support, love, resources, or maybe you to step forward and open your own arms and home. Some will say that abortion is better than giving birth and handing your baby to another family, but that's not true. God loves adoption. Jesus himself was raised by a man who wasn't his biological father. Every Christian has been adopted into God's family (Romans 8:15), which is why so many Christians love and support adoption itself. Make no mistake, that kind of love is work. Sacrificial work. Costly work. But Christlike work. Paul wrote,

"Therefore, as we have opportunity, let us do good to all people, especially to those who belong to the family of believers" (Galatians 6:10). Let's do good. Let's meet needs.

Soon after the apostles died, the early church had to navigate life in the Roman world. The Romans, as you may have heard, did not love children. Not only did they abort them; they also exposed them. During the first days after birth, people just took their kids and left them outside to die. If they were sick or handicapped or the "wrong" gender, they exposed them to the elements, to the animals. But guess who showed up? The Christians. The Christians picked up the babies, adopted them, and raised them as their own. In fact, this was so common that churches quickly became the place where the pagans abandoned their infants. Leave those little lives with the church. They'll love them. They are pro (every) life.

When Jesus died and rose, he made a promise that, through faith in him, God would adopt us as his own children. He promised that our Father would not abandon us as bastard sinners but would set the table with a place for us. He would leave the light on and the door unlocked so we could always come home, always have a room to rest, always have grace to come back to.

The sexually immoral and the selfish, the abortionist and the apathetic, all of us can come to Jesus and have every need met, every sin erased, every mistake covered so we might discover that God is pro-life, pro-your-life, pro-eternal-life. Romans 10:11 promises, "Anyone who believes in him will never be put to shame." Anyone—that's you—who believes in him—that's Jesus—will never be put to shame. We will always belong. Because Jesus was pro-you-and-God-together-forever life.

Call me a spiritual optimist, but I think that truth has changed you. I think you're willing to love everyone, to be pro (every) life.

STUDY QUESTIONS

1. Why is it common, even among Christians, to care more about the baby in the womb than about the other lives involved in an unplanned pregnancy?

2. Imagine if you were pregnant and didn't plan it (or you had gotten a woman pregnant without planning it). What would be your top three needs? How might a local church that truly cared about you help you meet those needs?

3. Meditate on 2 Corinthians 5:14,15. How does the gospel of Jesus' love for us affect the way we treat our neighbors, including those who are facing an unplanned pregnancy?

CONCLUSION

Imagine the apostle Paul as he walks through the big-city buzz of ancient Athens for the very first time. As he looks left, he sees the towering Parthenon, glittering with marble and promoting the worship of fabricated idols who have no eyes to see, hearts to love, or power to save. As he looks right, he spots one of the many brothels where prostitutes use their lips and hips to entice new customers through the perfumed door. First-century Athens is a moral mess.

Yet Paul doesn't run or hide. Instead, he talks. With love for the lost in his heart and the love for the Lord in his soul, Paul talks. He speaks words of grace and truth, of comfort and conviction.

I pray that this book has made you a little more like Paul, equipped not to run from tough topics but to talk about them with God's grace and truth.

The world around us seems to need God more than ever before. Our own hearts need him just the same. Thank God that the good Lord has not left us alone but instead inspired the Truth that equips us for every good work.

Friend, there is work to do and a world in need. May Jesus guide you to do his will.

"All Scripture is God-breathed and is useful for teaching, rebuking, correcting and training in righteousness, so that the servant of God may be thoroughly equipped for every good work" (2 Timothy 3:16,17).

ACKNOWLEDGMENTS

To the Holy Spirit—I'm not sure if the Holy Spirit is into shout-outs, but I'd like to shout out to the Spirit of God for inspiring the authors of the Bible to talk taboo. From the drunkenness of Noah to the lewdness of David, the intimacy of the Song of Songs to the racial struggles of the early church, I love that God's Word is filled with real sins and real grace. Holy Spirit, I praise you for being the first one in every Bible-based church to talk about what we all need to be talking about.

To Dr. John Parlow—When I was a teenager, you taught and modeled sermons that intersected with the highest highs and the lowest lows of our lives. Thanks for being pivotal in my life and my ministry.

To Tim Glende—Having a lead pastor who leads the way with courageous preaching is no small blessing. I thank God for you.

To the Time of Grace team—You are the hands and feet and strength and heart of this amazing ministry. Plus, you're just plain fun. Thanks to you, I'll never think of centaurs, Amanda Hugginkiss, Fabio, or Leeroy Jenkins the same way.

To Mandy Swiontek—You are the queen of editing, organization, kind-yet-quality feedback, and overall awesomeness. Most readers of this book won't know you, but I wish they would.

To Esther and the team at The Fedd Agency—Thanks for putting some wind in my sails as an author. Your words from our first-ever conversation will stick with me for a long time.

To our Supper Club—Kim and I love doing dinner with all y'all month after month, but we love infinitely more the chance to talk about anything and everything. But for the record, Kim and I are not quite ready to live on a deserted island with you.

To Kim—Giving your husband permission to talk about the real us takes trust and humility. I wouldn't be so open about our lives if it made you uncomfortable, but I am so grateful that you are comfortable allowing me to talk taboo. Also, I love you. In addition, date night is the best night of every week. In conclusion, to quote *Dumb and Dumber*, "I like you a lot."

To Brooklyn and Maya—It has to be weird sometimes to have a dad who talks about sex in church. To compensate for the awkwardness, I promise to buy you some Chick-fil-A the day you finish this book.

To you, the reader—I praise God that you value the blessings on the other side of awkward conversations. And I pray that I've convinced you to talk taboo too.

RESOURCES ON ABUSE

Need Help?

1. *Time of Grace* television series *Abuse: What Does God Say?* Find it at timeofgrace.org.

2. Your pastors—While your pastors are not trained/licensed counselors and should not replace a professional therapist, they are equipped to help you deal with the effects of sin on your soul, including those sins that have been committed against you. Their confidential, Christ-centered guidance can be one vital piece of your recovery and healing.

3. Christian Family Solutions (christianfamilysolutions.org)—CFS is a professional, Christian counseling organization that exists to help and heal people in need. CFS has many licensed counselors on staff who are trained to help individuals who have been abused. CFS clinicians can integrate an individual's Christian faith into therapy so that the healing power of the gospel is present during the treatment process. Appointments are available in person or through telehealth. Call 800.438.1772 for more information.

Websites

1. GRACE (Godly Response to Abuse in the Christian Environment; netgrace.org)—GRACE helps Christian ministries recognize, prevent, and respond to abuse in its various forms. I found this website to be a rich resource of videos and articles for anyone looking for biblical answers on sexual, emotional, verbal, and/or physical abuse.

2. Freedom for the Captives (freedomforcaptives.com)—This ministry was created to help protect children from abuse in addition to empowering abuse survivors. Filled with Scripture and free resources, Freedom for the Captives is a wonderful place for congregations to learn how to make their churches safe places for every child to worship Jesus.

Books

1. *Rid of My Disgrace: Hope and Healing for Victims of Sexual Assault* by Justin and Lindsey Holcomb—This was the first book that I ever read on the topic of abuse and, nearly a decade later, continues to be one of my favorites. This work focuses on sexual abuse and guides the reader to the cleansing, purifying, and restoring work of Jesus.

2. *The Body Keeps the Score: Brain, Mind, and Body in the Healing of Trauma* by Bessel van der Kolk—This book, recommended by Dr. Brandon Hayes of Christian Family Solutions, explores the connection between various types of trauma and our brains' ability to trust, practice self-control, and experience pleasure afterward. This pioneering work has become a *New York Times* bestseller.

3. *On the Threshold of Hope: Opening the Door to Healing for Survivors of Sexual Abuse* by Diane Mandt Langberg, PhD—This book, recommended by Sheryl Cowling of Christian Family Solutions, is written for men and

women who have been traumatized by sexual abuse and approaches healing from a Christian perspective. Cowling has twenty-five years' experience counseling children, teens, and adults. She is board certified as a professional Christian counselor, as an expert in traumatic stress, and in telemental health.

NOTES

Chapter 1

1. "Mental Health by the Numbers," National Alliance on Mental Illness, accessed March 30, 2023, https://www.nami.org/mhstats.

Chapter 2

1. Mary Leigh Keith, "To the Depressed Christian," CRU Singapore, accessed March 30, 2023, https://www.cru.org/sg/en/stories/life-and-relationships/emotions/to-the-depressed-christian.html.
2. Mary Leigh Keith, "3 Ways to Care for Your Depressed Friend," CRU, accessed March 30, 2023, https://www.cru.org/us/en/blog/life-and-relationships/emotions/3-ways-to-care-for-your-depressed-friend.html.

Chapter 6

1. "Statistics," National Sexual Violence Resource Center, accessed March 30, 2023, https://www.nsvrc.org/statistics.

Chapter 7

1. David Kinnaman and Gabe Lyons, *unChristian: What a New Generation Really Thinks About Christianity . . . and Why It Matters* (Grand Rapids: Baker Books, 2007), 26.
2. "When Foundations Tremble," *Leadership Journal*, January 1, 1993, http://www.christianitytoday.com/le/1993/93l2134.html?start=1.

Chapter 8

1. Mark Moring, "Jennifer Knapp Comes Out," *Christianity Today*, April 13, 2010, http://www.christianitytoday.com/ct/2010/aprilweb-only/jenniferknapp-apr10.html?start=1.
2. Gene Robinson, *God Believes in Love: Straight Talk About Gay Marriage* (New York: Vintage Books, 2012), 90.
3. Rosaria Champagne Butterfield, *The Secret Thoughts of an Unlikely Convert* (Pittsburgh: Crown & Covenant Publications, 2012), 493-495.

Chapter 11

1. "Report: How Many Adults and Youth Identify as Transgender in the United States?," UCLA Williams Institute, June 2022, https://williamsinstitute.law.ucla.edu/publications/trans-adults-united-states/.
2. Ashley Austin et al., "Suicidality Among Transgender Youth: Elucidating the Role of Interpersonal Risk Factors," *Journal of Interpersonal Violence* 37, no. 5-6 (March 2022), https://pubmed.ncbi.nlm.nih.gov/32345113/.

Chapter 12

1. Juliana Menasce Horowitz, Nikki Graf, and Gretchen Livingston, "Marriage and Cohabitation in the U.S.," Pew Research Center, November 6, 2019, https://www.pewresearch.org/social-trends/2019/11/06/marriage-and-cohabitation-in-the-u-s/.

2. Ibid.

Chapter 14

1. Gary Shriver and Mona Shriver, *Unfaithful: Hope and Healing After Infidelity* (Colorado Springs: David C Cook, 2009), 115.
2. Ibid., 45.

Chapter 20

1. David Landes, "Swedish Church Members 'Don't Believe in Jesus,'" The Local SE, updated June 15, 2011, https://www.thelocal.se/20110615/34370/.

Chapter 21

1. Matt Walsh, *The Unholy Trinity: Blocking the Left's Assault on Life, Marriage, and Gender* (New York: Image, 2017), 1.
2. Glen O'Brien, *John Wesley's Political World* (New York: Routledge, 2023).

Chapter 22

1. Paul Olson, "Wisconsin Drinks a Lot of Korbel Brandy," *Driving Inertia*, August 16, 2012, https://drivinginertia.com/3017/wisconsin-drinks/.

Chapter 23

1. Luke Gilkerson, "How Many Christians View Porn? A Lot, Actually," Covenant Eyes, December 23, 2015, https://www.covenanteyes.com/2015/06/26/how-many-christians-view-porn-a-lot-actually/.

Chapter 25

1. National Domestic Violence Hotline, accessed March 31, 2023, https://www.thehotline.org/identify-abuse/understand-relationship-abuse/.

2. "Fast Facts: How Big Is the Problem?," Centers for Disease Control and Prevention, accessed March 31, 2023, https://www.cdc.gov/violenceprevention/intimatepartnerviolence/fastfact.html.

Chapter 28

1. *New Encyclopedia Britannica*, 15th ed., vol. 14 (1974), s.v. "Pregnancy."
2. Dr. Willie Parker, *Life's Work: A Moral Argument for Choice* (New York: ATRIA Books, 2017), 12, 96.
3. Amelia Bonow and Emily Nokes, eds., *Shout Your Abortion* (Oakland: PM Press, 2018), 54.
4. Ibid., 77.
5. Ibid., 97.
6. Ibid., 88.
7. Abby Johnson with Cindy Lambert, *Unplanned: The Dramatic True Story of a Former Planned Parenthood Leader's Eye-Opening Journey Across the Life Line* (Carol Stream: Tyndale Momentum, 2014), 190.

Chapter 29

1. Luu D. Ireland, "Who Chooses Abortion? More Women Than You Might Think," *The Conversation*, July 27, 2018, https://theconversation.com/who-chooses-abortion-more-women-than-you-might-think-99982.
2. Ibid.

ABOUT THE AUTHOR

Mike Novotny pours his Jesus-based joy into his ministry as a pastor at The CORE in Appleton, Wisconsin and as the lead speaker for Time of Grace, a global media ministry that connects people to God through television, print, and digital resources. Unafraid to bring grace and truth to the toughest topics of our time, he has written numerous books, including *3 Words That Will Change Your Life*; *What's Big Starts Small*; *You Know God Loves You, Right?*; and *When Life Hurts*. Mike lives with his wife, Kim, and their two daughters, Brooklyn and Maya; runs long distances; and plays soccer with other middle-aged men whose best days are long behind them. To find more books by Mike, go to timeofgrace.store.